Second Edition

BEHAVIOR MODIFICATION IN THE HUMAN SERVICES

A Systematic Introduction to Concepts and Applications

Second Edition

BEHAVIOR MODIFICATION IN THE HUMAN SERVICES
A Systematic Introduction to Concepts and Applications

MARTIN SUNDEL
University of Texas at Arlington
and
SANDRA STONE SUNDEL
Behavior Therapist and Consultant
Arlington, Texas

PRENTICE-HALL, INC.   ENGLEWOOD CLIFFS, N.J. 07632

Library of Congress Cataloging in Publication Data

SUNDEL, MARTIN, 1940–
    Behavior modification in the human services.

    Bibliography: p.
    Includes index.
    1. Behavior modification. I. Sundel, Sandra Stone,
1948–   II. Title.
BF637.B4S9 1982   158′.3   81-21088
ISBN 0-13-073916-2   AACR2

Production editor: Dee Josephson
Manufacturing buyer: John Hall
Cover Design: Miriam Recio

Printed in the United States of America

10 9 8 7 6 5 4 3 2 1

Prentice-Hall International, Inc., *London*
Prentice-Hall of Australia Pty. Limited, *Sydney*
Prentice-Hall of Canada, Ltd., *Toronto*
Prentice-Hall of India Private Limited, *New Delhi*
Prentice-Hall of Japan, Inc., *Tokyo*
Prentice-Hall of Southeast Asia Pte. Ltd., *Singapore*
Whitehall Books Limited, Wellington, *New Zealand*

To Lil and Harry Stone
and
To the memory of Pauline and Louis Sundel

CONTENTS

6
SHAPING AND RESPONSE DIFFERENTIATION   57

7
STIMULUS CONTROL: DISCRIMINATION AND GENERALIZATION   67

8
ELEMENTS OF BEHAVIORAL ASSESSMENT   80

9
CONDUCTING A BEHAVIORAL ASSESSMENT   95

10
CONDITIONED POSITIVE REINFORCEMENT AND CHAINING   109

PREFACE

Our purpose in writing this book is to provide an introduction to behavior modification concepts, principles, and practices. The basic principles of behavior are systematically presented within a human-services context. Using a framework that integrates these behavioral principles with practical applications, we have placed special emphasis on the basic knowledge and skills required in behavioral assessment, intervention planning, and evaluation. In this way, the implementation of a behavioral-change program is considered with a planned, ethical strategy and with a rationale for intervention.

The book is designed for students and practitioners in social work, psychology, education, nursing, and allied health and human-service professions. In addition, parents, teachers, clergy, and others will find the principles, techniques, and examples in this book relevant to situations they encounter. Case examples are drawn from these diverse fields to illustrate the wide range of applications of behavior modification.

This second edition builds on the strengths of the first edition and includes many new features: (1) At the beginning of each chapter, a case excerpt illustrates a basic concept. (2) Many practical examples have been added throughout the book to amplify explanations of the principles and to illustrate their applications in a wide range of settings. (3) A summary of key points is provided at the end of each chapter. (4) References have been updated, although a number of the original ones have been retained because of their classic contributions to the field. (5) New material on assessment, evaluation, and recent developments in the field is presented.

Chapters 1 through 7 and 10 through 15 cover the basic principles of behavior modification. Chapters 8, 9, and 16 present a behavioral assessment, treatment planning, and evaluation framework for integrating the behavioral principles with practice. Thus, in addition to teaching the principles of behavior, this book provides a practice-oriented model for applying these principles. Charts, graphs, and other measuring instruments serve as aids in the analysis of case studies and examples.

Many case examples are provided to illustrate applications of the behavioral approach in a wide range of practice settings. The eight case studies referred to throughout the text are designed to help develop skills in specifying and analyzing client behaviors and their controlling conditions. These case studies also demonstrate how behavioral-change goals and intervention plans are formulated. They illustrate various principles and intervention techniques, and they show how criteria for evaluating behavioral programs can be applied. Throughout the book, you will be asked specific questions about the case studies to assess your comprehension of the subject matter and skill in applying behavioral concepts to practice situations.

The case studies are drawn from practice settings. They are based on actual experience in human service. In all case studies and examples used in this book, the real names of clients have been changed.

The course materials have been used extensively with students and practitioners from a variety of educational backgrounds and human-service settings. The questions and answers for all tests have been revised based on their performance. This book has benefited from the challenging comments and suggestions made by our students and colleagues, including those in our workshops and continuing-education programs. The major principles presented in this book are based on the operant conditioning approach of B. F. Skinner and his followers, the classical conditioning model of Ivan Pavlov, and social-learning theory developed by Albert Bandura and his associates. We are indebted to our many colleagues, too numerous to mention here, who have provided conceptual, empirical, and clinical foundations for the body of knowledge incorporated in this text. Many of their names will be found in the suggested readings.

We would like to acknowledge the following individuals who, over the years, have had an influence on our work in this field: Edwin Thomas, Eileen Gambrill, George Geis, Harry Lawrence, Richard Stuart, and William Butterfield. We would like to thank Ed Stanford, Sue Taylor, and Dee Josephson of Prentice-Hall for the many ways in which they helped make this a better book. We thank Dean Paul Glasser who has provided a supportive environment for this work. Thanks also to Donna Turner and Doris Cochran for their diligent and efficient typing of the manuscript, and to Cindy Viol and Judy Buckler for their assistance. Finally, special thanks to our children, Adam and Jenny, for being so patient with us all these months.

We hope that reading this book will be a positive reinforcing learning experience for you, and that you will be stimulated to explore further this exciting and promising field.

HOW TO USE THIS BOOK

COURSE MATERIALS

The book contains the following materials:

1. *Case Studies:* Eight case examples demonstrating the application of behavioral principles to practice problems. These case studies are located throughout the text and also in Appendix 1 for your convenience, and should be referred to wherever indicated.
2. *Course Pretest:* Twelve questions and answers, constituting a pretest for the total course of study. The questions are representative of the course post-test. The course pretest is found in Appendix 2. Answers to the course pretest are found in Appendix 3.
3. *Chapters:* Sixteen chapters presenting behavioral concepts and applications. Each chapter contains a list of objectives, a pretest, a teaching unit, a post-test, and answers to the pretest and post-test. Chapter pretest answers are found in Appendix 4. Chapter post-test answers are in Appendix 5. Each chapter builds on concepts and test items from previous chapters; therefore, we recommend that you work through the chapters in the order in which they are presented.
4. *Course Post-Test:* Thirty-five questions and answers, constituting a post-test for the course.

CASE STUDIES

The eight *case studies* are referred to throughout the text to illustrate the application of the behavioral principles. Questions on the course pretest and course post-test require answers based on the information found in these case studies. Chapter pretests and post-tests also frequently require answers based on the information from the case studies. In addition, references to specific cases are made at various points in the chapters.

THE COURSE PRETEST

After working through the *course pretest,* you will have obtained an overview or sampling of the course content. The purposes of the course pretest are (1) to orient you to the type of questions that you will be required to answer correctly upon completion of the course, and (2) to help you assess your entering knowledge of the course content. In addition, the course pretest provides you with a measure of your current level of behavioral knowledge in relation to a set of performance criteria. Your performance on the course pretest can also be compared later with your score on the course post-test. We recommend that you take the course pretest (Appendix 2) before reading any of the chapters. When you have answered all the questions, score the test by comparing your answers to those given in Appendix 3. You are not expected to achieve criterion score on the course pretest unless you have had prior exposure to behavioral concepts. If you achieve criterion score (that is, 90 percent) on the course pretest, you may take the course post-test (p. 210). If you also achieve criterion score on the course post-test, you have demonstrated mastery of the material and may only need to review or study certain parts of the text, if any.

THE CHAPTERS

Objectives are stated at the beginning of each chapter to indicate the results to be achieved after completing the chapter. Each chapter has a *pretest* that will orient you to the content presented in the chapter and determine your familiarity with it. Score the pretest before reading the chapter by comparing your answers to those given in Appendix 4. You are not expected to achieve criterion score on the chapter pretests. Taking the chapter pretests, however, will give you practice with the types of questions and answers included in the post-tests. If you achieve criterion score on the chapter pretest, you can take the chapter post-test without reading the chapter. If you also achieve criterion score on the chapter post-test, you should go on to the next chapter pretest. If you achieve less than criterion score on the chapter pretest, you should study the chapter. Each chapter covers the content necessary to meet its objectives. The *chapter post-test* is taken after you have studied the chapter. Score the chapter post-test by comparing your answers to those in given Appendix 5. If criterion score is not achieved, review the chapter and retake the test until you achieve criterion score.

Suggested readings are included at the end of each chapter. The references were selected according to their relevance for specific principles or applications and constitute a small sample of available literature. They provide theoretical foundations, case studies, and empirical research that can be consulted to further clarify and elaborate the concepts and applications presented.

THE COURSE POST-TEST

The *course post-test* is taken after you have completed the sixteen chapters. Answers to the course post-test follow it on pages 216–223. If you do not achieve criterion score, you should review the chapters related to the incorrect answers. When you achieve criterion score on the course post-test, you have mastered the content of this course.

A *summary of notational symbols and paradigms* used throughout the text is found in Appendix 6. The *glossary* contains definitions of technical terms which are introduced in boldface in the text.

Scoring

Many of the questions ask for examples that demonstrate application of course concepts; therefore, a number of different correct answers may be possible for a particular question. In these cases, criteria for correct answers are delineated. If your answer includes the criteria stated, you receive the maximum number of points. If your answer includes two out of three correct parts, for example, you receive two points for the question. If your answer does not include any of the stated criteria, you receive zero points for that question.

The tests make frequent use of open-ended questions, instead of true-false or multiple-choice questions. They are designed to help you develop skills in applying the principles, rather than merely identifying which of two or more answers is correct. Sample answers are given for each open-ended question that meet the criteria specified for a correct answer.

The following guidelines can be used in scoring certain kinds of questions that are asked frequently throughout the tests.

1. When a question asks for a description of a procedure, the answer should list the operations or steps required to carry out that procedure in a manner that could be replicated.
2. When a question asks for an example that describes a procedure or technique, the answer must include a specific example describing the steps involved in implementing that procedure or technique.
3. When the question asks for a paradigm of a procedure or technique, the correct symbols and their explanations must be included. If the question asks for a paradigm showing an example, the symbols of the paradigm must be drawn correctly, and the explanation of the symbols must be stated in relation to a specific example.
4. When a question asks for a description of the effects of a certain procedure, the answer must describe the expected results of using that procedure.
5. When a question asks for an example that describes the effects of a certain procedure, the results of that procedure must be stated in relation to information based on a specific example. When a case example is given, the answer must be stated in relation to information obtained from that example.
6. When a question asks for an evaluation of the effectiveness of a certain procedure or technique, the answer must state a specific criterion for determining whether or not the procedure or technique accomplished its intended goal.

The following presents several examples of completely correct, partially correct, and completely incorrect answers to the same question to illustrate some of the points discussed above.

Question: Describe the positive reinforcement procedure and its effect on the strength of a response. (2 points)

Correct answer: The presentation of an object or event following a response (procedure) that increases the strength of that response (effect). (2 points)

Partially correct answer: Present a positive reinforcer to someone immediately after he performs the target behavior (procedure). Its effect is to modify that behavior. (1 point)

Incorrect answer: 1. Indicate reinforcer before desired behavior to entice person to act in desired way. 2. Give positive reinforcer immediately after behavior as a reward. (0 points)

The value of each question reflects the number of components required for a complete answer. In the above example, the total number of points possible for a completely correct answer is 2—1 point for the correctly stated procedure and 1 point for the correctly stated effect. The first answer above received 2 points. The second answer was only half correct; therefore, it received 1 point. The third answer was incorrect and received 0 points. Point values are specified beside each question.

The acceptable score for each test was established as 90 percent of the questions answered correctly. This is indicated as the *criterion score* shown at the bottom of each test.

RECOMMENDATIONS FOR
INSTRUCTOR USE OF THIS BOOK

A variety of instructional formats can be utilized with this book. The instructor can use the book by itself or with supplementary readings. We recommend that chapters be assigned in sequential order to be completed by the student prior to class sessions. In some cases, however, instructors may assign chapters in a different order. For example, some instructors prefer to teach negative reinforcement after positive reinforcement. Since negative reinforcement is often a difficult concept for students to learn, we have presented it as Chapter 13, after the student has had a chance to master the other basic principles. In our experience, this order provides an effective way of teaching the principles.

The instructor can use class time to clarify, elaborate, and discuss the chapters and readings. Class time can also be used for demonstrations and practice skill sessions that allow students to participate in role-plays involving applications of principles and techniques.

Students can report their pretest and post-test scores each week and chart them over the period of the course. The instructor can require students to retake each deficient post-test until 90 percent criterion or better is achieved.

An alternative format requires students to complete chapter pretests and read the chapters outside of class. Students take the chapter post-tests in class, either scoring their own papers, exchanging papers for grading, or handing them in for scoring by the instructor.

The course pretest can either be administered during the first class session or be assigned for the students to complete outside of class. The course post-test can be used as a final exam for the course, either to be taken in class or completed at home.

The instructor can use additional readings in both basic and applied research to supplement this book and can draw from the suggested readings included at the end of each chapter.

INTRODUCTION

Mrs. Drake complained to a practitioner at a community mental health center that she found it impossible to discipline her nine-year-old son, Stephen. He frequently hit his younger sister, Dianne, making her cry and inflicting bruises. He sometimes broke her toys during these incidents. When Mrs. Drake intervened to stop Stephen from hitting Dianne, Stephen cursed and kicked Mrs. Drake. Verbal reprimands, threats, and attempts to physically punish Stephen failed to eliminate his undesired behaviors.

The practitioner instructed Mrs. Drake to observe and record situations in which the hitting occurred. Mrs. Drake reported that Dianne often teased or made faces at Stephen prior to his hitting her. Mrs. Drake's report also indicated that she spent most of her time in the evenings trying to discipline Stephen. She said that their family life was a shambles and she dreaded coming home from work.

Treatment consisted of Mrs. Drake telling Dianne to stop teasing and making faces at Stephen with the contingency arranged that if she teased and made faces, she would lose privileges for the day, such as watching television or having a bedtime snack. On two subsequent occasions, Dianne lost television privileges and a bedtime snack. After these two experiences, Dianne stopped teasing and making faces at Stephen.

The practitioner also instructed Mrs. Drake to tell Stephen to go to his room when he hit Dianne. If he refused to obey, Mrs. Drake would physically carry or move Stephen to his room, where he was required to remain by himself for 15 minutes. If he kicked or cursed Mrs. Drake, the time was extended five minutes. If he screamed or made loud noises while in his room, the time was also extended five minutes.

The first time Mrs. Drake took Stephen to his room, he kicked and cursed. He also screamed while in the room. Stephen remained in his room for 25 minutes. The same thing happened the second time. The third time Mrs. Drake instituted the procedure, Stephen stopped kicking and cursing her. The fourth time, Stephen went to his room by himself and remained there quietly until his time was up. After the fifth time the procedure was employed, Stephen no longer hit his sister.

1

In order to develop positive interactions between Mrs. Drake and Stephen, the practitioner instructed her to spend more leisure time with Stephen. Mrs. Drake identified activities that Stephen liked, such as playing cards with her. She played cards with him each evening. She also was instructed to spend more time doing fun things with Stephen and Dianne together. The goal was to balance the amount of time Mrs. Drake spent in pleasant activities with each child and the amount of time she spent with them as a family.

This case illustrates the application of the behavior modification approach to improve family relationships. Behavior modification is a humanistic approach that emphasizes

- positive behavioral changes, as well as reducing problematic behaviors;
- active participation of the individual in problem definition, goal setting, intervention planning, implementation, monitoring, and evaluation;
- accountability of the practitioner in working to improve the individual's situation;
- individualized behavioral-change programs; and
- assessment and evaluation measures that allow the individual and practitioner to determine the effects of the behavioral-change program.

Behavior modification has achieved tremendous popularity during the past decade. Its historical roots, however, can be traced to the early part of the century. Names like Pavlov, Watson, Skinner, and Wolpe have been associated with bold new approaches to understanding and influencing human behavior. Application of behavior-modification techniques has become increasingly widespread as practitioners in growing numbers acknowledge the place of this technology in solving human problems.

Behavior modification is the application of principles and techniques derived from the experimental analysis of behavior to a wide range of human problems. Behavior modification involves the systematic study of behavior and its determinants using objective techniques and empirically testing their effects. It is results-oriented, in that behaviors are monitored to determine the direction and extent of change. Behavior modification as presented in this book emphasizes the principles of operant conditioning, the concepts of social learning theory, and the methods of applied behavior analysis. The respondent or classical conditioning approach is also covered, but to a lesser extent.

The terms behavior modification and behavior therapy are often used interchangeably, and the distinction between them in much of the literature has become blurred. Historically, however, behavior therapy referred to treatment methods based primarily on classical conditioning, and the term behavior modification typically referred to behavioral change programs based on operant conditioning methods. In practice, the term behavior therapy connotes the provision of behavior modification services to individuals in a client-therapist setting. The term behavior modification refers to the application of behavioral analysis and change techniques to a broader range of problems and settings. It has been used in a variety of institutions and environments, including mental hospitals, community mental health centers, correctional facilities, family service agencies, child welfare agencies, industrial settings, schools, neighborhoods and other open community settings.

Behavior modification techniques have been applied to the entire spectrum of age groups, from infants to geriatric citizens. They have been used to remedy dysfunction in inpatient and outpatient treatment settings, as well as in preventive programs such as parent training, classroom management, cardiovascular risk reduction and promotion of healthy lifestyles. The current trend in self-help books based on behavioral interventions has expanded the resources available for individuals who wish to modify their own behaviors. It is too soon to draw conclusions regarding the effectiveness of these self-help materials, however. Nevertheless, these books represent the behavioral contribution to the exploding self-help movement.

A broad range of human problems has been subjected to behavioral analysis, including overeating, smoking, drug and alcohol abuse, stuttering, enuresis, encopresis, marital and family concerns, anxiety, depression, phobias, nail biting, child management problems in school and home, and sexual dysfunction. There has been considerable interest among the public in methods of improving self-control and personal effectiveness, especially in problems of interpersonal communication such as nonassertiveness. Relaxation methods based on the behavioral approach, including biofeedback, are being used for stress management and tension reduction. Behavioral medicine has emerged as an interdisciplinary field investigating and treating physical health problems such as asthma, insomnia, migraine headaches, hypertension, colitis, ulcers, and back pain.

Once concentrated primarily in closed institutions, behavioral practitioners can now be found in almost every kind of agency, organization, institutional, and community setting. This increased range of applied settings has been accompanied by greater sophistication and sensitivity of behavioral practitioners to organizational and agency policies, standards, and norms that can facilitate the integration and optimal use of these techniques.

The behavior modification approach differs from other psychotherapeutic approaches popular today. There are several distinguishing features of the behavioral approach:

1. Focus on the present. Examination of current behaviors and their controlling conditions are emphasized, as opposed to preoccupation with early historical or developmental events in the individual's life.

2. Assessment of the individual's behaviors and their controlling conditions. Analysis of the client's situation focuses on behaviors defined as deviant, maladaptive, inappropriate, undesired, or problematic. These target behaviors are delineated, along with relevant antecedents and consequences. Interpretations of the client's personality or character are not considered in a behavioral assessment.

3. Focus on altering environmental variables. Changes in the individual's behavior are brought about by influencing observable, measurable aspects of the environment, rather than trying to alter the individual's personality.

4. Emphasis on observable, measurable behaviors. Vague terms, diagnostic labels, and personality constructs are avoided unless they can be supported by observable, measurable behaviors.

5. Focus on relatively brief, time-limited intervention programs. Long-term, overdependent relationships between client and practitioner are generally discouraged.

6. Emphasis on accountability, evaluation, and measurement. Behavioral goals are delineated and progress toward their achievement is monitored. Evaluation of behavioral change is determined by comparing post-intervention measures with baseline data.

Human service workers are constantly on the front lines facing problems that require practical solutions. Increasing concern about the effectiveness of social services, mental health, mental retardation, education, corrections, and physical health programs has created a demand for innovative methodologies and approaches whose results can be systematically evaluated. Funding sources of social programs have placed greater emphasis on accountability and cost-effectiveness. The behavior modification approach addresses these concerns and has attracted many professionals who have been searching for both conceptual rigor and practical interventions.

The goals of behavior modification are both to improve the human condition and to advance the scientific knowledge base of human behavior and its determinants. Behavioral principles have been tested empirically with a variety of human problems and situations. The accumulated knowledge of these applications constitutes the current "state-of-the-art" in the field, and its basic features are encompassed in this book.

In this book, we present the basic principles of behavior modification in a wide range of human service applications. In addition, we provide a method for organizing these principles into an integrated framework for

- assessing an individual's problem or situation,
- formulating goals,
- planning and implementing a behavioral change program, and
- evaluating its effectiveness.

Integration of the behavioral principles with this problem-solving framework will facilitate the thoughtful, professional application of behavior modification techniques and procedures.

1

SPECIFYING BEHAVIOR

---

objectives

After completing this chapter, you should be able to:

1. describe events according to observable behaviors or responses,
2. discriminate between vague and behaviorally specific statements,
3. rewrite vague statements into behaviorally specific ones, and
4. rewrite a statement to include a frequency measure of response strength.

Shortly after the midterm grades came out, a teacher referred Harold to the school social worker, describing Harold as being 'inattentive in the classroom, poorly motivated, and having a negative attitude toward learning.'

PRETEST QUESTIONS

Chapter 1

(2) 1. State two essential criteria for specifying a response.

(6) 2. A. Indicate with a (+) which of the following statements are written in behaviorally specific terms and with a (−) statements which are vague and require further specification.

2. B.   After completing 2-A above, rewrite in specific terms only those statements in which the responses are not described behaviorally.

    a.   Ted saw three clients today and made four phone calls.

    b.   Bob is becoming a drug addict.

    c.   Bruce kissed Sally on the cheek.

    d.   She acted out her anger toward him.

(1) 3.   Name the most commonly used measure of response strength.

OBSERVABLE BEHAVIOR

The behavioral practitioner strives for specificity in describing the movements and actions of individuals. These activities are called **behaviors** or **responses,** terms which will be used interchangeably throughout the text. A response is defined as any observable, measurable movement or activity of an individual. Responses can be verbal or nonverbal. Examples of verbal responses are screaming, stuttering, saying "thank you," lecturing to an audience, and laughing. Nonverbal responses include smiling, trembling, throwing a baseball, and raising an eyebrow. We are interested in observable behaviors because we can describe them and measure them.

Human service practitioners frequently encounter problems that are presented in vague, nonspecific language. For example, Mrs. Foster complained that her husband was "hard to get along with because of his insecurity." The behavioral practitioner attempts to delineate the individual's problem in words that clearly specify verbal and nonverbal behaviors. Thus, Mrs. Foster was asked to describe her husband's speech and nonverbal behaviors that were related to his being "insecure." She specified his behaviors as follows: statements such as "I can't earn enough money to keep you happy" and "Everyone is getting promoted except me"; and nonverbal behaviors such as walking slouched with his head down and writing 25 letters each week in response to jobs advertised in the newspaper.

In order to clearly specify an event, the individual's behavior should be described in *positive, observable terms*. Negatively stated descriptions such as "Harold does not turn in his class assignments" are insufficient because they fail to describe what Harold *is* doing in the problematic situation. An appropriate description of Harold's problematic behavior might be, "Harold looks at comic books instead of writing his assignment."

A description of an individual's behavior in observable terms specifies what the person *says* or *does*. The use of unobservable constructs such as "ego impairment," "improved self-image," or "underlying hostility" is insufficient for measurably describing behavior. These terms do not contribute essential information about the behavior. If such terms are used, they should be accompanied by behaviorally specific descriptions of what the individual says or does that leads to their use. If a child is described as exhibiting "underlying hostility," it is unclear exactly what the child says or does, and his or her behavior is open to many interpretations. The label "underlying hostility" may be an interpretation or a conclusion drawn on the basis of the child's having set three fires, for example. The treatment issue could be formulated in terms of whether to modify behaviors related to the fire setting or to explore the "underlying hostility."

This book focuses on specification and analysis of the client's behavior and its controlling conditions, so that modification or treatment plans can be formulated on the basis of measurable, observable events. The use of hypothetical, unobservable constructs and inferences should be avoided. If such shorthand labels are used, they should be accompanied by behavioral descriptions.

CASE STUDY 1

Behavioral Assessment of Drug Abuse

Harold, a twelve-year-old junior high school student, started smoking marijuana six months ago at a party given by one of his friends. He enjoyed that experience and continued his experimentation with other drugs, including amphetamines and barbiturates. During the past few months, Harold has failed to complete his class assignments, sometimes handing in a blank sheet of paper. His midterm report card showed four Fs and one C in a crafts course. Harold's parents, Mr. and Mrs. Townsend, were concerned that he might drop out of school or not pass to the next level. About this time, Mrs. Townsend found a marijuana cigarette and some of her diet pills in Harold's desk drawer. When confronted with this evidence, Harold admitted to taking drugs, but argued that they did not interfere with his functioning in school or at home.

Shortly after the midterm grades came out, a teacher referred Harold to the school social worker, describing Harold as being "inattentive in the classroom, poorly motivated, and having a negative attitude toward learning." He was failing most of his classes.

Harold complained to the school social worker that his parents frequently grounded him, nagged him, withheld his allowance, and denied him privileges such as watching television and going out with his friends. Upon further questioning, Harold revealed that his parents' disciplinary measures were applied because of his failing grades. Harold admitted that he, too, was worried about flunking out of school, and conceded that his drug taking might be interfering with his studying. When asked to describe his drug taking, Harold indicated that he smoked pot regularly with his friends and took pep pills and downers occasionally. Harold indicated that when he started studying, his friends often invited him over to listen to records and get stoned. He also spent many evenings at his girlfriend's home, and they usually began the evening by taking some pills. When he was home alone, Harold would look in his notebook for his class assignments, smoke two or three joints before beginning them, and complete only part of his assignments or none of them at all.

After several sessions, Harold said that he was beginning to recognize the relationship between his poor school performance and drug taking.

CLARIFYING VAGUE TERMS AND
FUZZY LANGUAGE

In Case Study 1, the teacher complained that Harold was "inattentive and poorly motivated" in class. The social worker wanted to know in specific terms how Harold was "inattentive and poorly motivated." Did he walk around the room? Did he throw papers on the floor? Did he laugh at the teacher? Did he make faces? A more acceptable description would be, "Harold stared at the ceiling in class and completed only one out of ten math problems." Thus, a stranger reading this description is provided with a concrete, observable instance of Harold's "inattentive and poorly motivated" classroom behavior. Similarly, statements such as "Greg refused to take his medicine as prescribed" or "Jane denied spreading the rumor about Carol's affair" fail to describe what these individuals said or did in those situations. Refusing to take his medicine could mean that Greg said, "I refuse to take my medicine," or that he emptied the bottle of pills in the trash.

Vague language referring to an individual's actions should be defined in behaviorally specific terms. This usually requires reporting actual observations of the individual's behavior in the given situation. How precisely one should specify a response depends on the description required to set a goal for modifying it. An adequate description provides enough detail about the form or appearance of the response so that other individuals can accurately identify the response.

MEASURING RESPONSE STRENGTH

A precise description of a response includes a measure of **response strength.** The strength of a response indicates (1) how often the response occurs within a given time period (response rate), (2) how long the response lasts (duration), (3) how intense the response is (intensity), or (4) how long the interval is between presentation of an event and performance of the response (latency).

Response rate or frequency per time unit is the primary measure of response strength. Response rate or frequency indicates how often or how many times the response occurs within a given time period. For example, "Mrs. Jones washed her hands eight times in the past hour." Other measures of response strength include **duration** (how long a response lasts), **intensity** (the severity of a response), and **latency** (the interval between presentation of a certain event and occurrence of the response). For example, "The dinner bell rang and Bert came to the table within ten seconds" (latency); "Sam jogged for 20 minutes" (duration). Sometimes two or more of these measures are used to describe a particular response; for example, "Mrs. Lake cried in her room for over 30 minutes (duration) three times this week (rate)." Measures of response strength will be discussed further in Chapter 9.

SUMMARY

1. Response and behavior are equivalent terms.
2. A response is defined as any observable, measurable, verbal or nonverbal movement or activity.
3. An observable response specifies what an individual says or does in positive terms.
4. If vague terms are used in labeling unobservable events, behaviorally specific descriptions should be included.
5. Four measures of response strength are rate (frequency/time unit), duration, latency, and intensity.

POST-TEST QUESTIONS

(10) 1. A. Indicate with a (+) which of the following statements are written in behaviorally specific terms, and with a (−) the statements that are vague and require further specification.

    2. B. After completing 1-A above, rewrite in specific terms only those statements in which the responses are not described behaviorally.

    a. Eddy took two cans of beer from the refrigerator.

    b. Johnny expressed his feelings of inadequacy at the ball game.

    c. Norman showed hostile feelings toward his probation officer this week.

d. Mr. Smith asserted his authority over use of the car.

e. He thinks of his girlfriend often.

f. Mr. Foster said, "I can't earn enough money to make you happy."

(1) 2. In Case Study 1, pages 7–8, Harold is described as having a "negative attitude toward learning." Specify a behavior that might have led the teacher to describe him in that way.

(1) 3. Rewrite the following statement to include a frequency-per-time-unit (rate) measure of response strength: Mr. Foster ordered a drink from the bar.

2

POSITIVE REINFORCEMENT

objectives

After completing this chapter, you should be able to:

1. specify a target behavior and its appropriate baseline measure,
2. give an example illustrating the positive reinforcement procedure and its effect on the frequency of a response,
3. describe how baseline data are used to determine if a stimulus acts as a positive reinforcer,
4. indicate when a positive reinforcer should be delivered to maximize its effectiveness, and
5. draw a paradigm showing how positive reinforcement can be used to increase the frequency of a response.

Caseworker to his supervisor: My client, Mr. Mosley, keeps arriving late for his appointments. It's ruining my schedule.

Supervisor: What are you doing about it?

Caseworker: When he arrives, I tell him how glad I am to see him and then I add on extra time at the end of the session.

Supervisor: No wonder he keeps coming late!

Chapter 2

(1) 1. In order to maximize the effectiveness of a positive reinforcer for a specific response, when should the positive reinforcer be delivered?

(4) 2. List the four outcomes or directions in which a target behavior can be modified.

(1) 3. It has been demonstrated that presentation of a certain event following a behavior can increase the likelihood that the behavior will recur. Name the behavioral principle to which this statement refers.

(3) 4. In the example that begins this chapter, what behavior did the caseworker positively reinforce? What were the reinforcers?

REINFORCING STIMULI

A **stimulus** (plural, stimuli) can be any object or event. It can include physical features of the environment (for example, a telephone ringing), as well as an individual's own behavior or the behavior of others (for example, a smile). A stimulus can precede or follow a response. In this chapter, we are concerned with a **positive reinforcer,** the stimulus that follows a response and increases its strength or likelihood of occurrence.

Positive reinforcement is a procedure used to increase the strength of a response. A positive reinforcer is a stimulus presented after a response that increases the strength of the response. The reinforcer is presented *contingent on* performance of the response, that is, the response must be emitted or performed in order for the reinforcer to be delivered. Thus, the principle of positive reinforcement states that the strength of a behavior can be increased by certain consequences, namely, presentation of a stimulus that acts as a positive reinforcer. A response that is positively reinforced is more likely to be performed again under similar conditions.

A **behavioral paradigm** is a stimulus-response model using notational symbols to depict relationships between stimuli and responses. Behavioral paradigms are used throughout this book to provide schematic representations of behavioral concepts and procedures. Paradigms can be used to analyze client problems in behavioral terms. They visually depict relationships that may not be readily apparent from verbal descriptions.

The following behavioral paradigm depicts the positive reinforcement procedure:

Effect: The response (R) increases in strength.

The S^+ in the above paradigm indicates a stimulus (S) whose presentation increases (+) the strength of a response it follows. If frequency is the measure of response strength, the effect of the positive reinforcement procedure is that the response (R) increases in frequency.

Behaviors that are conditioned or learned in this manner are called **operant behaviors.** An operant behavior is controlled or governed by its consequences. The individual *operates* or acts on the environment to produce those consequences. This is in contrast with **respondent behavior,** which is elicited by a specific antecedent or event occurring prior to the response. Respondent behavior will be discussed in Chapter 14.

EXAMPLES OF POSITIVE REINFORCEMENT

You may have observed from your own experience that if someone performs a certain behavior and it is followed by a pleasant event, he or she will tend to perform that behavior on other similar occasions. For example, Fred tells jokes when he is with his friends. His friends laugh at his jokes. If Fred tells jokes again under similar circumstances, his friends' laughter served as a positive reinforcer for Fred's joke telling. In paradigm form the above example would look like this:

Effect: Fred's joke telling increases in frequency; that is, the likelihood is increased that he will tell jokes again.

Another example shows how parents can use positive reinforcement to increase performance of household chores. For the past three months, Gary has only washed the dinner dishes once each week. A plan is arranged whereby each time Gary washes the dinner dishes he receives 75¢. The money serves as a positive reinforcer for dishwashing if the frequency of Gary's dishwashing increases. The response in this example is Gary's washing the dinner dishes. As long as the money serves as a positive reinforcer, Gary will continue to wash the dishes. In subsequent chapters we will examine some of the factors involved in maintaining response strength without having to present the reinforcer each time the response occurs.

In the example at the beginning of this chapter, the caseworker positively reinforced Mr. Mosley's coming late. By greeting him warmly and adding extra time on to the session, the caseworker increased the likelihood that Mr. Mosley would arrive late again. The supervisor recognized the reinforcing effect of the caseworker's behaviors on the client's lateness.

Some common positive reinforcers include food, water, sex, attention, praise, and money. Although stimuli may differ in their ability to serve as positive reinforcers for different individuals, almost any object or event can act as a positive reinforcer for specific responses under certain conditions. Even stimuli that appear to be unpleasant can serve as positive reinforcers. For example, Ed and Charlie were climbing on the bed. Their grandmother came in and shouted, "Boys! Don't jump on that bed! You'll get hurt." Ed and Charlie laughed and started jumping. Grandmother repeated her warning and continued to shout at them while they kept laughing and jumping. In paradigm form the example would look like this:

$$R \xrightarrow{\text{is followed by}} S^+$$
Jumping on bed   is followed by   grandmother shouting

Effect: Jumping on the bed increases in frequency. The likelihood is increased that this behavior will be performed again.

REINFORCERS AND REWARDS

The term **reward** is sometimes inappropriately used as synonymous with the term positive reinforcer. A reward is an object or event that is identified as pleasant, satisfying, desirable, and that the individual will seek out or approach. Rewards can, and frequently do, serve as positive reinforcers. A stimulus is only called a positive reinforcer, however, if its presentation increases the strength of the response it follows. For example, suppose that Gary's dishwashing did not increase over the initial rate of once per week when he was paid 75¢. His mother would conclude that the money was not a positive reinforcer for Gary's dishwashing.

The paradigm below shows a response followed by a stimulus (S) that fails to serve as a positive reinforcer. The stimulus is neutral in regard to increasing the strength of the response.

$$R \xrightarrow{\text{is followed by}} S$$
Dishwashing   is followed by   75 ¢

Effect: Response rate remains the same. The money was not a positive reinforcer for Gary's dishwashing.

When Gary's mother followed his dishwashing with praise, however, Gary's dishwashing markedly increased. Praise was a positive reinforcer for dishwashing.

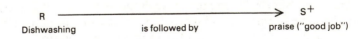

$$R \xrightarrow{\text{is followed by}} S^+$$
Dishwashing   is followed by   praise ("good job")

Effect: Gary's dishwashing increased in frequency.

FACTORS THAT INFLUENCE REINFORCER EFFECTIVENESS

A number of factors can influence the effectiveness of a positive reinforcer: timing, deprivation, satiation, size, amount, type, and quality.

When to Deliver a Positive Reinforcer. A positive reinforcer is most effective when delivered or made available *immediately after* the response to be increased. If you give Nathan an ice cream cone *before* he mows the lawn, it is less likely that he will mow the lawn than if you give him the ice cream cone *after* he mows the lawn. If you wait too long to give Nathan his ice cream cone for mowing the lawn, however, you might find him less willing to mow the lawn again. A delay in reinforcement could also result in unintentionally strengthening a behavior occurring at the time reinforcement is delivered, rather than strengthening the desired behavior. Therefore, in order to maximize the effectiveness of a positive reinforcer, the reinforcer should be presented not only *after* the response has occurred, but *immediately* after.

Deprivation and satiation. **Deprivation** refers to a condition in which a reinforcer has been unavailable to an individual for a specified period of time; for example, Sam has not had dessert for 8 days; Sheila has gone without sleep for 24 hours. **Satiation** refers to a condition in which a reinforcer has been continuously available to an individual until it loses its reinforcing effect.

For example, if you offer Nathan an ice cream cone for mowing the lawn and he has just eaten a triple scoop ice cream cone, the likelihood that he will mow the lawn will be low. He is satiated on ice cream. If, however, he has not been allowed to have ice cream for several days, the likelihood that he will mow the lawn for an ice cream cone will be higher. He has been deprived of ice cream. In general, a reinforcer is most effective in increasing the strength of a response when a high level of deprivation exists, and less effective during a low level of deprivation. A reinforcer is ineffective in increasing the strength of a response when the individual is satiated with regard to that reinforcer.

Size, amount, type, and quality of the reinforcer. The effectiveness of a stimulus as a positive reinforcer may be related to its size, amount, type, or quality. A candy bar may increase the frequency of 10-year-old Tom's pulling weeds, but it probably will not increase the frequency of 14-year-old Harry's doing the same job. The type of reinforcer that is appropriate for a 10 year old may not be appropriate for a 14 year old.

The importance of size or amount of reinforcement becomes evident when we observe that Tom pulls weeds for a candy bar, but one candy bar will not serve as a positive reinforcer for harder jobs such as raking and bagging leaves or shoveling snow from the driveway. For $15.00, however, the likelihood is greatly increased that Tom will rake leaves or shovel the snow. An individual's estimate of the effort required to perform a response can influence the effectiveness of the reinforcer. For ex-

15

ample, most people probably would not walk from downtown Los Angeles to Santa Monica for $15.00, although many would eagerly attempt to do so for $15,000. On the other hand, a cross country runner might accept $5.00 to walk this route.

HOW TO IDENTIFY POTENTIAL REINFORCERS

Before attempting to increase the strength of a behavior through positive reinforcement, you must determine what stimulus to use as a positive reinforcer. There are several ways to identify stimuli that could act as positive reinforcers for an individual: (1) observe what the individual does when choosing an activity, (2) ask the individual what stimuli have served as positive reinforcers in the past, and (3) give the

FIGURE 2-1   Reinforcement survey schedule (RSS)[a]

NAME   DATE

The items in this questionnaire refer to things and experiences that may give joy or other pleasurable feelings. Check each item in the column that describes how much pleasure it gives you nowadays.

	Not at All	A Little	A Fair Amount	Much	Very Much
1. Eating					
a. ice cream					
b. candy					
c. fruit					
2. Beverages					
3. Alcoholic Beverages					
4. Beautiful Women					
5. Handsome Men					
6. Solving Problems					
7. Listening to Music					
a. classical					
b. country western					
c. jazz					
8. Watching Sports					
a. football					
b. baseball					
c. basketball					
9. Looking at Interesting Buildings					
10. Looking at Beautiful Scenery					
11. TV, Movies, Radio					
12. Like to Sing					
13. Being Praised					
14. Peace and Quiet					

[a]Reprinted with permissions of authors and publisher from: Cautela, J. and Kastenbaum, R.A. "A Reinforcement Survey Schedule for Use in Therapy, Training, and Research." *Psychological Reports,* 1967, *20,* 1115-1130.

FIGURE 2-1 (cont'd.)

Situations I Would Like to Be In

How much would you enjoy being in each of the following situations?

1. You have just completed a difficult job. Your superior comes by and praises you highly for a job well done. He also makes it clear that such good work is going to be rewarded very soon.
   not at all ( )   a little ( )   a fair amount ( )   much ( )   very much ( )

2. You are walking along a mountain pathway with your dog by your side. You notice attractive lakes, streams, flowers, and trees. You think to yourself, "It's great to be alive on a day like this, and to have the opportunity to wander alone out in the countryside."
   not at all ( )   a little ( )   a fair amount ( )   much ( )   very much ( )

3. You are sitting by the fireplace with your loved one. Music is playing softly on the phonograph. Your loved one gives you a tender glance and you respond with a kiss. You think to yourself how wonderful it is to care for someone and have somebody care for you.
   not at all ( )   a little ( )   a fair amount ( )   much ( )   very much ( )

Now place a check next to the number of the situation that appeals to you most.

List things you do or think about more than

5 TIMES A DAY	10 TIMES A DAY	15 TIMES A DAY	20 TIMES A DAY

individual a form to complete such as a reinforcement survey schedule. Excerpts from two such forms (Cautela & Kastenbaum, 1967; Cautela, 1977) are found in Figures 2-1 and 2-2. These forms list specific stimuli that have served as positive reinforcers for individuals, for example, various foods, entertainment, sports, hobbies, and so on. The person is asked to rate the attractiveness of each item on the reinforcement schedule. These ratings are considered in selecting stimuli that are likely to serve as positive reinforcers for the individual.

TARGET BEHAVIOR

The **target behavior**(s) is the behavior(s) to be observed or counted; it is the focus of modification. Depending on the desired behavioral change, there are four outcomes or directions in which a target behavior can be modified. Modification techniques can be applied so that a behavior is (1) acquired or established, (2) increased or strengthened, (3) maintained at a particular rate or pattern of occurrence, or (4) decreased or weakened. For example, in Fred's case, joke telling was the target behavior that was increased by his friends' laughter. Gary's dishwashing was the target behavior to be increased by paying him. With Ed and Charlie, the target behavior was jumping on the bed, which was strengthened by their grandmother's shouting.

17

FIGURE 2-2 Children's reinforcement survey schedule (CRSS)[a]

Directions:
    This is a list of many different things or activities. Explain how much you like each choice by making an "X" in the appropriate box.

    If you dislike the choice, make an "X" in the box under Dislike:

    If you like the choice, make an "X" in the box under Like:

    If the choice is something which you like very, very much, make an "X" in the box under Like Very Much:

	Dislike	Like	Like Very Much
			X

		Dislike	Like	Like Very Much
1.	Do you like candy?			
2.	Do you like fruit?			
3.	Do you like cooking?			
4.	Do you like to drink soda?			
5.	Do you like to make models?			
6.	Do you like to play with model cars and trains?			
7.	Do you like to draw and paint?			
8.	Do you like football?			
9.	Do you like basketball?			
10.	Do you like kickball?			
11.	Do you like camping?			
12.	Do you like listening to music?			
13.	Do you like singing?			
14.	Do you like fixing broken things?			
15.	Do you like having a birthday party and getting presents?			

16.	If your friend is sick, do you like to take some things to your friend's house to make your friend feel happier?			
17.	Do you like someone to take care of you when you are scared?			
18.	If you are sick, do you like people to take care of you?			

19. What do you think is the best thing about you?

_____

_____

20. What do you daydream about?

_____

_____

21. What do you do for fun?

_____

_____

22. What would you like for your birthday?

_____

_____

23. Do you have any collections? _____ If so, what do you collect?

_____

_____

ªExcerpted from Cautela, J.R., *Behavior Analysis Forms for Clinical Intervention.* Champaign, Illinois: Research Press, 1977. Reprinted with permission from Research Press. Developed in collaboration with Linda Brion-Meisels.

In this book you are learning to apply a **behavioral assessment framework** to a wide variety of situations. This framework includes specifying target behaviors, formulating goals, developing and implementing an intervention plan, and evaluating progress. The first step in behavioral assessment is to specify the target behavior in behaviorally specific terms. In the last chapter you learned how to specify behaviors that were stated in vague terms.

OBTAINING BASELINE DATA

The second step in behavioral assessment, carried out after specification of the target behavior, is to collect **baseline data.** Baseline data include specific measures of response strength that can be used in formulating goals and an intervention plan. They also provide criterias for evaluating progress in measurable terms.

Response rate or frequency of the response (per unit of time) is typically obtained as a baseline measure, and this will serve here as the focus of our discussion. For example, "Dennis completed two out of five home visits scheduled this week"; "Gary washed the dinner dishes once per week." These data are obtained during assessment and indicate the baseline rate of Dennis's completing home visits and of Gary's dishwashing, that is, the rates at which these behaviors occurred prior to the implementation of an intervention plan.

The following chart can be used to record baseline data.

DAYS	DESCRIPTION OF RESPONSE	RESPONSE STRENGTH:[a] FREQUENCY/TIME UNIT
Sun.		
Mon.		
Tues.		
Wed.		
Thurs.		
Fri.		
Sat.		
		Total: Average:

[a]Specify measure of response strength to be used. In this case, specify response strength in terms of frequency per time unit. Place a vertical mark (|) to indicate each occurrence of the target response.

A chart showing one week of Gary's baseline data would look like this:

DAYS	DESCRIPTION OF RESPONSE	RESPONSE STRENGTH: FREQUENCY/DAY
Sun.	washed dinner dishes	0
Mon.	washed dinner dishes	0
Tues.	washed dinner dishes	0
Wed.	washed dinner dishes	I
Thurs.	washed dinner dishes	0
Fri.	washed dinner dishes	0
Sat.	washed dinner dishes	0
		Total: 1 Average: 1/week

Another way of charting Gary's baseline rate of washing dinner dishes looks like this:

WEEKS	DESCRIPTION OF RESPONSE	RESPONSE STRENGTH: FREQUENCY/WEEK
1	washed dinner dishes	l
2	washed dinner dishes	l
3	washed dinner dishes	l
		Total: 3 Average: 1/week

The effect of a reinforcer on a target behavior can be evaluated by comparing the baseline rate of the behavior with its rate after delivery of the reinforcer. For example, Donna was instructed to exercise her leg every 2 hours for 12 hours each day to regain full use of the leg after surgery. Since exercising the leg was painful, Donna had only been exercising it once or twice each day. To increase Donna's exercising, her mother decided to give her stars on a chart as reinforcers for leg exercises. These stars could then be traded in for something Donna would choose.

To determine if the stars were reinforcers for Donna's exercising, her baseline rate of exercising would be compared with her exercise rate after Donna received stars. The baseline rate indicated that Donna exercised her leg only once a day over a 7-day period prior to receiving stars. The chart below shows one week of baseline data recorded for Donna's exercising:

DAYS	DESCRIPTION OF RESPONSE	RESPONSE STRENGTH: FREQUENCY/DAY
Sun.	exercised her leg	l
Mon.	exercised her leg	ll
Tues.	exercised her leg	l
Wed.	exercised her leg	0
Thurs.	exercised her leg	l
Fri.	exercised her leg	l
Sat.	exercised her leg	l
		Total: 7 Average: 1/day

After receiving stars for exercising, Donna exercised her leg 5 times a day over a 3-week period. These data provided measures of the effectiveness of stars as positive reinforcers for Donna's exercising. A chart of Donna's exercising after receiving stars for doing so looked like this:

DAYS	DESCRIPTION OF RESPONSE	RESPONSE STRENGTH: FREQUENCY/DAY
Sun.	exercised her leg	ЦНТ
Mon.	exercised her leg	ЦНТ
Tues.	exercised her leg	ЦНТ I
Wed.	exercised her leg	ЦНТ
Thurs.	exercised her leg	ЦНТ
Fri.	exercised her leg	IIII
Sat.	exercised her leg	ЦНТ
		Total: 35 Average: 5/day

A weekly chart of Donna's exercising with reinforcement over a 3-week period looks like this:

WEEKS	DESCRIPTION OF RESPONSE	RESPONSE STRENGTH: FREQUENCY/WEEK
1st	exercised her leg	ЦНТ ЦНТ ЦНТ ЦНТ ЦНТ IIII ЦНТ
2nd	exercised her leg	IIII ЦНТ ЦНТ ЦНТ I IIII ЦНТ I
3rd	exercised her leg	ЦНТ I ЦНТ I ЦНТ ЦНТ ЦНТ I ЦНТ I ЦНТ I
		Total: 104 Average: 35/week

The above charts show that stars served as reinforcers for Donna's exercising.

REINFORCEMENT OF BEHAVIOR: SOCIAL, TANGIBLE, AND SELF-INITIATED

Some people have learned to reinforce their own behaviors with praise ("I did a good job") or other positive statements about themselves ("That was a difficult task, but I did it.") For others, completing a job is the most important reinforcer. These individuals appear to require fewer external reinforcers than others to maintain desired behaviors. They are often described as self-starters, high achievers, highly motivated, or as deriving great satisfaction from their work.

Other people seem to require frequent external approval or tangible demonstrations of their worth, or their productivity decreases. For example, some children have difficulty paying attention to the teacher in school. Points, privileges, praise, or tangible reinforcers can be effective in teaching these children to attend to their teachers so they can learn in school. Other children find schoolwork itself reinforcing, so that task completion and teacher feedback are their major reinforcers. These differences in reinforcer effectiveness for various behaviors may be related to the reinforcement practices of parents and others, as well as individual differences.

SUMMARY

1. A stimulus can be any object or event. It can include physical features of the environment, as well as an individual's own behavior or the behavior of others.

2. A positive reinforcer is a stimulus presented after a response that increases the strength of the response. Frequency per time unit is the most common measure of response strength. A response that has been increased in frequency or strengthened through reinforcement is more likely to be performed again under similar conditions.

3. A stimulus serves as a positive reinforcer for a particular response only if it increases the strength of that response.

4. Positive reinforcement is a procedure to increase the strength of a response. The positive reinforcement procedure consists of presenting a positive reinforcer contingent on the performance of a response.

5. A stimulus that serves as a positive reinforcer for one person's behavior may be ineffective when used with someone else. Stimuli that appear rewarding may not be positively reinforcing for particular responses. Stimuli that appear aversive or unpleasant, on the other hand, may serve as positive reinforcers.

6. The effectiveness of a stimulus as a positive reinforcer is influenced by the following factors: timing, deprivation, satiation, size, amount, type, and quality.

7. The first step in behavioral assessment is to specify the target response in behaviorally specific terms. The second step is to collect baseline data, such as response rate. Baseline data should be systematically recorded to obtain measures of response strength, prior to intervening.

8. Modification techniques can be applied so that a behavior is (1) acquired or established, (2) increased or strengthened, (3) maintained at a particular rate or pattern of occurrence, and (4) decreased or weakened.

SUGGESTED READINGS

BACHRACH, J., ERWIN, W. J., and MOHR, J. P., "The Control of Eating Behavior in an Anorexic by Operant Conditioning Techniques," in Ullmann, L. P., and Krasner, L. (Eds.), *Case Studies in Behavior Modification* (New York: Holt, Rinehart & Winston, 1965), pp. 153–163.

CAUTELA, J. R., "Reinforcement Survey Schedule (RSS)," in J. R. Cautela, *Behavior Analysis Forms for Clinical Intervention* (Champaign, Ill.: Research Press, 1977), pp. 45–52.

CAUTELA, J. R., "Children's Reinforcement Survey Schedule (CRSS)," in J. R. Cautela, *Behavior Analysis Forms for Social Intervention* (Champaign, Ill.: Research Press, 1977), pp. 53–62.

CAUTELA, J. and KASTENBAUM, R. A., "A Reinforcement Survey Schedule for Use in Therapy, Training and Research," *Psychological Reports,* 20 (1967), 1115–1130.

GEWIRTZ, J. L., and BAER, D. M., "Deprivation and Satiation of Social Reinforcers as Drive Conditions," *Journal of Abnormal and Social Psychology,* 57 (1958), 165–172.

HAUGHTON, E., and AYLLON, T., "Production and Elimination of Symptomatic Behavior," in Ullmann, L. P., and Krasner, L. (Eds.), *Case Studies in Behavior Modification* (New York: Holt, Rinehart & Winston, 1965), pp. 94–98.

PHILLIPS, D., FISCHER, S.C., and SINGH, R., "A Children's Reinforcement Survey Schedule," *Journal of Behavior Therapy and Experimental Psychiatry,* 8(2) (June 1977), 131–134.

SKINNER, B. F., *Behavior of Organisms.* (Englewood Cliffs, N.J.: Prentice-Hall, Inc., 1938), Chapter 8, 308–340.

SKINNER, B. F., *Science and Human Behavior* (New York: Free Press, 1953), Chapter 6, 91–106.

POST-TEST QUESTIONS

(2) 1. Define the positive reinforcement procedure and its effect on the strength of a response.

(2) 2. Give one example of an object or event that you think acts as a positive reinforcer for you. State your proof.

(3) 3. From Case Study 1, pages 7–8, draw a paradigm showing how positive reinforcement could be used to increase the frequency of Harold's completing his class assignments, labeling the appropriate components. What evidence could be used to evaluate the effect of this procedure?

(4) 4. Rewrite the following statements, specifying the target behaviors and indicating the baseline rates.

    a.   Hank is always annoying his brother.

    b.   Mary was often depressed.

(2) 5. Correct these statements so that the effectiveness of the candy bar and the movies as positive reinforcers can be maximized.

    a.   Mrs. Jones gave Edward a candy bar and asked him to take her dog for a walk.

    b.   Harvey washed his father's car and his father took him to the movies three weeks later.

(1) 6. Lillian goes shopping immediately after she completes her housework. How could baseline data be used to determine if going shopping served as a positive reinforcer for doing housework?

EXTINCTION

objectives

After completing this chapter, you should be able to:

1. give an example of a behavior that decreases in frequency through application of an extinction procedure,
2. determine if a given stimulus serves as a positive reinforcer for a specific response,
3. given a case example, describe how positive reinforcement strengthens both desired and undesired behaviors,
4. describe the effect of extinction on the rate of a target response, and
5. describe how spontaneous recovery is considered in an intervention plan.

When Carla's mother told her to put her toys away, Carla screamed. Mrs. Hernandez would attempt to placate her by promising to buy her new clothes and putting Carla's toys away herself.

Mrs. Hernandez was instructed to stop making promises to Carla when she screamed about putting away her toys, and to walk away from Carla when she did this. She was told that Carla's screaming might get worse before it got better, but that if she held firm, Carla's screaming would gradually decrease. Mrs. Hernandez carried out these instructions for five days, during which time Carla's screaming gradually decreased. By the sixth day, Carla no longer screamed when told to put her toys away.

Chapter 3

(4) 1. Renumber the following steps so that they are in the correct order to carry out the procedure that you would use to determine if a specific stimulus served as a positive reinforcer for a target behavior.

   ____ 1. Withhold the stimulus continuously, that is, each time the target response occurs.

   ____ 2. Determine the frequency of target behavior.

   ____ 3. Observe decrease in frequency of target behavior.

   ____ 4. Present stimulus after the target behavior occurs and observe an increase in its frequency.

(2) 2. What are two practical difficulties you might encounter in applying an extinction procedure to decrease the frequency of an undesired response?

(1) 3. What is spontaneous recovery?

(2) 4. Describe the extinction procedure and its effect.

DECREASING RESPONSE STRENGTH

In the previous chapter, we described positive reinforcement as a procedure to increase the strength of a response. This chapter is concerned with decreasing the strength of a response by applying a procedure called **extinction,** an example of which is given in Case Study 2, p. 30. Like positive reinforcement, the extinction procedure alters the consequences of a behavior. By systematically withholding the reinforcing consequences for a behavior, we can decrease its frequency.

The extinction procedure consists of withholding the positive reinforcer continuously, that is, each time the target response is performed. The positive reinforcer should be withheld immediately after the response occurs. The extinction effect is a decrease in the frequency of the response to zero (0) or to a prespecified level. A response that decreases to zero has been extinguished and is unlikely to be emitted again under similar conditions.

The extinction procedure is shown in paradigm form as follows:

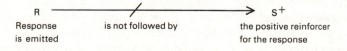

R	is not followed by	S⁺
Response is emitted		the positive reinforcer for the response

Effect: Response decreases in frequency to zero or a prespecified rate.

The symbol ⟶／⟶ in the above paradigm indicates that the positive reinforcer (S^+) is withheld continuously (no longer presented) until the frequency of the response (R) decreases to the designated level.

The effect of the extinction procedure is that the target response decreases in frequency to: (1) zero or a prespecified level; or (2) its baseline rate, that is, the rate prior to reinforcement. For example, in the previous chapter we found that the baseline rate of Donna's exercising was 1 time a day. When she received stars contingent on exercising, the frequency increased to 5 times per day. The positive reinforcement paradigm for Donna's exercising looks like this:

R ⟶ S^+
Exercising   is followed by   star on a chart

Effect: Exercising increased in frequency over its baseline rate.

After one week of this program, Donna's mother stopped giving her stars for exercising. When the stars were withheld, the rate of Donna's exercising decreased to its baseline rate of 1 time a day. In paradigm form, this extinction procedure can be depicted as follows:

R ⟶／⟶ S^+
Exercising   is not followed by   a star on a chart

Effect: Donna's exercising decreased in frequency to its baseline rate.

This example demonstrates the effect of extinction in decreasing the frequency of exercising. It also demonstrates the effectiveness of stars as positive reinforcers for Donna's exercising. If the stars were not the positive reinforcers, withholding them would not decrease Donna's exercising. In this example, we could reinstate Donna's exercising by giving her stars again (see Figure 3-1).

EVALUATION DESIGN FOR CASE STUDIES:
A-B-A-B

The graph in Figure 3-1 represents an example of the A-B-A-B experimental design for case studies. A refers to the baseline and B refers to the intervention. A_1 is the baseline measure of the response, recorded before any intervention is made. B_1 refers to the measure of the response after the intervention has been implemented. A_2 refers to a return or reversal to baseline conditions, that is, the intervention is removed. B_2 refers to reinstatement of the intervention. The A-B-A-B design is used to evaluate the effectiveness of the intervention in producing the behavior change (see, for example, Hersen and Barlow, 1976).

In Figure 3-1, A_1 is the baseline rate of Donna's exercising. B_1 refers to the response rate after reinforcement was delivered contingent on exercising. The rate of Donna's exercising increased. A_2 is a return to baseline conditions by removal of positive reinforcement for exercising (extinction). The rate of Donna's exercising decreased to its baseline level. B_2 refers to reinstatement of reinforcement contingent on exercising. The rate of Donna's exercising again increased. These data show that reinforcement was responsible for the increase in Donna's exercising.

APPLYING EXTINCTION TO DECREASE
UNDESIRED BEHAVIORS

In real life, behavioral practitioners do not always have the opportunity to develop a behavior, extinguish it, and reinstate it. Often we are asked simply to eliminate or decrease an undesired behavior to a desired, prespecified frequency—for example, Sally's excessive giggling in class. In this situation, we must determine what the reinforcing consequences are for Sally's giggling in class.

Three steps are typically followed in implementing an extinction procedure. The first step is to observe what happens when Sally giggles in class and then to try to identify the positive reinforcer for giggling. For example, we observe that other students laugh when Sally giggles.

Second, we count the number of times Sally giggles during a given time period to determine her rate of giggling. We decide to count each occurrence of giggling as a separate giggling response if it lasts 5–10 seconds. We find that Sally giggles an average of 6 times an hour.

Third, we remove the social consequences of her giggling in class. We instruct the other students to continue working, to turn their faces away from Sally, and to remain silent when she giggles. If our initial observation that the students'

FIGURE 3-1   Graph of Donna's exercising

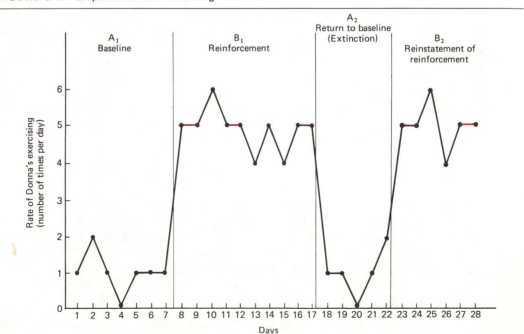

laughter reinforced Sally's giggling is accurate, removing this reinforcer should result in a decrease in giggling. If the children's laughter is not a reinforcer for Sally's giggling, its removal will have little or no effect on the rate of Sally's giggling in class.

In Figure 3-2, A_1 is the baseline rate of Sally's giggling. B_1 is the intervention, extinction. The rate of Sally's giggling decreased after an initial increase. A_2 is a return to the baseline condition by removing the intervention, that is, allowing positive reinforcement for giggling. The rate of Sally's giggling increased. B_2 refers to reinstatement of the intervention. Sally's giggling again decreased. These data show that the intervention, extinction, was responsible for the decrease in Sally's giggling.

Besides decreasing the frequency of Sally's giggling, we have also determined that the positive reinforcer for her giggling was the laughter of other students. We could reinstate Sally's giggling by telling the children to laugh at Sally when she giggles in class. We could again decrease Sally's giggling by telling the children to turn their faces away and remain silent when she giggles in class.

CASE STUDY 2

Decreasing Tantrum Behaviors

In a group of parents who were learning child management skills, Carla's mother, Mrs. Hernandez, told the social worker that almost every time she told Carla to put her toys away, Carla screamed. Mrs. Hernandez would attempt to placate her by promising to buy her new clothes and by putting Carla's toys away herself.

Mrs. Hernandez was instructed to stop making promises to Carla when she screamed about putting away her toys, and to walk away from Carla when she did this. She was told that Carla's screaming might get worse before it got better, but that if she held firm, Carla's screaming would gradually decrease. Mrs. Hernandez carried out these instructions for five days, during which time Carla's screaming gradually decreased. By the sixth day, Carla no longer screamed when told to put her toys away.

The social worker had also instructed Mrs. Hernandez to praise Carla and give her reinforcers, such as gum or cookies, when she put her toys away. Mrs. Hernandez followed these instructions and Carla began putting her toys away more frequently.

In Case Study 2, it was determined that Carla's mother was positively reinforcing Carla's screaming by putting the toys away herself and promising to buy her new clothes. Mrs. Hernandez was instructed to use an extinction procedure to decrease Carla's screaming. This involved withholding the positive reinforcers maintaining Carla's screaming. By walking away from Carla when she screamed, Mrs. Hernandez was allowing the screaming to occur with no reinforcement. Thus, Carla's screaming was observed to decrease over a few days.

ETHICAL CONSIDERATIONS

There are ethical considerations involved in reinstating reinforcement for undesired behaviors (for example, Sally's case) and removing reinforcement for desired behaviors (for example, Donna's case). Behaviors that are harmful to the individual or others should not be reinstated after extinction simply to demonstrate the effectiveness of the procedure. Similarly, behaviors that are beneficial to the individual or others should not be extinguished. Sometimes it may be appropriate to reinstate reinforcement or remove reinforcement in a carefully controlled research study that attempts to develop new knowledge about the effects of certain stimuli on behavior, determine the effects of novel interventions, or assess the effects of interventions on different behaviors. In such research studies, the informed consent of the individual or significant other should always be obtained. The rationale indicating the benefit for the individual or future clients should be stated. Because it is not always ethical to use the A-B-A-B reversal design, other evaluative approaches are available that do not involve returning to baseline conditions. Multiple baseline designs, for example, do not require reversal to baseline. Other experimental designs that do not involve reversal to baseline include changing-criterion, simultaneous-treatment, and multi-element designs. Detailed treatment and examples of these alternative designs can be found elsewhere (Hersen & Barlow, 1976; Kazdin, 1980; Martin & Pear, 1978).

EFFECTS OF EXTINCTION

The target response usually does not disappear immediately. The initial effect of extinction is often a sharp increase in the strength of the target behavior. For example, during the first 3 hours that students ignored Sally's giggling, she giggled 38 times (see Figure 3-2). Disruptive or "emotional" responses such as kicking, hitting, or complaining might also be observed. For example, when you put money in a vending machine for a soft drink and nothing comes out, you might kick the machine, especially if you have been reinforced by vending machines in the past. Similarly, the first day Gary is not paid for washing the dishes, he might complain or mumble under his breath. If reinforcement is continuously withheld, however, the target behavior will gradually decrease until it reaches its baseline or prespecified level. Our measure for effective reduction of Sally's giggling would be the teacher's estimate of a reasonable frequency for that behavior under appropriate circumstances. Extinction, then, is judged to be effective when the target behavior decreases to a prespecified level.

Many behaviors are reinforced by social consequences such as attention, praise, recognition, conversation, and expressions of interest or concern from other individuals. In withholding such social reinforcement to extinguish undesired behavior, the behavior modifier should ignore the individual by turning away, avoiding eye contact, and refraining from conversation. The behavior modifier should not scowl, grimace, or exhibit other facial or verbal behaviors that could possibly reinforce the response to be extinguished.

CONSISTENCY AND CONTROL OF REINFORCEMENT

Two practical difficulties might be encountered in implementing an extinction procedure: (1) ensuring consistency of nonreinforcement for undesired

FIGURE 3-2   Graph of Sally's giggling in class

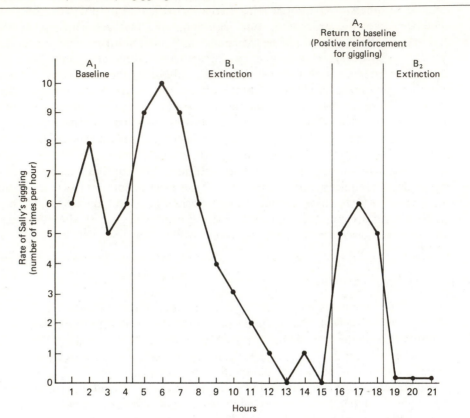

behaviors, and (2) preventing the delivery of reinforcement by others for undesired behaviors. In implementing an extinction procedure, you should consistently withhold the reinforcer for the response. There is often a tendency to "give in" or reinstate the reinforcer, especially during the period of increased responding or disruptive behavior that can occur at the beginning of extinction. "Giving in" reinforces exactly that response which is to be decreased, making it more difficult to extinguish.

For example, Mrs. Smith, who was hospitalized, pressed the call button for a nurse 10 times or more per hour. When a nurse answered the call, Mrs. Smith would say, "I just want to make sure you gals are doing your job." Her roommates complained to the nurses about Mrs. Smith's loud talking every time a nurse entered. Her nurses and doctors discussed these disruptive behaviors with her to no avail.

The nurses decided to implement an extinction program to decrease the frequency of Mrs. Smith's unnecessary calls. After two calls went unanswered, the nurses heard Mrs. Smith complaining loudly to her roommates about the poor quality of nursing care. After two more calls went unanswered, the nurses heard Mrs. Smith shouting and throwing things on the floor. They agreed to go in to see Mrs.

Smith, and when one nurse entered the room, Mrs. Smith stopped screaming and said, "Just want to make sure you gals are doing your job." In this case, the nurses reacted prematurely to Mrs. Smith's "emotional" behaviors at the beginning of extinction and reinstated the reinforcer for her undesired behavior.

The second major difficulty in implementing an extinction program is preventing the delivery of reinforcement by others for the undesired behavior. When we are not in control of the individual's reinforcing environment, someone else could reinforce the behavior that we are attempting to extinguish. For example, nurses on another shift might continue to answer Mrs. Smith's calls, thereby making the response more difficult to extinguish. Such unauthorized reinforcement for undesired behavior has been referred to as "bootleg" reinforcement.

POSITIVE REINFORCEMENT OF INCOMPATIBLE BEHAVIOR

As we have seen, the extinction procedure is used to decrease the strength of a response. For example, Donna's exercising decreased when she no longer received stars. Sally's giggling decreased when her classmates stopped laughing. In each of these cases the target response decreased when the positive reinforcer was withheld. In practice, however, when we extinguish an undesired behavior, we should also positively reinforce desired behaviors in the problematic situation. When we extinguish Sally's giggling, therefore, we should positively reinforce appropriate classroom behaviors that are incompatible with giggling; that is, they cannot occur at the same time. Behaviors incompatible with giggling include reading quietly, talking at appropriate times to other students and to the teacher, reading aloud for the class, and answering questions asked of her by the teacher. Similarly, when extinguishing Mrs. Smith's inappropriate calls to the nurses, the nurses should also reinforce appropriate behaviors Mrs. Smith performs when she is not calling them. Examples of appropriate behaviors that the nurses could reinforce with attention and praise include talking about feeling better, conversing with her roommates, and taking her medication.

SPONTANEOUS RECOVERY

An additional feature of extinction that is important to the behavior modifier is **spontaneous recovery.** Frequently, after a behavior has been extinguished, it will recur even though it has not been reinforced for some time. The behavior could recur when the individual is in a situation similar to the one in which the behavior was reinforced. Individuals participating in the extinction procedure should be instructed to continue to withhold the reinforcer if the response recurs.

For example, at bedtime 5-year-old Jerry would plead with his father for more television time, and his father always agreed. Jerry's bedtime got later and later, and it was becoming very difficult to wake him up in the morning. Jerry's parents tried to get him to bed earlier, but Jerry always got his way. In order to extinguish Jerry's pleading, his father was instructed to turn off the television, tell him there would be no more TV that evening, and ignore his pleading. At first, Jerry's pleading increased in frequency and he threw his toys on the floor. Jerry's father turned off the television at Jerry's bedtime each night until Jerry's pleading gradually decreased in frequency, duration, and intensity. By the seventh night, he no longer pleaded at bedtime. Jerry's father continued this procedure successfully for two weeks. One evening the following week, Jerry's mother turned off the television at his bedtime. Jerry pleaded, but the television remained off. His mother's turning off the television and leaving it off when Jerry pleaded constituted another extinction trial in which reinforcement was withheld for Jerry's pleading.

In implementing the extinction procedure, it is essential to identify those individuals who have control over the availability or delivery of reinforcement in the client's environment. These individuals must consistently follow the designated modification plan. In Jerry's situation, both his mother and father, as well as baby-sitters and relatives, must turn off the television and leave it off at the designated time, so that Jerry's pleading is not reinforced.

In anticipation of the possible spontaneous recovery of Jerry's pleading, Jerry's parents were instructed to remain firm in leaving the television off if he pleaded on future occasions. They were also instructed to inform anyone else who would be responsible for turning the television off at Jerry's bedtime to ignore his pleading should it occur.

SUMMARY

1. Extinction is a procedure for decreasing response strength or the likelihood that a response will be performed again under similar conditions.
2. The extinction procedure consists of withholding the positive reinforcer for a response until the response decreases to a prespecified level or to its baseline rate. The positive reinforcer should be withheld immediately after the response is performed and each time it occurs.
3. Positive reinforcement involves the presentation of reinforcing consequences contingent on a response; extinction involves withholding the reinforcing consequences contingent on a response.
4. In order to decrease a response, one must determine: (1) the positive reinforcer for the response, (2) the response rate, and (3) if withholding the positive reinforcer continuously results in a decrease in response rate.
5. The extinction procedure can be used to determine if a stimulus has served as a positive reinforcer for a specific response.
6. The A-B-A-B experimental design is used in the evaluation of case studies. Ethical considerations should be taken into account when using this design in an applied setting.
7. The initial effect of extinction may be a sharp increase in the rate of a target response and disruptive or "emotional" responses.
8. Lack of consistency in withholding reinforcement and inability to prevent delivery of reinforcement by others are two practical difficulties encountered in implementing the extinction procedure.

9. When an undesired behavior is extinguished, a desired behvavior, incompatible with the undesired behavior, should be reinforced.

10. The possible spontaneous recovery of an extinguished response should be anticipated and a plan arranged for continued extinction of the response.

SUGGESTED READINGS

ALLEN, K. E., TURNER, K. D., and EVERETT, P. M., "A Behavior Modification Classroom for Head Start Children with Problem Behaviors," *Exceptional Children,* 1970, *37,* 119–127.

AYLLON, T., and MICHAEL, J., "The Psychiatric Nurse as a Behavioral Engineer," *Journal of the Experimental Analysis of Behavior,* 1959, *2,* 323–334.

BRISCOE, R. V., HOFFMAN, D. B., and BAILEY, J. S., "Behavioral Community Psychology: Training a Community Board to Problem Solve," *Journal of Applied Behavior Analysis,* 8 (1975), 157–168.

HERSEN, M. and BARLOW, D. H., *Single Case Experimental Design* (Elmsford, N.Y.: Pergamon Press, 1976).

KAZDIN, A. E., *Behavior Modification in Applied Settings,* rev. ed. (Homewood, Illinois: The Dorsey Press, 1980).

MARTIN, G. and PEAR, J., *Behavior Modification: What It Is and How to Do It* (Englewood Cliffs, N.J.: Prentice-Hall, Inc., 1978).

PINKSTON, E. M., REESE, N. M., LeBLANC, J. M., and BAER, D. M., "Independent Control of a Pre-school Child's Aggression and Peer Interaction by Contingent Teacher Attention," *Journal of Applied Behavior Analysis,* 1973, *6,* 115–124.

WILLIAMS, C. D., "The Elimination of Tantrum Behavior by Extinction Procedures," *Journal of Abnormal and Social Psychology,* 1959, *59,* 269.

WOLF, M., BIRNBRAUER, J., LAWLER, J., and WILLIAMS, T., "The Operant Extinction, Reinstatement, and Re-extinction of Vomiting Behavior in a Retarded Child," in R. Ulrich, T. Stachnick, and J. Mabry (Eds.), *Control of Human Behavior,* vol. 2 (Glenview, Ill.: Scott, Foresman, 1970), 146–153.

POST-TEST QUESTIONS

(3) 1. Describe the procedure for extinguishing a response by giving an example in which you specify the response and its reinforcer.

(3) 2. After observing a mother hug her son when he cried, what would you do to determine whether or not the mother's hugging served as a positive reinforcer for the child's crying?

(1) 3.   Describe the effects of extinction on the rate of a target response.

(2) 4.   Using the information from Case Study 2, page 30, indicate how positive reinforcement played a part in the following:

   a.   Increasing the frequency of an undesired behavior.

   b.   Increasing the frequency of a desired behavior.

(1) 5.   How is spontaneous recovery considered in a treatment plan?

4

POSITIVE REINFORCEMENT CONTINGENCIES

objectives

After completing this chapter, you should be able to:

1. give an example of a positive reinforcement contingency,
2. compare self-control reinforcement contingencies with accidental contingencies,
3. define and give an example of the Premack Principle,
4. indicate when it is appropriate to use a continuous schedule of reinforcement,
5. state two advantages of using an intermittent schedule of reinforcement rather than a continuous schedule of reinforcement, and
6. compare resistance to extinction for a response maintained on a continuous versus an intermittent schedule of reinforcement.

Betty Jones frequently invites her friends for coffee in the morning, but she rarely gives her children breakfast. She can increase the frequency of giving her children breakfast if inviting her friends over is made contingent on making breakfast for her children.

Chapter 4

(4) 1. Which of the following are statements of positive reinforcement contingencies? (Circle the correct ones.)

    a. Finish your math assignment and you may play outside.

    b. If you wash the dishes, I'll give you an ice cream cone.

    c. If you fight with your brother, you will get a spanking.

    d. He completed his chores in three hours.

(1) 2. Briefly describe how superstitious behavior is acquired.

(3) 3. Give an example of a positive reinforcement contingency you could establish to help Harold (Case Study 1) complete his class assignments.

(1) 4. Intermittent reinforcement makes a well-learned response more resistant to extinction. (Circle one.)

    a. True

    b. False

(1) 5. When is it more appropriate to use continuous reinforcement rather than intermittent reinforcement?

BEHAVIORAL CONTINGENCIES AND POSITIVE REINFORCEMENT

        We have discussed positive reinforcement and extinction, two procedures for modifying a response by altering its consequences. In positive reinforcement, the reinforcer is presented *contingent on* performance of the response. In extinction, the positive reinforcer is withheld contingent on performance of the response.

A **behavioral contingency** specifies the behaviors to be performed in order for certain consequences to follow. A positive reinforcement contingency is one type of behavioral contingency. Self-control reinforcement contingencies, accidental contingencies, punishment contingencies, and negative reinforcement contingencies are other types of behavioral contingencies.

A **positive reinforcement contingency** indicates that a behavior must be performed in order for a positive reinforcer to become available. The contingency is stated in positive terms, with clear specification of the behavior, the reinforcer, and the circumstances under which reinforcement will occur. Examples of positive reinforcement contingencies include: "If you trim the hedges, we will go fishing"; "After you finish your piano lesson, Diane, you may go shopping with Sherry." The positive reinforcer is more likely to be effective when it immediately follows the desired behavior than when it is delayed.

Positive reinforcement contingencies can be stated explicitly, as above, or they can serve as rules that control an individual's behavior without his or her awareness or ability to describe them. In a marital relationship, for example, one partner may be unaware of the positive reinforcement contingencies that exist between the behaviors that she or he emits and the affection (reinforcers) given by the spouse.

CONTINGENCY CONTRACTING

Behavioral contracts have been used to facilitate behavior change by stating explicitly, in writing, the contingencies between behaviors and their consequences. A contract specifies the behavior change desired and the reinforcers to be given for performing the desired behaviors. It also states the negative consequences or punishers to be presented for not fulfilling the terms of the contract. **Contingency contracting** has been used to modify a wide range of behaviors such as to increase positive interactions between delinquent teenagers and their parents, to reduce disruptive classroom behaviors and increase on-task performance, to reduce smoking, to decrease overeating, and to increase positive marital interactions.

A major advantage of contingency contracting is that it requires the participation of all parties involved in a behavior change program. Terms of the contract can and should be negotiated in order to ensure active pursuit of behavioral change goals. Typically, the practitioner negotiates the conditions of a behavioral contract so that they are satisfactory to all parties. Although the contract is signed, it should be flexible enough to be renegotiated if necessary.

For example, Mr. and Mrs. Gregory would like their 14-year-old daughter, Sue, to be home by 10:00 P.M. each week night. They have been arguing over this issue for weeks, and Sue frequently gets home after midnight. The practitioner who has been counseling this family helped negotiate a behavioral contract that focused on Sue's curfew. The parents wanted Sue home by 10:00 P.M. Sunday through Thursday nights. Sue wanted extra spending money and permission to invite her girlfriends to her house more often.

FIGURE 4-1   Behavioral contract between Sue and Mr. & Mrs. Gregory

SUE AGREES TO:	MR. & MRS. GREGORY AGREE TO:
Be in the house by 10:00 P.M. each week night (Sunday through Thursday). Put a check mark on a chart for each night she is home by 10:00 P.M.	Give Sue $1.00 for each check mark.

BONUS: If Sue compiles 10 check marks in two weeks, Mr. & Mrs. Gregory will allow her to have a girlfriend stay over one Friday or Saturday night.

PENALTY: For every week night Sue comes home after 10:00 P.M., she will have to be in the house by 6:00 P.M. for the next two nights.

Signed:
Sue Gregory _____

Mr. & Mrs. Gregory _____

_____

Date: _____

According to the terms of the contract they signed, each night Sue came home by 10:00 P.M. she would give herself a check mark on a chart. At the end of the week, she would receive $1.00 for each check mark. Sue could earn a total of $5.00 per week. There was a bonus clause included so that if she compiled 10 check marks in two weeks, she could have a girlfriend stay over one Friday or Saturday night. For every night that Sue came home after 10:00 P.M., she would not be allowed to leave the house after 6:00 P.M. for the next two nights. Figure 4-1 is the agreement Sue and her parents signed.

A contingency contract can be an effective aid to behavioral change because the desired behavior and the consequences—reinforcers as well as punishers—are specified in advance. All parties involved know what to expect as a result of performing the designated behaviors. The behaviors and consequences need to be monitored, however, to be sure that the terms of the contract are being carried out. If difficulties arise, they should be discussed and the contract renegotiated, if necessary.

ACCIDENTAL CONTINGENCIES

A response can be conditioned by delivery of a positive reinforcer that is *accidentally* associated with the response. **Superstitious behavior** is often the result of an accidental or coincidental relationship between a response and a reinforcer; that is, an individual makes a response that is followed by a noncontingent reinforcer that coincidentally strengthens the response. The delivery of the reinforcer is not contingent on performance of the response. For example, a gambler twirls his "lucky" ring while playing blackjack, and he wins. He attributes his win to the twirl-ing of the ring. An event other than twirling the ring produced the reinforcer of win-ning, but the ring-twirling response accidentally became associated with the rein-forcer. The gambler twirls his ring again while playing blackjack, although this behavior cannot produce the reinforcer. Winning is not contingent on ring twirl-ing. The gambler would have drawn the winning cards on a reinforcing occasion whether or not he twirled his ring. Many strange behaviors have been reinforced by gamblers and others on the basis of an accidental contingency between a behavior and a reinforcer.

SELF-CONTROL REINFORCEMENT CONTINGENCIES

Positive reinforcement contingencies can be applied in a self-control pro-gram. In this way, the individual can increase the strength of desired behaviors by self-administered reinforcement. For example, a student was in danger of flunking statistics because he completed only a few of his assignments. He spent a lot of his time playing basketball. By arranging to play basketball only after completing his sta-tistics homework, the student increased the frequency of completing those assign-ments. Another example is a social worker who made sure he recorded a client inter-view before taking a coffee break. In these situations, the individuals arranged condi-tions so that the desired responses were followed by self-administered reinforcement.

THE PREMACK PRINCIPLE

The **Premack Principle** refers to a specific kind of positive reinforcement contingency that is named for its originator (Premack, 1959; 1965). The Premack Principle states that a response, R_1, occurring more frequently (with higher probability) than another response, R_2, can serve as a reinforcer for the response that occurs less frequently (with lower probability). In other words, R_1, the high-probability response can increase the frequency of R_2, the low-probability response. This is accomplished by allowing R_1 to occur only after R_2 has been performed. R_1 is made contingent on performance of R_2.

You can identify high-frequency responses for yourself by monitoring and recording how you spend your free time. These high-frequency responses are poten-tial reinforcers for low-frequency responses you wish to strengthen. For example, Jane frequently talked to her friends on the phone but rarely practiced the flute. According to the Premack Principle, talking on the phone could serve as a reinforcer for practicing the flute if talking on the phone was made contingent on practicing the flute. In another case, Betty Jones frequently invited her friends over for coffee in the morning, but she rarely gave her children breakfast. The Premack Principle indicates that inviting her friends over could act as a reinforcer for Betty's making breakfast for the children if inviting her friends over was made contingent on making breakfast. In these cases, the effect of using the Premack Principle was an increase in the frequency of Jane's practicing the flute and in Betty's giving her children breakfast.

CONTINUOUS AND INTERMITTENT
REINFORCEMENT

In the previous chapters on positive reinforcement and extinction, the contingencies described for increasing or decreasing a behavior specified that reinforcement be given or withheld continuously, that is, each time the response occurred. According to those contingencies, the responses were strengthened on a **continuous reinforcement schedule** (CRF) and weakened or extinguished on a continuous schedule of nonreinforcement. A **schedule of reinforcement** is a contingency that specifies the conditions under which reinforcement is delivered for a response.

We discussed the use of continuous reinforcement to increase the frequency of Donna's exercising her leg. After a response is well established, however, it is not always necessary to provide positive reinforcement each time the response occurs. The response can be maintained on a less-than-continuous or **intermittent schedule of reinforcement.** Chapter 5 describes various kinds of intermittent reinforcement schedules and their behavioral patterns and effects.

Intermittent reinforcement has at least four advantages over continuous reinforcement:

(1) Fewer reinforcements are required to maintain the behavior, resulting in more efficient use of available reinforcers.

(2) A response maintained on intermittent reinforcement is more resistant to extinction. **Resistance to extinction** refers to the number of responses emitted during extinction of the response. Thus, a response maintained on an intermittent schedule

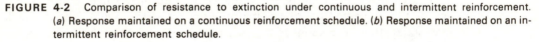

FIGURE 4-2 Comparison of resistance to extinction under continuous and intermittent reinforcement. (*a*) Response maintained on a continuous reinforcement schedule. (*b*) Response maintained on an intermittent reinforcement schedule.

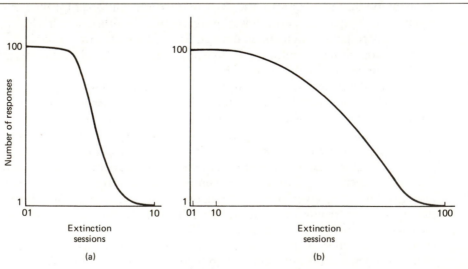

of reinforcement will take longer to extinguish than a response maintained on a continuous schedule of reinforcement, as shown in Figure 4-2 (Skinner, 1938).

(3) The reinforcer is effective for a longer time because satiation occurs gradually.

(4) Intermittent reinforcement more closely resembles reinforcement patterns that occur in the individual's environment.

It is advantageous to use continuous rather than intermittent reinforcement to establish a response or to strengthen one that occurs with low frequency. Attempting to establish a response with intermittent reinforcement could lead to extinction of the response before the relationship between the response and the reinforcer is established. After the response is well established, it is appropriate to introduce an intermittent schedule of reinforcement. Not only will this procedure require fewer reinforcements and make the response more resistant to extinction, but it resembles most reinforcement schedules operating in the individual's environment.

SUMMARY

1. A positive reinforcement contingency indicates that a behavior must be performed in order for a positive reinforcer to become available. The reinforcer is made contingent on performance of the behavior.

2. Superstitious behavior is the result of an accidental contingency. In an accidental contingency, a reinforcer follows a response, but delivery of the reinforcer is not contingent on performance of the response. Thus, the reinforcer accidentally increases the likelihood that the response will be performed again under similar circumstances.

3. A self-control reinforcement contingency allows an individual to arrange behavioral contingencies so that self-administered reinforcement is made contingent on desired behavior.

4. The Premack Principle states that a high-probability response can serve as a reinforcer for a low-probability response. A behavior that occurs with low frequency, therefore, can be reinforced with a high-frequency behavior.

5. Continuous reinforcement is reinforcement delivered each time a response occurs. Continuous reinforcement, rather than intermittent reinforcement, is used to establish a response or strengthen one that occurs with low frequency.

6. Intermittent reinforcement is delivered on a less-than-continuous schedule. Intermittent reinforcement is used to maintain a well-established response.

7. Intermittent reinforcement has four advantages over continuous reinforcement once the response has been established: (a) fewer reinforcements are required to maintain the response, so that more efficient use is made of available reinforcers, (b) the reinforcer is effective for a longer time because satiation occurs more gradually, (c) the response is more resistant to extinction, and (d) the reinforcement schedules more closely resemble those in the individual's environment.

SUGGESTED READINGS

HOMME, L. E., CSANYI, A. P., GONZALES, M. A., and RECHS, J. R., *How to Use Contingency Contracting in the Classroom* (Champaign, Ill.: Research Press, 1969).

KAZDIN, A. E., and POLSTER, R., "Intermittent Token Reinforcement and Response Maintenance in Extinction," *Behavior Therapy,* 1973, *4,* 386–391.

MAHONEY, M. J., and THORESEN, C. E., *Self-control: Power to the Person* (Belmont, Calif.: Brooks/Cole, 1974).

O'BANION, D. R. and WHALEY, D. L., *Behavior Contracting: Arranging Contingencies of Reinforcement* (New York: Springer Publishing Co., 1980).

PREMACK, D., "Reinforcement Theory," in Levin, D. (Ed.), Nebraska Symposium on Motivation: 1965 (lincoln, Nebraska: University of Nebraska, 1965) pp. 123–180.

PREMACK, D., "Toward Empirical Behavioral Laws: I. Positive Reinforcement," *Psychological Review,* 1959, *66,* 219–233.

SKINNER, B. F., "Contingencies of Reinforcement in the Design of a Culture," *Behavioral Science,* 1966, *2,* 159–166.

SKINNER, B. F., "Superstition and the Pigeon," *Journal of Experimental Psychology,* 1948, *38,* 168–172.

SKINNER, B. F., *Science and Human Behavior* (New York: Free Press, 1953), Chapter 15, pp. 227–241.

STUART, R. B. (Ed.), *Behavioral Self-Management: Strategies, Techniques, and Outcomes* (New York: Brunner/Mazel, 1977).

VATTANO, A. J., "Self-management Procedures for Coping with Stress," *Social Work,* 1978, 113–119.

POST-TEST QUESTIONS

(2) 1. Reexamine Case Study 1 on pages 7–8. State a positive reinforcement contingency related to Case Study 1 that you could use to help Harold complete his class assignments. Specify a reinforcer and a response.

(2) 2. As described in this chapter, self-control reinforcement contingencies are more desirable than accidental contingencies. What is the difference between an accidental contingency and a self-control reinforcement contingency?

(1) 3. When is it more appropriate to use continuous reinforcement rather than intermittent reinforcement?

(1) 4. What evidence indicates that intermittent reinforcement makes a response more resistant to extinction than continuous reinforcement?

(3) 5. State three advantages of using intermittent reinforcement over continuous reinforcement.

(3) 6. Define the Premack Principle and give an example of its use and effect.

5

SCHEDULES OF REINFORCEMENT

objectives

After completing this chapter, you should be able to:

1. identify the characteristics of ratio and interval schedules of reinforcement,
2. give an example of straining the ratio, and
3. describe how to schedule the delivery of reinforcement to maintain a response once it has been established, given a case example.

A teacher established a positive reinforcement contingency for a child who scribbled on his math work sheets instead of solving the problems. On the first day of the procedure, she gave the child a gold star immediately after he completed each math problem. The child earned twelve gold stars. The second day of the procedure, she required that he complete ten math problems in order to receive one gold star. On that day, the child completed three problems and scribbled on the rest of the work sheet.

(1) 1. What is the effect of increasing a ratio too quickly on a fixed-ratio schedule?

(2) 2. In fixed-interval and variable-interval schedules, what two events are required in order for reinforcement to be delivered?

(2) 3. State two characteristics of responses maintained on ratio schedules.

(1) 4. State one way in which fixed-ratio and variable-ratio schedules generate different behavior patterns.

(4) 5. Match the following schedules in Column A with their examples in Column B.

A	*B*
1. fixed-ratio _____	a. deadlines
2. variable-ratio _____	b. piece work
3. fixed-interval _____	c. slot machines
4. variable-interval _____	d. waiting for a taxi

INTERMITTENT REINFORCEMENT SCHEDULES

We usually are not reinforced every time we perform a particular response. We do not get an answer every time we ring a doorbell, nor are we positively reinforced every time we offer our advice, suggestions, or opinions to others. Nevertheless, we continue to call on our friends, give advice and suggestions, and state our opinions.

A schedule of reinforcement is a contingency that specifies the conditions under which reinforcement is delivered for a response. An intermittent schedule of reinforcement is typically used after a response has been established and occurs consistently. After a response has been established, reinforcement can be gradually shifted from a continuous to an intermittent schedule. If intermittent reinforcement is applied before the response occurs consistently, the response may extinguish.

The purpose of this chapter is to present the major intermittent schedules of reinforcement and their effects on response rates and patterns. Four types of intermittent schedules are described: **fixed-ratio (FR)**, **variable-ratio (VR)**, **fixed-interval (FI)**, and **variable-interval (VI)**.

Fixed-Ratio Schedules

The first intermittent schedule we will discuss is the **fixed-ratio (FR) schedule.** In the FR schedule, a prescribed number of responses must be performed in order for reinforcement to be delivered. For example, an FR 2 schedule indicates that two responses must be emitted before reinforcement will be delivered. An FR 10 schedule requires that 10 responses be emitted for reinforcement. A continuous reinforcement (CRF) schedule is the same as FR 1 because reinforcement is delivered after each response.

The FR schedule typically generates high rates of responding with minimal hesitation between responses until the ratio is completed. A *postreinforcement pause* is associated with the FR schedule. This means that after the reinforcer is presented, the individual pauses or takes a short break from responding. An example of an FR schedule would be a worker paid on a piecework basis, receiving $5.00 for every 10 boxes loaded. An individual on this schedule generally performs at a high, consistent rate, taking little time off until he or she completes the ratio (loads 10 boxes). After reinforcement is obtained, the worker rests for a brief period (postreinforcement pause), then begins the ratio again.

When using an FR schedule, the ratio or number of responses required for reinforcement should be increased gradually. If the response does not receive adequate reinforcement, it will extinguish. The more drastic the increase in the ratio, the more likely the response will extinguish. For example, in teaching a retarded child to dress herself, reinforcement was initially given after she buttoned each button; this initial continuous reinforcement (CRF) schedule represents FR 1. The teacher, wanting to strengthen this response, increased the ratio to FR 2, FR 3, and then FR 4; the latter schedule required the child to button four buttons in order to receive reinforcement. If the teacher had shifted from CRF immediately to FR 4, the child would probably not have buttoned four buttons, reinforcement would not have been delivered, and the response would have extinguished. This rapid shift from CRF to an FR that is too large to support the response is called **straining the ratio.** The same effect could have occurred had the teacher shifted from FR 2 or FR 3 to FR 8. The eight responses required on the last reinforcement schedule would probably have been too many, so that the response would have extinguished.

Mr. Calvin, a patient in a mental hospital, was taught to shave himself every day. The response that was reinforced consisted of using an electric shaver until clean-shaven. A continuous reinforcement schedule (CRF) was used to develop this behavior until it occurred consistently for two weeks. Ward staff wanted to maintain his shaving without reinforcing him with a token each time he shaved. During the third week they reinforced him every other time he shaved, using an FR 2 schedule. The fourth week they reinforced him once for every three shaves, FR 3. The fifth week they changed the reinforcement schedule to FR 5. After that they reinforced him once a week, FR 7.

In order to maintain Mr. Calvin's daily shaving, the ward staff gradually increased the ratio schedule from FR 1 to FR 7 over a four-week period. If they had shifted from FR 1 immediately to FR 7, Mr. Calvin probably would not have shaved the seven days required for reinforcement, and Mr. Calvin's shaving probably would have extinguished.

Variable-Ratio Schedules

A second type of intermittent reinforcement schedule is the **variable-ratio (VR) schedule.** In VR schedules, reinforcement is delivered after an *average* number of responses is emitted. The ratio is randomly varied around a given value. Thus on a VR 10 schedule, reinforcement will be delivered after an average of ten responses has been emitted. This means that reinforcement can occur after one response, after ten responses, or after twenty responses, as long as the average (mean) number of responses producing reinforcement is ten. Similarly, a VR 12 schedule indicates that a reinforcer is delivered after an average of twelve responses has been emitted. This means that reinforcement could occur after one response, twelve responses, or twenty responses, as long as the average number of responses producing reinforcement is twelve. VR schedules, like FR schedules, generate extremely high rates of responding with minimal hesitation between responses. In fact, VR schedules generate the highest rates because unlike the FR schedule, there is no postreinforcement pause.

Slot machines are typically programmed to deliver reinforcement on a VR schedule. Since a gambler never knows exactly what ratio is required for reinforcement, he or she inserts coins and pulls the handle at a high rate, with minimal hesitation between responses. Unfortunately for the gambler, the slot machine is programmed on a high VR schedule to take more of the gambler's money than it pays out. The persistent behavior of a door-to-door salesperson on commission is similar to behavior generated by VR schedules. The salesperson knocks on doors or makes telephone calls but never knows in advance which contact will result in the reinforcement of a sale. Past experience indicates the "average" number of contacts required to make a sale.

CASE STUDY 3

Conditioning Verbal Behavior

Mr. Clark was a 45-year-old patient who had been on a back ward of a mental hospital for eleven years. He was described by ward staff as mute and withdrawn. He spent much of the day sitting in a chair looking at the floor or pacing up and down the halls of the ward. Mr. Clark remained silent when spoken to and did not initiate conversation with patients or staff.

The treatment procedure consisted of placing Mr. Clark in a room where slides of animals, people, and landscapes were shown to him through a slide projector. Mr. Clark was asked to talk about the pictures when he saw a green light appear on a panel. When the green light was off, the psychologist spoke about the pictures and Mr. Clark was asked to silently look at them. When the green light was turned on, Mr. Clark was instructed to speak. When Mr. Clark made any speech sound he was given a piece of candy. A counter registered one point for each sound that Mr.

Clark made. In addition, the psychologist said "good" immediately after each sound. An automatic recorder counted each second of speech as one response.

Mr. Clark made no speech sounds during the initial treatment session, only 5 responses the second session, and 48 responses during the fifth session. During the tenth treatment session, Mr. Clark said 76 words, such as "boy and girl," "cat," "house and yard." During the next five sessions, the psychologist asked Mr. Clark specific questions about the content of the slides and gave Mr. Clark hints that facilitated correct responding. On the fifteenth session Mr. Clark appropriately described a slide as follows: "A boy and girl are playing on the swing."

After 15 sessions, ward staff reported that for the first time in many years Mr. Clark had spoken to several persons and had made short replies to comments directed to him by staff.

Scheduling Reinforcement

Mr. Clark in Case Study 3 was taught to respond verbally to slides through a reinforcement program designed to increase his speech. Initially, his speech was reinforced on a CRF schedule. After a consistent rate of speaking was established on CRF, reinforcement was shifted to a small FR schedule, FR 2. The FR schedule was gradually increased to larger FR schedules, including FR 3, FR 4, FR 6, FR 8. In order to approximate reinforcement available in his environment, reinforcement was then shifted to VR schedules, including VR 4, VR 7, VR 10. Because VR schedules generate high response rates, Mr. Clark's speech was strengthened by gradually shifting the schedule of reinforcement in progression from CRF to FR to VR.

Fixed-Interval Schedules

The next intermittent reinforcement schedule we will discuss is called **fixed interval** (FI). In FI schedules, reinforcement becomes available when a response is made after the passage of a specified period of time. For example, an FI 2-minute schedule means that 2 minutes must pass before a response can be reinforced. The FI schedule requires that not only must the time interval pass, but the response must also be emitted after this period of time has elapsed. If the reinforcement required only the passage of time, any behavior occurring at the end of the interval could be inadvertently reinforced.

Fixed-interval schedules generate response patterns with an initial low rate of responding and a terminal high rate of responding. This means that as the interval draws to an end, the frequency of responses increases. An example of an FI schedule would be any situation involving a deadline. For example, if examinations are scheduled for the end of the month, a student might exert little effort in studying the first few days of that month, somewhat more, perhaps, around the middle of the month, but, by the last few days before the exam, the student's study behaviors would increase up to the day of the exam. A similar pattern was found when the behavior of the U.S. Congress over a 21-year period was studied (Weisberg & Waldrop, 1972). The number of bills passed at the beginning of the session was low. As the session moved toward the end, however, a greater number of bills was passed. In analyzing these data, each session of Congress was shown as an interval. The findings indicated an initial low rate of responding at the beginning of the interval (few bills passed). As the session moved toward adjournment (reinforcement), an increasing number of responses were made (more bills were passed).

Another example of an FI schedule is shopping at a department store that closes at 9:00 P.M. and opens at 10:00 A.M. This is an FI 13-hour schedule because any response of going to the store before 10:00 A.M., that is, before the interval has elapsed, is not reinforced. The first response made after 10:00 A.M. is reinforced by the store being open. As the time gets closer to 10:00 A.M., people become more likely to go to the store, even though they have to wait outside. On a sale day, especially at popular stores, people have been known to line up as early as 7:00 A.M. for a 10:00 A.M. opening.

If visiting hours at a prison or correctional facility are from 7 to 9 P.M., a response of going there to visit an inmate before 7:00 P.M. will not be reinforced. A response made after 7:00 P.M. will be reinforced by a visit with the inmate. Since a response made after 9:00 P.M. will not be reinforced, this type of schedule is called **fixed-interval with limited hold** (FI-LH). This means that after the interval has elapsed, the reinforcer is available for only a limited amount of time. The response, therefore, must be emitted after the interval has elapsed but before the availability of reinforcement is terminated. This schedule is an FI 22-hour–LH 2-hour schedule. The department store example also represents an FI-LH schedule since the store is only open from 10 A.M. until 9 P.M. The schedule is an FI 13-hour–LH 11-hour schedule.

Variable-Interval Schedules

The next schedule we will describe is the **variable-interval** (VI) **schedule.** In variable-interval schedules reinforcement is delivered for a response made after an average (mean) amount of time has passed. The interval is randomly varied around a given time value. Thus, VI 4 minutes indicates that reinforcement is made available for a response emitted after an average of 4 minutes has passed. The individual could be reinforced for making a response after one minute, after 10 minutes, or after 12 minutes, as long as the average amount of time that passed was 4 minutes. Again, remember that not only does the designated time period have to elapse, but the response must also be emitted in order for reinforcement to occur.

Variable-interval schedules typically generate a consistent, moderate response rate with no postreinforcement pause. Most waiting behavior appears similar to the response pattern generated by a VI schedule. For example, a woman standing on a corner waiting for a taxi cab, a man looking out the window waiting for the mail to arrive, or waiting for a baseball to be hit in your direction are governed by VI schedules, since the amount of time one must wait for each reinforcement varies.

A VI schedule was used to establish task-oriented behavior in a school-age child who frequently left his seat in class. Using a timer to signal the end of an interval, the behavior modifier varied the amount of time required for the child to attend to a specific task. When the timer signalled the end of the interval, the child had to be attending to the task in order to receive a gold star and praise. For example, the child was instructed to work on a puzzle at the table. He was told that if he was working when the buzzer sounded, he would receive a gold star. A VI 5 minute schedule was used. The interval varied around an average of 5 minutes. Since the child didn't know exactly when the timer would signal availability of reinforcement, he worked at the task until the end of the interval. The schedule was increased to VI 10 minutes and then gradually to longer intervals. The gradual, progressive shifting to larger VI schedules required the child to work puzzles for increasingly longer periods of time and generated a stable rate of task-oriented behavior.

COMPARISON OF SCHEDULES

Figure 5-1 shows cumulative response graphs of the four major intermittent schedules of reinforcement. They illustrate the characteristic patterns associated with each type of schedule.

Figure 5-1(a) illustrates a fixed-ratio schedule. The graph shows a high response rate with little hesitation between responses, and a postreinforcement pause when the ratio is completed. This graph is an example of an FR 3 schedule, such as a person on a piecework wage who receives $1.00 for every three shirt collars sewn.

Figure 5-1(b) illustrates a variable-ratio schedule. The graph shows a very high response rate with little hesitation between responses and no postreinforcement pause. This graph is an example of a slot-machine schedule (VR 75).

FIGURE 5-1(a)   Cumulative record of an FR 3 schedule. The slash (╲) marks indicate delivery of reinforcement. A indicates post-reinforcement pause.

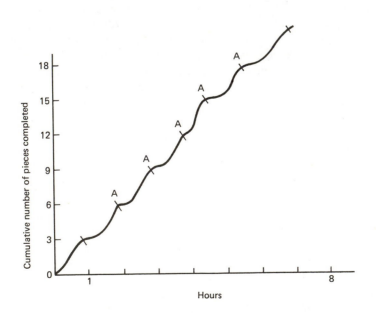

FIGURE 5-1(b) Hypothetical slot-machine schedule, VR 75. The slash marks (╲) indicate delivery of reinforcement.

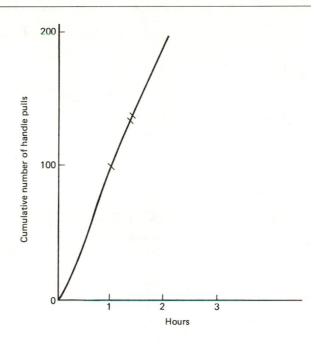

FIGURE 5-1(c) Cumulative record of three months study behavior with exams at the end of each month (FI 1 month). A is initial low rate of responding; B is terminal high rate of responding. The slash marks (╲) indicate delivery of reinforcement.

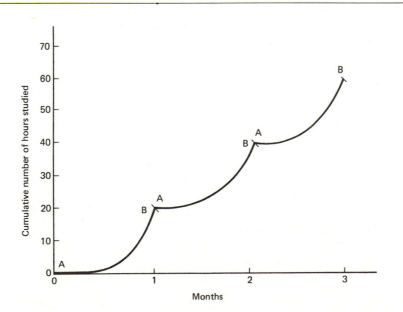

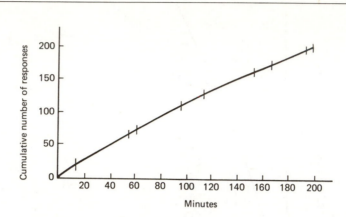

Figure 5-1(c) illustrates a fixed-interval schedule. This graph shows an initial low rate of responding and an increasingly higher rate of responding as the interval nears the end. The scallop is characteristic of this schedule. This graph is an example of three months of an individual's study behavior when there was an exam at the end of each month (FI one month).

Figure 5-1(d) illustrates a variable-interval schedule. This graph shows a moderate, but consistent rate of responding. It is an example of a person waiting for a fish to bite, with the interval varying around 20 minutes (VI 20 minutes).

A continuous reinforcement schedule is used to establish a behavior or strengthen one that occurs with low frequency. Responses reinforced on CRF

TABLE 5-1 Characteristics of four schedules of reinforcement

FIXED-RATIO (FR)	VARIABLE-RATIO (VR)	FIXED-INTERVAL (FI)	VARIABLE-INTERVAL (VI)
High response rate with minimal hesitation between responses	Highest response rate with minimal hesitation between responses	Initial low rate of responding; terminal high rate of responding	Consistent, moderate rate of responding
Postreinforcement pause	Highly resistant to extinction	Scallop	Highly resistant to extinction
Piecework	Slot machines	Limited hold possibility	Waiting for an expected event
		Deadlines	

schedules will extinguish faster than those maintained on intermittent schedules. Variable schedules, both ratio and interval, produce behaviors that are the most resistant to extinction. Table 5-1 compares characteristics of the four schedules of reinforcement discussed in this chapter.

In applying schedules of reinforcement to human behavior, we have attempted to illustrate how they can be relevant for the human services. In everyday life, however, there may be more than one schedule operating, as well as additional reinforcers and other variables influencing a behavior. For example, it is difficult to find precise examples of variable schedules that are naturally programmed as such in the environment. Further research is necessary to determine more adequately the potential for applying reinforcement schedules as they relate to human service problems.

SUMMARY

1. A continuous reinforcement (CRF) schedule is used to establish a response or strengthen one that is performed with low frequency. After the response has been established and is emitted consistently, an intermittent schedule of reinforcement is used in order to maintain the response without reinforcing it each time it occurs.
2. There are four major types of intermittent reinforcement schedules: (1) fixed-ratio (FR), (2) variable-ratio (VR), (3) fixed-interval (FI), and (4) variable-interval (VI).
3. The fixed-ratio (FR) schedule requires that a certain number of responses be performed in order for reinforcement to be delivered. The FR schedule generates a high response rate with minimal hesitation between responses. A postreinforcement pause is characteristic of a fixed-ratio schedule.
4. If a fixed-ratio schedule is increased too rapidly, the response may extinguish. This is called straining the ratio. The more drastic the increase in ratio, the more likely that the response will extinguish.
5. In a variable-ratio schedule, reinforcement is delivered after an average (mean) number of responses is emitted. The ratio is randomly varied around a given value. Variable-ratio schedules generate the highest response rates, with minimal hesitation between responses.
6. A fixed-interval schedule requires that a response be performed after a specified period of time has elapsed in order for reinforcement to be delivered. Fixed-interval schedules generate a low initial rate of responding and a high terminal rate of responding. This means that as the interval of time draws to an end, the frequency of responses increases.
7. In a variable-interval schedule, reinforcement is delivered when a response is made after an average amount of time has passed. The interval is randomly varied around a given time value. Variable-interval schedules generate consistent, moderate response rates.

SUGGESTED READINGS

COMMONS, M. and NEVIN, J. (Eds.), *Quantitative Analysis of Behavior: Discriminative Properties of Reinforcement Schedules* (Cambridge, Mass.: Bollinger, 1981).

FERSTER, C. B., and SKINNER, B. F., *Schedules of Reinforcement* (Englewood Cliffs, N.J.: Prentice-Hall, Inc., 1957).

SEMB, G., and SEMB, S., "A Comparison of Fixed-page and Fixed-time Reading Assignments in Elementary School Children," in E. Ramp, and G. Semb (Eds.) *Behavior Analysis: Areas of Research and Application* (Englewood Cliffs, N.J.: Prentice-Hall, Inc., 1975), pp. 233–243.

WEISBERG, P., and WALDROP, P., "Fixed-interval Work Habits of Congress," *Journal of Applied Behavior Analysis,* 5, 1972, 95–97.

POST-TEST QUESTIONS

(1) 1. Give an example of straining the ratio.

(3) 2. Using the information from Case Study 3, pages 49–50, how could you schedule reinforcement to maintain Mr. Clark's increased vocalizations after session 15?

(10) 3. Match the schedules in Column A with their characteristics from Column B. (Items from Column B can be used 0, 1, or more times in Column A and each schedule in Column A can have 1 or more characteristics from Column B.)

Column A	*Column B*
Fixed-interval _____	1. Initial low rate of responding, terminal high rate of responding.
Variable-interval _____	2. Postreinforcement pause.
	3. Consistent, moderate rate of responding; no postreinforcement pause.
Fixed-ratio _____	4. Characteristic slot-machine schedule.
Variable-ratio _____	5. Very high response rate with minimal hesitation between responses.
	6. Scallop.
	7. Initial burst of responding, tapering off to low rate of responding.
	8. Deadlines.
	9. Piecework.
	10. Waiting for a taxi.

6

SHAPING AND RESPONSE DIFFERENTIATION

objectives

After completing this chapter, you should be able to:

1. define a response class and give an example of one,
2. give an example of response differentiation,
3. describe how the DRO procedure can be used to decrease the frequency of a response,
4. describe the use of a DRO procedure to test the effectiveness of a reinforcer, and
5. describe the steps involved in shaping a behavior.

When Joe tried to talk with his stepfather about his problems in school, his stepfather turned on the television and turned away from Joe. When Joe talked about sports, however, his stepfather looked at him, listened to what he said, and discussed the topic with him. Joe and his stepfather have long conversations about sports but rarely discuss the problems Joe is having at school.

Chapter 6

(1) 1. In Case Study 3, pages 49–50, Mr. Clark's speech could be developed by (circle one correct answer):

   a. extinction

   b. intermittent reinforcement

   c. shaping with successive approximations

   d. differential reinforcement of approximation of incompatible responses

(1) 2. In order to shape a new behavior, you would not use differential reinforcement. (Circle one.)

   a. True

   b. False

(2) 3. For the response class "talking about sports," name two responses.

(2) 4. How are positive reinforcement and extinction involved in differential reinforcement?

(2) 5. Give an example of a DRO procedure that could be used to decrease Carla's screaming (Case Study 2).

DIFFERENTIAL REINFORCEMENT

We have defined operant behavior as behavior that is controlled by its consequences. The individual *operates* or acts on the environment to produce those consequences. The positive reinforcement procedure is used to increase the strength of an operant response. The extinction procedure is used to weaken or decrease the strength of an operant response. **Differential reinforcement** involves the use of both positive reinforcement and extinction. In this procedure one response is reinforced while reinforcement is withheld from other responses. When the reinforced response occurs frequently, to the exclusion of responses from which reinforcement is withheld, we say that the response has become differentiated.

For example, when Joe tried to talk to his stepfather about his problems at school, his stepfather turned on the television and turned away from Joe. When Joe talked about sports, however, his stepfather looked at him, listened to what he said, and discussed the topic with him. Thus, responses related to talking about sports were positively reinforced with attention, while responses related to talking about problems at school were extinguished. It should come as no surprise, then, to learn that Joe's conversations with his stepfather were almost exclusively about sports. Responses related to talking about sports had become differentiated, that is, they occurred with greater frequency than verbal responses dealing with other topics.

Differential reinforcement produces the highly skilled responses of artists, musicians, public speakers, and professional athletes. For example, compare the refined backhand responses of a tennis champion with those of a novice, or the bowing technique of a concert violinist with that of a beginner. In both cases, the skilled responses of the experts have become highly differentiated or refined through differential reinforcement of an increasingly narrow range of desired responses. Similarly, through training, supervision, and experience, the beginning practitioner learns to become more skillful in interviewing clients to obtain assessment data and in formulating intervention plans.

RESPONSE CLASS

Variability is a basic feature of operant behavior because a behavior is rarely repeated in exactly the same form. When a response is emitted and followed by a reinforcer, it becomes more likely that the response will be performed again. The reinforcer also increases the frequency or likelihood of occurrence of other responses that have the same or similar effect on the environment as the reinforced response. Thus, not only is a single response reinforced, but a class or group of responses is also reinforced. This group of operant responses—each member or response producing the same or similar effect on its environment (e.g., reinforcement)—is called a **response class.**

In Joe's case, the response class that was consistently reinforced by his stepfather was "talking about sports." The responses associated with talking about sports were more likely to occur because, whenever one member of the response class was reinforced, all other members were also reinforced. For example, there are many responses Joe could make that would be members of the reinforced response class "talking about sports." He could talk about any sport, individual athletes, last night's game, or a historical sports event. Talking about any one of these subjects with his stepfather would increase the likelihood of occurrence of any of the others.

Differential reinforcement can be applied to narrow the range of reinforced responses within a response class. For example, if Joe's stepfather only reinforced talking about baseball, soon Joe and his stepfather would talk only about baseball to the exclusion of other sports. There are still many responses involved in talking about baseball, however, and when any one of these responses is reinforced, this increases the likelihood that every other response will be emitted. When Joe talked to his stepfather about the Texas Rangers and was reinforced, for example, all responses included as members of the "baseball talk" response class were reinforced.

Figure 6-1 is a set of paradigms of the differential reinforcement procedure depicting Joe's responses. From the paradigms, you can see how an increasingly narrow range of responses becomes differentiated. The above example also demonstrates that the words "response" and "behavior" refer to a class of responses rather than to one discrete response. Similarly, one member of a response class represents a sub-class of responses, not a single, discrete response.

THE DRO PROCEDURE

Differential reinforcement can be used to decrease the frequency of an undesired behavior by reinforcing behaviors *other than* the undesired behavior. Using the **DRO** (Differential Reinforcement of Other) **procedure,** the undesired behavior is extinguished, and desired behaviors are reinforced. For example, in Case Study 2, the social worker told Carla's mother to reinforce Carla when she put her toys away. The worker could also have instructed the mother to reinforce any appropriate behavior Carla engaged in *other than* screaming, such as helping her mother put groceries on the shelf, fixing a broken toy, or playing quietly by herself. In this use of the DRO procedure, reinforcement is withheld for undesired behavior and appropriate responses are strengthened.

DRO has been used to decrease the frequency of a child's self-injurious scratching (Allen & Harris, 1966). When the child engaged in any behavior other than scratching, her mother praised her and gave her gold stars and tangible reinforcers. In a case involving sibling conflict (Leitenberg, et al., 1977), the children were reinforced with pennies and parental praise after each one-minute interval during which no conflict (for example, hitting or name calling) occurred. In these cases, differential reinforcement was given contingent on any behavior other than the undesired behaviors of scratching and physical and verbal attacks. The DRO procedure reduced the child's scratching and the sibling conflict. Pleasant interactions also increased in both studies.

USING DRO TO TEST REINFORCER EFFECTIVENESS

There is another way Differential Reinforcement of Other (DRO) can be applied. The DRO procedure can be used to determine if a stimulus serves as a reinforcer for a target response.

In order to conduct this test, follow these steps:

1. Determine the rate of the target response.
2. Identify the stimulus intended to serve as a reinforcer for the target response.
3. Withhold the stimulus for the target response, and present the stimulus after any response other than the target response.

FIGURE 6-1

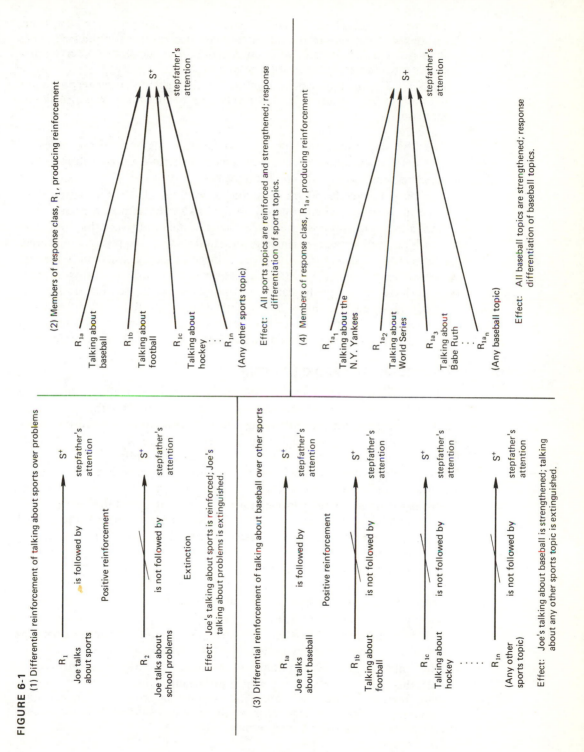

(1) Differential reinforcement of talking about sports over problems

R₁
Joe talks
about sports
→ is followed by → S⁺
stepfather's
attention

Positive reinforcement

R₂
Joe talks about
school problems
is not followed by → S⁺
stepfather's
attention

Extinction

Effect: Joe's talking about sports is reinforced; Joe's talking about problems is extinguished.

(2) Members of response class, R₁, producing reinforcement

R₁ₐ
Talking about
baseball

R₁ᵦ
Talking about
football

R₁c
Talking about
hockey
. . .

R₁ₙ
(Any other sports topic)

→ S⁺
stepfather's
attention

Effect: All sports topics are reinforced and strengthened; response differentiation of sports topics.

(3) Differential reinforcement of talking about baseball over other sports

R₁ₐ
Joe talks
about baseball
is followed by → S⁺
stepfather's
attention

Positive reinforcement

R₁ᵦ
Talking about
football
is not followed by → S⁺
stepfather's
attention

R₁c
Talking about
hockey
is not followed by → S⁺
stepfather's
attention

. . . . .

R₁ₙ
(Any other
sports topic)
is not followed by → S⁺
stepfather's
attention

Effect: Joe's talking about baseball is strengthened; talking about any other sports topic is extinguished.

(4) Members of response class, R₁ₐ, producing reinforcement

R₁ₐ₁
Talking about the
N. Y. Yankees

R₁ₐ₂
Talking about
World Series

R₁ₐ₃
Talking about
Babe Ruth
. . .

R₁ₐₙ
(Any baseball topic)

→ S⁺
stepfather's
attention

Effect: All baseball topics are strengthened; response differentiation of baseball topics.

4. Record the rate of the target response as well as the rate of the other responses. If the rate of the target response decreases while the rate of the other responses increases, you can conclude that the stimulus served as a positive reinforcer for the target response.
5. *Optional.* Present the positive reinforcer following the target response and withhold it for any other response. The rate of the target response should increase.

The fifth step should not be used to increase the rate of an undesired response, except perhaps under carefully controlled experimental conditions where the undesired response would also be extinguished.

Now turn to pages 49–50 and reexamine Case Study 3. The DRO procedure could be used to determine whether candy and points served as positive reinforcers for Mr. Clark's speaking. Suppose the psychologist wanted to be sure that the attention Mr. Clark received in the experimental situation was not the positive reinforcer for speaking. (1) Mr. Clark would be given a piece of candy and points for any behavior *other than* speaking. (2) If Mr. Clark's speech decreased and behaviors other than speaking increased, then the candy and points served as reinforcers for Mr. Clark's speech. (3) The psychologist could further demonstrate the effectiveness of the candy and points as reinforcers for Mr. Clark's speech by once again presenting them after he spoke. If his speaking increased in frequency, they acted as reinforcers.

SHAPING WITH SUCCESSIVE APPROXIMATIONS

Differential reinforcement, as previously discussed, is a technique for increasing the frequency of selected responses already occurring within a response class. To develop a response that differs significantly from an existing response, we can shape the new behavior using differential reinforcement. The shaping procedure involves the use of differential reinforcement to strengthen members of one response class. When these responses are performed consistently, the criterion for reinforcement is shifted to the next response class.

Shaping with successive approximations is a procedure used to develop a new behavior or one that rarely occurs. Since a client can seldom perform the desired behavior at the beginning of treatment, we establish a series of intermediate behaviors or successive approximations to the desired, terminal behavior.

The following steps can be implemented to shape a behavior:

1. Specify the terminal response (desired behavior).
2. Specify the positive reinforcer(s) to be used.
3. Specify initial and intermediate responses. The initial response to be reinforced must bear some resemblance to the terminal behavior.
4. Differentially reinforce the initial response until it is performed consistently.
5. Shift the criterion for reinforcement from the initial response to an intermediate response. Intermediate responses must approximate the terminal response; that is, the criterion for reinforcement is shifted to responses that are increasingly similar to the terminal response.

6. Reinforce the intermediate response until it is performed consistently. Steps 5 and 6 of this procedure are repeated until the terminal behavior is performed.
7. Reinforce the terminal behavior.

For example, shaping with successive approximations was used to reinstate Mr. Clark's speech (Case Study 3):

1. The terminal behavior was for Mr. Clark to speak in sentences about slides that he was shown.
2. The positive reinforcers given Mr. Clark were candy, points, and verbal praise from the psychologist.
3. The initial response criterion included any speech sound. Intermediate responses included words, phrases, and answers to questions about the slides.
4. Initially, any speech sound made by Mr. Clark was reinforced.
5. When Mr. Clark made speech sounds consistently, the criterion for reinforcement was shifted to words. This meant that any vocalization would no longer meet the criterion for reinforcement. Mr. Clark was required to speak words before receiving the candy, points, and praise.
6. When Mr. Clark was saying words consistently, the criterion for reinforcement was shifted to yet another intermediate response—phrases—which was the next approximation to the terminal behavior. Speaking in phrases was reinforced until Mr. Clark consistently spoke in phrases. This process of reinforcing a response until it was performed consistently, then shifting the criterion for reinforcement to the next intermediate response, was continued until the terminal response was performed.
7. Mr. Clark was reinforced for speaking in sentences about slides that he was shown.

Shaping with successive approximations was also employed by a nurse to teach a physically handicapped girl to use crutches for walking instead of using a wheelchair:

1. The terminal response was walking 50 steps on crutches.
2. Positive reinforcers were points and praise ("very good").
3. The initial response was movement toward the crutches, which were placed within her reach. Intermediate responses included touching the crutches with her hands, holding the crutches in her hands, using the crutches to raise herself from the wheelchair, standing up with the crutches properly positioned, and taking from 1 to 49 steps on the crutches.
4. Initially, when the girl made any movement toward the crutches, she was reinforced.
5. When she reached out toward the crutches 5 times, the criterion for reinforcement was shifted to the next intermediate response, touching the crutches.

6. Touching the crutches was reinforced until she touched them consistently. This procedure of reinforcing one response until it was performed consistently, then shifting the criterion for reinforcement to the next intermediate response, continued until the terminal behavior was performed.

7. She was reinforced for walking 50 steps on crutches.

Shaping with successive approximations involves a gradual process in which a response must be developed at one level before reinforcement is shifted to the next level of approximation. When the desired response is performed, it should be reinforced immediately to ensure that reinforcement is given only for the appropriate behavior. If the criterion for reinforcement is shifted to the next level too quickly, or if insufficient reinforcement is given, the response could extinguish. On the other hand, if one response receives too much reinforcement, it becomes difficult to alter the individual's responses in the direction of the next approximation. The shaping procedure relies on reinforcing responses the individual is currently performing and on gradually shifting the criterion for reinforcement until the desired response is established.

Instructions and prompting are often used with shaping to facilitate the acquisition of new behaviors. Although shaping alone is useful with individuals who do not follow instructions, the shaping procedure becomes much more effective when instructions are given at each step. Demonstrations of the terminal behavior by a role model can also be used to promote rapid development of desired behaviors (see Chapter 11).

SUMMARY

1. Differential reinforcement involves the use of both positive reinforcement and extinction. One response is positively reinforced and increases in frequency or likelihood of occurrence, while other responses are extinguished and decrease in frequency or likelihood of occurrence.

2. Response differentiation is the result of differential reinforcement, that is, selectively reinforcing certain responses and extinguishing others. The reinforced responses become differentiated, that is, they are performed frequently to the exclusion of the extinguished responses.

3. A response class refers to a group of behaviors, each member or response producing the same or similar effect on its environment.

4. When one response in a response class is reinforced, other responses in that class are also reinforced. The words "response" and "behavior" refer to a class of responses rather than a single response. One member of a response class, therefore, represents a sub-class of responses, rather than a single, discrete response.

5. The differential reinforcement of other (DRO) procedure can be used to decrease undesired behaviors by reinforcing any behaviors other than the undesired one.

6. DRO can also be used to test the effectiveness of a reinforcer for a specific response.

7. Shaping with successive approximations is a procedure for establishing a new behavior or one that rarely occurs.

8. Shaping with successive approximations involves using differential reinforcement to strengthen members of one response class and then shifting the criterion for reinforcement to other response classes until the terminal behavior is performed. Intermediate behaviors are reinforced and developed as successive approximations to the terminal behavior.

SUGGESTED READINGS

ALLEN, K. E., and HARRIS, F. R., "Elimination of a Child's Excessive Scratching by Training the Mother in Reinforcement Procedures," *Behaviour Research and Therapy,* 4, 1966, 79–84.

AYLLON, T., and AZRIN, M. H., "The Measurement and Reinforcement of Behavior of Psychotics," *Journal of the Experimental Analysis of Behavior,* 8, 1965, 357–383.

FERSTER, C. B., "The Use of the Free Operant in the Analysis of Behavior," *Psychological Bulletin,* 50, 1953, 263–274.

HOMER, A. L., and PETERSON, L., "Differential Reinforcement of Other Behavior: A Preferred Response Elimination Procedure," *Behavior Therapy,* 4, 1980, 449–471.

ISAACS, W., THOMAS, J., and GOLDIAMOND, I., "Application of Operant Conditioning to Reinstate Verbal Behavior in Psychotics," *Journal of Speech and Hearing Disorders,* 25, 1960, 8–12.

LEITENBERG, H., BURCHARD, J., BURCHARD, S., FULLER, E. J., and LYSAGHT, T. V., "Using Positive Reinforcement to Suppress Behavior: Some Experimental Comparisons with Sibling Conflict," *Behavior Therapy,* 8, 1977, 168–182.

SKINNER, B. F., *Science and Human Behavior* (New York: Free Press, 1953), Chapter 6, pp. 91–106.

POST-TEST QUESTIONS

(4) 1. Define a response class and give an example of one, describing two of its members.

(7) 2. The seven steps involved in shaping a behavior are listed below. Fill in the specific responses and/or reinforcers related to each step, using your own example of shaping a motor (nonverbal) behavior.

                                                                                  Fill in with examples

1. Specify terminal response.   1.
2. Specify reinforcer(s).   2.

3. Specify initial and intermediate responses directed toward achieving terminal response.   3.

4. Differentially reinforce initial response until it occurs consistently.   4.

5. Shift criterion for reinforcement to next intermediate response.   5.

6. Continue the procedure of differential reinforcement and shifting the criterion for reinforcement until the terminal behavior is performed.   6.

7. Reinforce terminal behavior.   7.

(2) 3. Two second-grade students fight whenever they are together in school. Describe how a DRO procedure can be used to decrease the frequency of their fighting.

(3) 4. Give an example of response differentiation, specifying a response class, the differentiated response, and the reinforcer.

(2) 5. Using the information from Case Study 3, pages 49–50, describe how the psychologist could use a DRO procedure to determine if it was the candy and points that served as reinforcers for Mr. Clark's increased speech and not the attention he received in the experimental situation.

7

STIMULUS CONTROL: DISCRIMINATION AND GENERALIZATION

objectives

After completing this chapter, you should be able to:

1. describe the use of reinforcement and extinction in discrimination training,
2. give an example of stimulus fading,
3. describe a procedure for establishing a discrimination using two antecedent stimuli, one response, and a reinforcer, and
4. specify two criteria for achievement of stimulus control.

In her interviews with Mrs. Munsen, the marriage counselor determined that Mr. and Mrs. Munsen rarely discussed topics of mutual interest. In order to initiate changes in the focus of their interactions from complaints and arguments to more pleasant conversation, the counselor instructed Mrs. Munsen to make a list of topics that she should discuss with her husband (List A). These topics included his work, the two children, and camping. Mrs. Munsen made a second list of topics that she should not discuss with her husband (List B). Topics on List B included complaints about such things as his staying out late at night, watching television at his friends' homes, not taking Mrs. Munsen shopping or to the movies, and not spending time with his family.

In the counselor's office, when Mrs. Munsen discussed topics from List A, the counselor praised her and engaged in conversation with her. When Mrs. Munsen discussed topics on List B, the counselor did not reply. Mrs. Munsen's talking about topics on List A increased in frequency, while her talking about topics on List B decreased in frequency.

Chapter 7

(2) 1.   What is an S^D for a response? What is an S^Δ?

(1) 2.   What is the effect of a discrimination procedure involving two discriminative stimuli (S^D and S^Δ) and one response?

(1) 3.   In Case Study 3, what function did the green light serve?

(6) 4.   In the following examples, identify the discriminative stimulus, the response, and the reinforcer by labeling the S^D, R, and S^+, in the paradigms.

   a.   Bob sees Joe walking down the street. Bob says "hello," and Joe says, "good morning."

$$\left[\begin{array}{l} S^D \\ R \end{array}\right. \longrightarrow S^+$$

   b.   Shirley hears the ice cream truck, asks her aunt for a quarter, and buys an ice cream cone.

$$\left[\begin{array}{l} S^D \\ R \end{array}\right. \longrightarrow S^+$$

(1) 5.   True or False. When a response is reinforced in the presence of one S^D, it will not occur in the presence of other similar stimuli.

ANTECEDENTS

   The previous chapters focused on relationships between operant behaviors and their consequences. The presentation of a reinforcer after a response increases the likelihood that the response will be performed again under similar conditions. Similarly, the withholding of a reinforcer for a response decreases the likelihood that the response will be performed again. We have shown that by changing the schedule of reinforcement, we can influence the rate and pattern of a response. We have described how a behavior can be refined using differential reinforcement, and how a new response can be shaped by shifting the criterion for reinforcement in successive approximations to the terminal behavior. In summary, we have shown how consequences can be applied: (1) to establish a new behavior by shaping with successive approximations; (2) to increase the strength of a behavior by positive reinforcement; (3) to decrease the strength of a behavior by extinction; (4) to selectively increase one response while extinguishing others through differential reinforcement; and (5) to maintain a behavior at a certain frequency or pattern by employing a particular reinforcement schedule.

This chapter focuses on the relationships between a particular behavior, its consequences, and its antecedents. **Antecedents** refer to stimulus events that precede or accompany responses and which influence their performance. It is necessary to consider both the antecedents and consequences of a target behavior in order to determine its controlling conditions. This also allows the practitioner to choose from a wider range of procedures for modifying behavior than would be possible if only consequences were examined.

CASE STUDY 4

Stimulus Control of Marital Interaction

Mrs. Munsen consulted a marriage counselor about her marital difficulties. Her husband refused to see the counselor with her. Mrs. Munsen complained that her husband ran around town drinking with his male friends during the evenings and spent little time with her and their children. They rarely went to the movies or to other entertainment, and Mrs. Munsen did all the food shopping by herself. She had stopped making his breakfast as a result of their frequent arguments before he left for work.

Mrs. Munsen berated her husband for going out with his friends, for not helping her around the house, and for not spending time with her and their children. Mr. Munsen responded to her criticism by swearing at her and telling her to mind her own business. Mrs. Munsen became so upset during these arguments that she ran into her room and locked the door, remaining there until Mr. Munsen left the house.

In her interviews with Mrs. Munsen, the marriage counselor determined that Mr. and Mrs. Munsen rarely discussed topics of mutual interest. Their conversations revolved around Mrs. Munsen's complaints and Mr. Munsen's abusive responses to them. Mrs. Munsen said that she would like to have more satisfying conversations with her husband and felt that improvement in this area was her primary concern.

In order to initiate changes in the focus of their interactions from complaints and arguments to more pleasant conversation, the counselor instructed Mrs. Munsen to make a list of topics that she should discuss with her husband (List A). These topics included his work, the two children, and camping. Mrs. Munsen made a second list of topics that she should not discuss with her husband (List B). Topics on the second list included complaints such as his staying out late at night, watching television at his friends' homes, not taking Mrs. Munsen shopping or to the movies, and not spending time with his family. Mrs. Munsen was also instructed to greet Mr. Munsen with a kiss when he came home from his job, and to ask him how his work had gone.

In the counselor's office, when Mrs. Munsen discussed topics from List A, the counselor praised her and engaged in conversation with her. When Mrs. Munsen discussed topics on List B, the counselor did not reply. Mrs. Munsen's talking about topics on List A increased in frequency, while her talking about topics on List B decreased in frequency.

THE DISCRIMINATION TRAINING PROCEDURE

Discriminative stimuli are antecedents that exert control over the performance of a response. There are two kinds of discriminative stimuli: the S^D (pronounced "ess-dee") and the S^Δ (pronounced "ess-delta"). The S^D and S^Δ are alternatively presented so that a discrimination can be formed between these stimuli. A response made in the presence of an S^D is followed by reinforcement. The S^D signals or *sets the occasion for* a response to be reinforced. The S^Δ signals that a response made in its presence will not be followed by reinforcement. If the response is emitted in the presence of S^D, reinforcement will follow and increase the frequency of the response. A response emitted in the presence of S^Δ is not followed by reinforcement and decreases in frequency.

Discrimination training is a procedure used to reinforce a response in the presence of S^D and to extinguish it in the presence of S^Δ. The reinforced response is referred to as a discriminated response. In paradigm form, the discrimination training procedure looks like this:

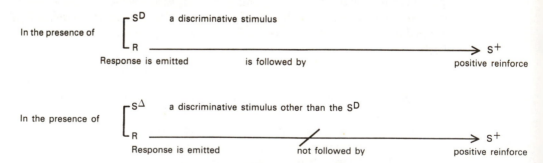

Effect: The frequency of the response performed in the presence of S^D increases; the frequency of the response performed in the presence of S^Δ decreases.

For example, a telephone ringing serves as the S^D for the response of answering it (for example, picking up the receiver and saying "hello"), which is followed by the reinforcer of a reply. If the telephone does not ring (S^Δ) and you lift the receiver and say "hello," no reinforcer will be delivered; that is, no one will reply. Thus, answering the telephone when it rings occurs with high frequency, whereas answering the telephone when it does not ring occurs with low frequency.

In Case Study 3 (see pages 49–50), the green light *on* served as the S^D for Mr. Clark's speaking about the slides. If Mr. Clark spoke when the green light was on, he received candy, points, and praise. The green light *off* was the S$^\triangle$ for speaking about the slides. If Mr. Clark spoke when the light was off, positive reinforcement was withheld. In paradigm form, this example of discrimination training would look like this:

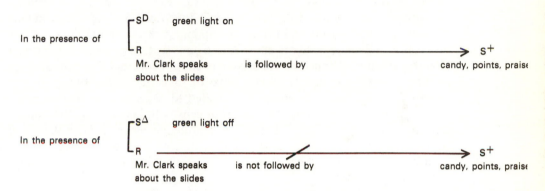

Effect: Mr. Clark's speaking about the slides when the green light was on increased in frequency; Mr. Clark's speaking about the slides when the green light was off decreased in frequency.

The green light on was the S^D for Mr. Clark to speak in order to be reinforced. In other words, the green light on served as the signal or cue indicating that speaking would be reinforced. Both positive reinforcement and extinction are involved in the discrimination training procedure. Thus, responses performed when the green light was on (S^D) were reinforced and strengthened. Verbal responses made when the green light was off (S$^\triangle$) were not followed by positive reinforcement and, therefore, were weakened. In teaching this discrimination, the response was reinforced only when it was performed in the presence of S^D. A response must initially be performed under both the reinforced S^D condition and the unreinforced S$^\triangle$ condition, however, so that the discrimination between responding in S^D and S$^\triangle$ can be formed.

STIMULUS CONTROL

When the response occurs to S^D and never or rarely to S$^\triangle$, we say that the response is under **stimulus control.** An additional characteristic of stimulus control is that the response is emitted with short latency after presentation of the S^D. Latency refers to the amount of time transpiring between presentation of the S^D and performance of the response. A short latency, therefore, means that the response is performed immediately or very soon after the S^D is presented. Mr. Clark's speech was under stimulus control when he spoke only when the green light was on and began to speak as soon as it went on.

Many of our behaviors are under the control of antecedents. Clocks and watches are S^Ds for getting up in the morning and for arriving at appointments and other important events on time. Calendars also serve as S^Ds for responses such as giving birthday presents, sending anniversary cards, and preparing for important meetings or professional events. Other people's speech, smiles, and other nonverbal behaviors serve as S^Ds or cues for our responses to them. For example, when someone smiles at you, it usually signals that an appropriate response from you will be reinforced by that individual. When someone says, "Right this way," this serves as an S^D for your response of following that person's directions. Waving your arm and calling "Taxi!" is an S^D for the taxi driver to stop and pick you up. Giving the usher your ticket is an S^D for the usher to show you to your seat. Instructions and directions are S^Ds that often exert considerable control over our behaviors. Prompts and other cues also serve as S^Ds that signal or set the occasion for certain behaviors.

Joe learned a discrimination related to discussing his school problems at home. When he talked about school problems with his mother (S^D), she provided reinforcement in the form of attention and discussing his concerns with him. His stepfather was an S^Δ for discussing school problems, however, because Joe was not reinforced for talking about them in his presence. In paradigm form, the example would look like this:

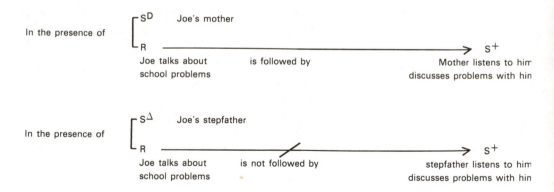

Effect: Joe discusses his school problems with his mother; Joe does not discuss these problems with his stepfather.

Stimulus control is a significant concept in behavioral analysis and modification for a number of important reasons:

1. Some individuals have acquired faulty discriminations. For example, a supervisor frequently phoned a caseworker at home in the evening to discuss agency matters that could have been dealt with during office hours. The caseworker usually accepted the calls and talked to the supervisor, thus reinforcing these calls.

The inappropriate calls can be analyzed as a problem of faulty discrimination on the part of the supervisor. Discussing agency business (R), unless urgent, should occur during office hours (S^D) and not occur outside of these hours (S^Δ). Since the supervisor was usually reinforced for calling the caseworker at home, the faulty discrimination was maintained.

If the caseworker wanted to help the supervisor make the proper discrimination, he would withhold the reinforcer of conversing with the supervisor when she called him at home. If the caseworker sometimes reinforced these calls and sometimes did not, the supervisor's responding during S^Δ would be intermittently reinforced, making it difficult to extinguish.

2. Some individuals have developed behaviors which are under the control of inappropriate stimuli. For example, obese people often overeat because they eat in the presence of many stimuli other than hunger (food deprivation), such as shopping in the grocery store, driving in the car, and watching food commercials on TV. Although eating is an appropriate response, it can become a problem when it occurs in the presence of inappropriate S^Ds.

3. Some people lack the skills necessary to perform appropriate responses in the presence of appropriate S^Ds. For example, a restaurant waiter overcharged Jack by one dollar. Jack was embarrassed to say anything so he paid the additional amount. In this example, Jack did not demonstrate the necessary assertive skills to respond appropriately to the S^D of a one-dollar overcharge.

4. Some individuals do not provide proper S^Ds that could signal or set the occasion for appropriate behaviors. For example, a woman feeds her family a diet lacking in essential nutrients because she does not keep the proper foods at home. This woman also has a problem in faulty discrimination, because she buys junk food at the store instead of nutritious food. The junk foods serve as S^Ds for her buying them, and the nutritious foods serve as S^Δs, when it should be the reverse.

STIMULUS FADING

Stimulus fading is a procedure to transfer stimulus control of a behavior from an original S^D to a novel antecedent stimulus without errors. The stimulus-fading procedure builds on a discrimination already learned. The individual responds in the presence of S^D and is reinforced. The S^D is gradually altered along a particular dimension (for example, color, size, loudness) until it resembles the new antecedent stimulus, which then acquires a discriminative function as an S^D for the response. The individual responds in the presence of the changing S^D until the response is emitted in the presence of the novel antecedent stimulus. The response continues to be emitted to a gradually changing S^D with no errors. This procedure is also called errorless learning because the individual makes the correct response throughout the procedure, never responding in the presence of S^Δ. Possible disruptive extinction effects due to incorrect, unreinforced responses are, therefore, avoided.

The stimulus-fading procedure builds on discriminations that the individual has previously acquired. The following steps are involved in implementing a stimulus-fading procedure: (1) identify the appropriate discrimination and the relevant stimuli S^D, S^Δ and the novel stimulus; (2) specify the stimulus dimension to be varied gradually or faded; (3) specify the correct response and its reinforcer; and (4) reinforce the individual's correct responses while changing the original S^D to the new stimulus.

For example, Jim, a retarded teenager, did not discriminate the men's restroom sign from the ladies' sign; that is, he sometimes walked into the ladies' restroom, sometimes into the men's. A stimulus-fading procedure to teach Jim this discrimination was used as follows:

1. The S^D was the men's restroom sign written in large letters; the S^Δ was the ladies' restroom sign written in small letters. The novel stimulus was the men's sign in small letters.
2. Letter size was selected as the stimulus dimension to be varied. Jim had been taught previously to discriminate large letters from small letters; that is, when shown two words, one written in small letters and one written in large letters, Jim chose the word written in large letters. The counselor showed Jim two signs, the men's restroom sign written in very large letters (S^D) and the ladies' restroom sign written in small letters (S^Δ).
3. When Jim chose the men's sign, the counselor praised him and gave him a token.
4. The size of the letters of the men's restroom sign was gradually decreased until the letters were the same size as those on the ladies' sign. Jim continued to choose the men's sign and was reinforced. Thus, Jim made the correct discrimination with no errors because he had learned to discriminate between large and small letters, and his behavior very gradually came under the control of the form of the letters (M-E-N) rather than the size (large letters). The stimulus-fading procedure was continued with Jim until he was able to discriminate the men's sign from other signs that could be used for restrooms, for example, "women."

Stimulus-fading techniques have been applied in situations where verbal instructions or cues are used to teach complex verbal or mechanical skills. Initially, the individual performs appropriately only in the presence of these cues. The cues are gradually faded out in a manner that allows the individual to continue responding to changes in the S^D. For example, an actor learning his or her lines on stage may rely on prompts or cues from the prompter. These cues are gradually faded out until the actor responds to the S^Ds provided by the spoken lines of the other actors on stage. Similar applications of fading techniques have been used in linear-programmed instruction such as:

"A reinforcer is a stimulus that increases the strength of a response."
"A reinforcer is a stimulus that increases the strength of a _____."
"A reinforcer is a stimulus that _____ the strength of a_____."
"A reinforcer is a stimulus that _____ the _____ of a_____."
"A reinforcer is a _____ that _____ the _____ of a_____."

Both fading and shaping procedures are used to establish new behaviors or to increase behaviors that occur with low frequency. In shaping, the form of the response is gradually changed by alteration of the reinforcing *consequences*. In contrast, fading involves gradual alteration of the *antecedent* stimulus or S^D that sets the occasion for the response to be performed. The fading procedure does not require changes in the initial response; the response remains the same throughout the procedure but is emitted in the presence of gradually varied stimulus conditions. Shaping, however, results in a terminal response that has become differentiated from and bears little resemblance to the initial response.

STIMULUS GENERALIZATION

Stimulus generalization is the opposite of discrimination. We have discussed how discrimination training can be applied to achieve stimulus control; that is, the response is performed in the presence of S^D but not S^Δ. According to the principle of **stimulus generalization,** a response reinforced in the presence of one stimulus, S^D, will subsequently be performed in the presence of other similar stimuli. For example, a child has learned to use the word "car" when she sees a four-wheeled vehicle. The child now calls every four-wheeled vehicle she sees "car." The word "car" *generalized* to all such vehicles.

In Figure 7-1, S^D_1 is the original stimulus that signals or sets the occasion for the response R_1 to be reinforced. S^D_2, S^D_3, and S^D_4 are three stimuli similar along some dimension to S^D_1. Stimulus generalization takes place when R_1 is emitted in the presence of S^D_2, S^D_3, or S^D_4.

For example, Lee copied answers (R_1) from a nearby student's paper (S^D_1) during a math exam. Lee passed the exam with the highest grade he ever received in math (S^+). On subsequent exams in that class, Lee copied answers (R_1) from other nearby students (S^D_2, S^D_3, etc.) whose papers he could see. Figure 7-2 shows this example of stimulus generalization in paradigm form.

Stimulus generalization is significant for human adaptation because we are often required to perform behaviors in new situations that we learned in other situations. Otherwise we would have to learn how to respond to every new situation. For example, most people learn to read from books in school. Reading thereafter generalizes to: (1) other reading material such as newspapers, magazines, and cereal boxes, and (2) other places such as libraries, doctors' offices, and buses. A person who learns to drive one standard-shift automobile can usually drive other standard-shift automobiles with little or no difficulty. These examples involve stimulus generalization because the responses associated with reading and driving that were learned in the original classroom and automobile have transferred or generalized to other places and automobiles.

A person treated in a mental hospital may learn appropriate social skills in this setting. Treatment is not complete, however, until the individual can also perform these behaviors outside the hospital. In other words, performance of appropriate social behaviors must generalize from the stimulus conditions (S^Ds) in the

FIGURE 7-1   Stimulus generalization paradigm

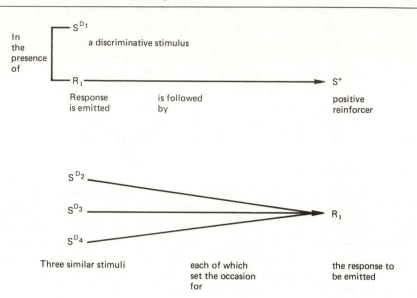

Effect: R_1 increases in frequency in the presence of S^{D_1}. The likelihood of R_1 occurring in the presence of S^{D_2}, S^{D_3}, and S^{D_4}, also increases.

FIGURE 7-2   Stimulus generalization example

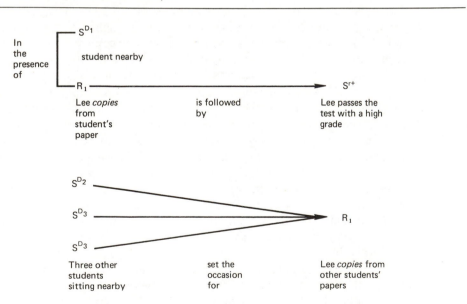

Effect: Lee is more likely to copy from student S^{D_1}. The likelihood that Lee will copy from students S^{D_2}, S^{D_3}, and S^{D_4} also increases.

hospital to the individual's environment. Chapter 15, "Transfer of Change," will cover this topic in more detail.

In the last chapter, we learned that the term *response* actually refers to a response class, rather than a single, discrete response. Each member of a response class produces the same or similar effect on its environment. Similarly, the term *stimulus* refers to a stimulus class or group of stimuli, rather than a single, discrete stimulus. Each member of a stimulus class serves the same function for a response, for example, as an S^D setting the occasion for a response to be reinforced.

The more similar a stimulus is to the original S^D, the more likely it is that the response will be performed in its presence. The frequency of responding is greatest in the presence of the original S^D and decreases in frequency as the stimulus becomes less similar to the original S^D. Stimulus similarity can include properties such as size, color, form, and other physical characteristics.

For example, Johnny was positively reinforced by his mother for swearing, although she intended to discourage this behavior. The mother served as the S^D for the response of swearing, and the reinforcer was the attention she paid him by her facial expressions and saying, "Johnny, now please don't talk that way!" Mother's attention was observed to increase rather than decrease Johnny's swearing. Johnny sometimes used swear words with his aunts, female teachers, and other women, but rarely with his male teachers or his father. Johnny's swearing was observed to occur most frequently in his mother's presence and with decreasing frequency as the stimuli became less similar to his mother.

Sometimes a practitioner encounters a client who is similar in some respect to a significant individual in the practitioner's life, such as a parent, friend, spouse, or child. The practitioner might respond to the client in the same way that he or she has behaved toward the significant individual. Stimulus generalization in such cases could be detrimental to the client, if the practitioner fails to consider this factor.

SUMMARY

1. Antecedents are stimulus events that precede or accompany responses and influence their performance.
2. Discriminative stimuli are antecedents that exert control over the performance of a response. There are two kinds of discriminative stimuli: the S^D and the S^Δ.
3. The S^D signals or sets the occasion for a response made in its presence to be reinforced. The S^Δ signals that a response made in its presence will not be reinforced.
4. A response performed in the presence of an S^D is reinforced and increases in frequency. A response performed in the presence of S^Δ is extinguished and decreases in frequency.
5. The discrimination-training procedure reinforces a response made in the presence of S^D and extinguishes a response made in the presence of S^Δ. The effect of this procedure is stimulus control: the response occurs to S^D and never or rarely to S^Δ. An additional feature of stimulus control is short latency between presentation of the S^D and performance of the response.

6. Stimulus fading is a procedure used to transfer stimulus control from an original S^D to a novel antecedent stimulus. The stimulus-fading procedure is called errorless learning because the individual emits the appropriate response under gradually changing S^Ds with no errors or responses to S^Δ.

7. The principle of stimulus generalization states that a response reinforced in the presence of one stimulus, S^D, will also be performed in the presence of similar S^Ds. The more similar the stimulus is to the original S^D, the more likely it is that stimulus generalization will occur.

8. The term stimulus actually refers to a stimulus class in the same way that the term response refers to a response class. Thus, each member of a stimulus class can serve the same function for a response, for example, as an S^D.

SUGGESTED READINGS

BARLOW, D. H., and AGRAS, W. S., "Fading to Increase Heterosexual Responsiveness in Homosexuals," *Journal of Applied Behavior Analysis,* 6, 1973, 355–366.

GOLDIAMOND, I., "Self-control Procedures in Personal Behavior Problems," *Psychological Reports,* 17, 1965, 851–868.

SANOK, R. L. and STRIEFEL, S., "Elective Mutism: Generalization of Verbal Responding Across People and Setting," *Behavior Therapy,* 10 (3), 1979, 357–371.

SHORKEY, C., and TAYLOR, J. "Management of Maladaptive Behavior of a Severely Burned Child," *Child Welfare,* 52, 1973, 543–547.

SKINNER, B. F., *Science and Human Behavior* (New York: Free Press, 1953), Chapters 7 & 8, 107–140.

SUNDEL, M., BUTTERFIELD, W., and GEIS, G., "Modification of Verbal Behavior in Chronic Schizophrenics," *Michigan Mental Health Research Bulletin,* 3, 1969, 37–40.

TERRACE, H. S., "Stimulus Control," in W. K. Honig (Ed.), *Operant behavior: Areas of Research and Application* (Englewood Cliffs, N.J.: Prentice-Hall, Inc., 1966), pp. 271–344.

POST-TEST QUESTIONS

(3) 1. Using the information from Case Study 4, pages 69–70, answer the following: (1) Describe the discrimination-training procedure that was used. (2) How were reinforcement and extinction involved in this procedure? (3) Describe the effects of this procedure.

(3) 2. Jim, a retarded teenager, does not discriminate the men's restroom sign from the ladies' sign; that is, he sometimes walks into the ladies' restroom, sometimes into the men's. Give an example of a stimulus-fading procedure you could use to teach Jim the appropriate discrimination.

(5) 3. Describe a procedure for establishing a discrimination. In your example, include one S^D, one S^Δ, and one response. Specify the reinforcer. How would you know when stimulus control has been achieved?

8

ELEMENTS OF BEHAVIORAL ASSESSMENT

objectives

After completing this chapter, you should be able to:

1. describe a target behavior in measurable terms,
2. give examples of deficit and excess problematic behaviors,
3. identify antecedents of a target behavior and negative consequences of that behavior, given a sample case, and
4. identify a target behavior, its antecedent, and the reinforcing consequences, given a sample case.

An intake interview in a social agency revealed the following information: Shirley's boss frequently asks her to work late. Last week, he made four such requests. When her boss makes these requests, Shirley holds her head down and says, 'Okay.' Shirley had unpleasant arguments with her husband twice over her working late, and on another night they arrived late to a play.

The student caseworker wondered how to use this information in a behavioral assessment.

PRETEST QUESTIONS

Chapter 8

(2) 1. Rewrite the following sentences so that the strength of the response is stated in measurable terms.

a. Hortense has repeatedly phoned the adoption agency.

b. Roger rarely kisses his wife.

(2) 2. In Case Study 8 (see Appendix 1), what were the behavioral excesses shown by Mrs. Gomez and Mr. Terry?

(2) 3. What were the negative consequences of these behaviors?

(3) 4. From the information given in the following paragraph, identify Henry's target response(s), the antecedent, and the negative consequences.

When someone comes over to talk to Henry or ask him a question, he mutters and speaks in a low voice so that the person has difficulty hearing what he is saying. The person typically stops talking and walks away from Henry soon after he begins to mutter.

(2) 5. State two criteria that can be used in establishing problem priorities for treatment.

INTRODUCTION TO BEHAVIORAL ASSESSMENT

The purpose of this chapter is to present major concepts and procedures of behavioral assessment. We have thus far covered various behavioral principles and procedures, illustrating their applications to a variety of situations. These principles will now be considered within a behavioral-assessment framework. **Behavioral assessment** is the method used to evaluate a client's problem(s) or circumstances so that goals and an appropriate intervention plan can be formulated. The behavioral-assessment framework presented here is applicable to most community and institutional settings.

Human service practitioners frequently encounter clients who lack effective problem-solving skills or complain about unmanageable "anxiety" or "depression." Traditional psychodynamic approaches usually involve lengthy diagnostic workups based on early developmental experiences of the client. These procedures typically lead to classification of the client according to standardized categories of mental disorder, such as "paranoid-schizophrenic," "obsessive-compulsive neurosis," or "antisocial personality." These labels often fail to provide the basis for an explicit treatment plan designed to ameliorate the conditions they represent. In addition, clients given the same label often exhibit different maladaptive behaviors. Diagnostic labels can establish or reinforce clients' beliefs or fears that they have a permanent pathological condition that cannot be altered. Such labels may have further detrimental consequences for some clients even after the maladaptive behaviors no longer occur. For example, they may experience difficulty in being hired for certain jobs.

Behavioral assessment involves systematic data gathering that focuses on current target behaviors and their controlling environmental conditions. Rather than resulting in diagnostic labels, behavioral assessment leads to specification of the client's problematic behavior(s), its controlling antecedents and consequences, and formulation of behavioral change goals. The behavioral change goals indicate the direction in which the target behavior(s) is to be modified. The intervention plan is based on these goals and involves selection of intervention techniques directed toward goal achievement. The focus on target behavior and its controlling stimuli in the environment provides the client with the expectation that the problematic situation can be measurably improved.

TREATMENT CONTRACT

When an individual goes to a social agency for help, an initial interview is conducted to determine the individual's interest in receiving assistance and the agency's suitability for providing that help. When the individual decides to seek service from this source, and the agency worker decides that appropriate service can be provided for this individual, this forms the basis for an agreement that can be formalized in a service or treatment contract. The **treatment contract** defines the roles of the client and worker so that each agrees to perform certain activities that can lead to attainment of the client's goals. In many cases, this agreement is verbal and informal.

ELEMENTS OF BEHAVIORAL ASSESSMENT

A thorough behavioral assessment should be carried out prior to implementing a behavioral-change program, so that intervention techniques are appropriately applied to the client's situation. This assessment includes baseline measures for evaluating the effectiveness of the behavioral-change program. In crisis situations, however, the practitioner may have to intervene prior to carrying out a thorough behavioral assessment, in order to provide the client with necessary resources, referrals, or direct assistance. Such emergencies include situations where the client is suicidal, requires immediate hospitalization, or where immediate action is required to provide food, housing, medical care, or physical protection.

Behavioral assessment involves consideration of the following elements: (1) problem area, (2) problem selection, (3) target behavior, (4) response strength, and (5) controlling conditions (antecedents and consequences).

Problem Area

The practitioner initiates the behavioral-assessment procedure by obtaining from the client a listing of major problem areas. Various problem checklists and questionnaires can be used in conjunction with interviewing to help identify major areas of difficulty. Figure 8-1 is the Problem Inventory, a checklist that helps individuals identify their major areas of concern. The items on this checklist represent areas of functioning for which an individual might seek help, for example, food, housing, job, health concerns. This inventory can help the worker narrow down the individual's complaints into general categories. Then, if it is apparent that the in-

FIGURE 8-1   Problem inventory

Below are some things that may be a problem for you. If you have concerns in any of these areas, please check the box next to it.

Rank order the three problems that most concern you by writing 1, 2, and 3 in the space next to those three problems.

☐ Food
☐ Clothing
☐ Housing
☐ Money
☐ Job
☐ School
☐ Physical Health
☐ Mental Health
☐ Feeling Lonely
☐ Sex
☐ Police or Courts
☐ Drugs

☐ Alcohol
☐ Trouble Sleeping
☐ Nervousness, Anxiety
☐ Physical Violence
☐ Get Confused about Things
☐ Difficulty Showing Emotions
☐ Can't Make Decisions
☐ Overeating
☐ Smoking
☐ Headaches
☐ Feeling Down or Blue
☐ Other (Specify)

dividual needs a referral, the worker will be able to identify the professional or agency that can be of help. In ranking the problems, the client is helped to zero in on the ones that are of most concern.

A problem area is often manifested in the role or position in which the individual experiences difficulty—for example, as a father, as a teacher, as an employee, or as a husband. Thus, problem areas might include discipline of children, for a father; classroom management, for a teacher; social skills, for an employee; or marital relations, for a husband. The Problem Checklist in Figure 8-2 can be used to help the client specify problem roles. Nineteen roles are listed. From these, the client identifies the roles he or she finds difficult to perform. Following this initial identification, the client is provided with sample problem descriptions to use as a guide in writing his or her problem statements in behaviorally specific terms.

Problem selection

If the client identifies more than one problem area, the practitioner should help the client select one problem for immediate attention. Using the following four criteria, the practitioner and client prioritize the problems presented:

1. The problem of immediate concern to the client and/or significant others (for example, family, friends, teachers).
   Examples: Mr. Foster wants to stop drinking. Mrs. Hernandez seeks help in managing her diabetic son's diet.

FIGURE 8-2　Problem checklist

In which of the following roles do you experience difficulty? Check (√) the role(s) which you have trouble performing.

Circle the role that *most* concerns you.

_____ Mother	_____ Classmate
_____ Father	_____ Teacher
_____ Sister	_____ Friend—same sex
_____ Brother	_____ Friend—opposite sex
_____ Son	_____ Employee
_____ Daughter	_____ Co-worker
_____ Step-relative	_____ Subordinate
_____ Other relative (specify)	_____ Neighbor
_____ Employer or supervisor	_____ Myself
	_____ Other (specify)

For each of the roles you circled, what are the one or two problems you are having that most concern you? Look at the examples below before you write your own. The examples indicate the kind of information that you should include in defining your problem(s).

2. The problem that has severe aversive or negative consequences for the client, significant others, or society if not handled immediately.

    Examples: Herman will be fired from his job unless he can start working cooperatively with co-workers. Sally will be expelled from school unless she attends more frequently.

3. The problem that can be corrected most quickly, considering resources and obstacles.

    Example: Bob and Jean Jones decide to work on resolving their arguments over financial matters before dealing with their more complicated sexual problems.

4. The problem that requires handling before other problems can be treated.

    Example: Mr. and Mrs. Smith decide that they must resolve their child-rearing disagreements before developing a program to modify their children's behavior problems.

Target Behavior

The client's target behavior(s) is stated in terms that clearly specify his or her responses. Responses are described in observable terms, without attaching labels or judgments such as "inadequate personality" or "passive-aggressive." Even labels such as anxiety or fear can be described in terms of the client's verbal behaviors or avoidance of the feared situation (see Chapter 13). Measurement of physiological

EXAMPLES:

Role	Problem
1. Spouse–husband	My wife and I are constantly quarreling. She usually sleeps in the children's room instead of with me.
2. Father	When I ask my oldest son to do his homework, he ignores me and shuts himself up in his room. He often teases and hits his younger sister.
3. Employee-speech therapist	When I disagree with my co-workers about a case presented at a staff meeting, I remain silent and do not state my disagreement.

PROBLEM OF MAJOR CONCERN TO ME

Role	Problem

Adapted from the Sundel-Lawrence Problem Checklist from "Behavioral Group Treatment with Adults in a Family Service Agency," by Martin Sundel and Harry Lawrence in *Individual Change Through Small Groups* by P. Glasser, R. Sarri, and R. Vinter (Eds.). Reprinted with permission of The Free Press, a Division of Macmillan Publishing Co., Inc., copyright 1974.

changes such as heart rate, temperature, muscle tension, and blood pressure can also be obtained. Other unobservable responses such as an individual's thoughts, feelings, and attitudes, although experienced subjectively, can be included if they are described in terms of the person's observable motor or verbal responses.

Problematic behaviors can be classified as either behavioral excesses or behavioral deficits. **Behavioral excess** refers to the high frequency of inappropriate behaviors emitted by the client. **Behavioral deficit** refers to the absence or low frequency of appropriate behaviors. Examples of behavioral excesses include overeating, drug and alcohol abuse, and telling lies. Examples of behavioral deficits include failure to speak up for one's rights, to attend work regularly, or to turn in class assignments. Behaviors can also be considered problematic when they are under faulty stimulus control. An individual performs a response that is inappropriate in certain situations, although the same response is appropriate under other circumstances. For example, yelling "Fire!" or breaking the fire alarm box is appropriate when there is a fire (S^D), but it is inappropriate and potentially dangerous when there is no fire ($S^\triangle$). Other words used to describe problematic target behaviors include "maladaptive," "deviant," "inappropriate," and "undesirable."

Response Strength

The strength of the target response is determined by measures of frequency per time unit (rate), duration, latency, and/or intensity. Frequency is the most commonly used measure of response strength. The number of times the target behavior is performed within a given time period is counted and recorded as baseline data. Recording each occurrence of the target behavior provides a continuous record. **Continuous recording** is particularly appropriate for self-management programs in which the individual records such target behaviors as the number of arguments per day, number of candy bars eaten per week, or number of home visits completed per week. Other target behaviors appropriate for continuous recording include the number of times per day a person agrees to do something and fails to follow through, the number of times a child practices a musical instrument per week, or the number of times a child says "no" per hour.

Continuous recording is not always feasible or efficient, for example, when recording high-frequency behaviors or monitoring several behaviors of one or more individuals. Interval recording and time sampling are two ways of recording behaviors noncontinuously. **Interval recording** involves selecting a block of time during which the target behavior will be observed (for example, 15 minutes), and further dividing this block into brief intervals (for example, 10 seconds). If the target behavior occurs during the brief interval, the observer records a check mark for that interval. If the target behavior is not emitted at all during the interval, the observer records zero for that interval. The behavior must be performed at least once during the interval in order to be recorded. Regardless of the number of times the behavior occurs during the interval, a check mark is recorded for that interval. At the end of the block of time, the number of intervals in which the target behavior occurred is counted. Interval recording is most reliable when an external event, such as a tape-recorded tone, signals the end of each interval. A headset with a prerecorded tone or

FIGURE 8-3   Interval record of Sam's out-of-seat behavior

Date ___11/15_____

Time __10:15 – 10:30__ (Social Studies)

Subject ___Sam P._____

Target Behavior ___out of seat_____

✓ = out of seat   0 = in seat

Intervals

1	✓	16	✓	31	✓	46	✓	61	✓	76	0
2	✓	17	✓	32	✓	47	0	62	✓	77	0
3	✓	18	✓	33	✓	48	0	63	0	78	0
4	✓	19	✓	34	0	49	0	64	0	79	0
5	0	20	✓	35	0	50	0	65	0	80	0
6	✓	21	✓	36	0	51	0	66	0	81	0
7	✓	22	0	37	0	52	0	67	0	82	0
8	✓	23	0	38	0	53	0	68	0	83	0
9	0	24	0	39	✓	54	0	69	0	84	0
10	✓	25	0	40	✓	55	0	70	0	85	0
11	0	26	0	41	✓	56	0	71	✓	86	✓
12	✓	27	0	42	✓	57	0	72	✓	87	✓
13	0	28	✓	43	✓	58	0	73	✓	88	✓
14	0	29	✓	44	✓	59	✓	74	✓	89	✓
15	0	30	✓	45	✓	60	✓	75	✓	90	0

TOTAL: 72/90 = 47% out of seat

Observer's initials _____

signal can be worn by the observer. Figure 8-3 shows a sample interval record of a student's out-of-seat behavior during his social studies class.

Interval recording is most appropriate for behaviors that occur with high frequency, such as facial tics, head banging, and inappropriate classroom talking. The interval record can provide an accurate reflection of the rates of these behaviors without having to count each occurrence.

Time sampling can also be used to record frequency data. Time sampling involves recording whether or not the target behavior is performed at certain times of the day. For example, a teacher can record the cooperative play behaviors of several nursery school children. He or she observes them at specified intervals—for example, at the end of every thirty minutes—and records the presence or absence of the target behaviors at those times (see Figure 8-4). Like interval recording, time sampling can be used to monitor high-frequency behaviors. It is also useful when monitoring several behaviors of one or more individuals. Time sampling requires less time and involvement on the part of the observer than continuous or interval recording. Further discussion of recording procedures and related issues is available (for example, Gambrill 1977; Martin & Pear 1978).

Target behaviors should be clearly specified so that the observers are likely to

FIGURE 8-4   Time-sampling record for cooperative play behaviors of nursery school children

Date   12/2

Subjects   Jan, Stewart

Target Behavior   Cooperative play*

+ = cooperative play   0 = no cooperative play

Time	Jan	Stewart
9:00 a.m.	0	0
9:30	+	+
10:00	0	+
10:30	+	+
11:00	0	0
11:30	0	+
12:00	0	+
12:30	+	+
TOTAL	3/8 = 38% time observed in cooperative play	6/8 = 75% time observed in cooperative play

*Cooperative play behaviors

1. using same toy with another child (sharing)
2. talking to another child
3. sitting next to another child waiting for a turn
4. giving something to another child
5. helping another child

agree on their independent observations. This means that each observer records the data independently of the other, that is, without consulting or signaling each other. The extent of agreement between observers is determined to insure that the behaviors have been adequately specified and recorded. In Figure 8-4, for example, the responses comprising cooperative play are listed on the recording form to aid the observers in identifying the appropriate behaviors to record.

Interobserver agreement or reliability can be determined by comparing the number of observations recorded the same way by each rater. For example, one observer recorded 38 intervals as + and another observer recorded 40 as +. The observers agreed on 38 intervals. They disagreed on two.

Interobserver agreement (IA) is computed by dividing the number of identical observations (IO) by the number of identical observations plus the number of different observations (IO + DO).

$$IA = \frac{IO}{IO + DO}$$

Interobserver agreement is expressed in terms of a percentage. In this example,

$$IA = \frac{IO}{IO + DO} = \frac{38}{38 + 2} = 95\%$$

Kazdin (1980) has suggested that estimates of interobserver reliability should be 80%–100%. A reliability figure lower than 80% indicates significant errors in recording. A major source of these errors could be inadequate specification of the responses to be observed.

Where applicable, the duration of the target behavior is recorded in addition to its rate. For example, "Sally giggled in class for 15 minutes three times per day"; "Fred talked for 30 minutes during the staff meeting 5 times last week." Another measure of response strength that is recorded when applicable is latency. The latency of a response is measured by the interval of time that transpires between presentation of the S^D and performance of the response. For example, Pedro's father called him to the dinner table and he came immediately (short latency). The nurse told the patient to put on a robe and he did so 20 minutes later (long latency).

The intensity or severity of behaviors such as hitting, teasing, kicking, or crying is often difficult or impractical to measure. The problematic feature of these behaviors involves the aversive consequences or effects that they have for the client or significant others. Individuals differ in their tolerance for the behaviors of others as well as in their own reactions to physical and social stimulation. Examining the aversive or negative consequences of the target behavior for the client and significant others provides an indicator for judging the intensity of the behavior. For example, the degree of "noisiness" of Dick's playing his stereo in the house is determined by a neighbor who complains to the police; the intensity of Sam's "tapping" a classmate on the arm is indicated by the victim's bruises or complaints to a teacher.

In assessing problems that occur infrequently, such as violent arguments between marital partners, the therapist should attempt to discover specific episodes that offended either partner. These episodes might not have been reported by the couple, although they often preceded major blow-ups. The frequency of these less violent but problematic interchanges should be obtained, and the motor and verbal responses of both partners in these situations should be delineated.

Controlling Conditions (Antecedents and Consequences)

In behavioral assessment, the practitioner attempts to specify the antecedent and consequent conditions maintaining the target behavior. Antecedents refer to events that precede, signal, or trigger a specific behavior. For example, an antecedent condition for Roger punching Charlotte with his fist was Charlotte calling Roger "stupid." A second antecedent was her refusal to have sexual intercourse with him.

It is sometimes difficult to identify the controlling antecedents that signal or set the occasion for target behaviors. The practitioner should describe in specific terms when and where the behavior is performed, who is present, and what is said or done by whom prior to performance of the behavior. As a rule, the practitioner focuses on current events that appear to be closely associated with the target behavior. In some instances, however, the practitioner might explore earlier antecedent events to determine their influence on the client's current behavior.

Reinforcing consequences refer to events that follow a target response and strengthen it. For example, when Maria breaks into line ahead of the other children, she is positively reinforced by receiving ice cream before them.

Aversive or negative consequences refer to events following a target behavior that are undesirable or unpleasant to the individual or significant others. Aversive consequences can decrease the likelihood that the response will be performed again under similar conditions. Aversive consequences that decrease response strength are called punishers (see Chapter 12). For example, when Frances was caught cheating, the professor tore up her paper and gave her a zero.

Sometimes there are both reinforcing and aversive consequences for the same behavior. In the above example, Maria was positively reinforced for breaking in line ahead of the other children. Breaking into line also had aversive consequences for Maria, however, when her mother scolded her and sent her home alone after she got her ice cream cone.

Immediate or short-term reinforcing consequences often have a stronger effect in maintaining a behavior than long-term negative consequences exert in suppressing or preventing the behavior from occurring. Sometimes we wonder why certain behaviors continue to occur in spite of severe negative consequences that eventually follow them. For example, a teenager steals a pen at the grocery store, even though he was taken to the police station last month for a similar offense. The immediate benefits of passing a test by cheating may offset possible negative consequences of being caught and disciplined. Staying in bed a few minutes longer may consistently result in arriving late to work and being criticized by the boss. The immediate pleasure of an extramarital affair may be offset later by the consequences of being discovered and the resulting conflicts that develop among family members.

Many individuals continue to engage in short-term pleasurable activities, although they risk significant health impairment in the long run. For example, considerable evidence exists that demonstrates the relationship between smoking and lung diseases, obesity and cardiovascular impairment, and drinking and liver disease. Short-term reinforcers exert greater control over these health-risking behaviors than the severe negative consequences that are further removed in time. Practitioners in the rapidly growing field of behavioral medicine are treating various health problems using behavioral principles (for example, Davidson & Davidson, 1980).

OBTAINING ASSESSMENT INFORMATION

Accurate, systematic data collection and recording are essential features of behavioral assessment and modification programs. Data indicating strength of the target behaviors are recorded, along with relevant antecedents and consequences. These measures constitute baseline data and should be obtained prior to formulation and implementation of the intervention plan. Response data are recorded before treatment, during treatment, and at follow-up periods, thus providing an ongoing basis for evaluating the effectiveness of the interventions. The practitioner uses these data to determine if target behaviors have increased or decreased in strength and if problematic antecedents and/or consequences have been altered.

The practitioner's observations can be validated by interviewing individuals associated with the client's problem. Sources of validation can include parents, relatives, neighbors, teachers, and peers as well as the client. A description of the client's problem as perceived by these individuals can be obtained, so that their roles in relation to the client's problem are made clear. Significant individuals can also be instructed to observe and record target behaviors and the conditions under which they are performed. Frequently, this monitoring procedure reveals the monitor's role in generating or maintaining the target behavior—that is, how he or she provides problematic antecedents or consequences related to performance of the target behavior.

Client self-reports, reports of significant others, direct observations of a client's behavior, behavioral questionnaires and checklists may be used to obtain assessment information. The Problem Inventory and Problem Checklist were discussed earlier in this chapter. The Fear Survey Schedule (Wolpe & Lang, 1964) is used to identify events that are anxiety producing for an individual. The Reinforcement Survey Schedule (Cautela & Kastenbaum, 1967) identifies stimuli that can be considered as potential reinforcers for specific individuals. The Marital Precounseling Inventory (Stuart & Stuart, 1973) and the Sundel Assertiveness Scale (Sundel & Sundel, 1980) are other examples of assessment instruments. These instruments provide the practitioner with information that otherwise could require extensive interviewing or observation. Other behavioral questionnaires and diagnostic instruments, such as the Life History Questionnaire (Wolpe & Lazarus, 1966), are available.

SUMMARY

1. Behavioral assessment is a method used to evaluate a client's problem or circumstances so that appropriate goals and an intervention plan can be formulated.

2. Behavioral assessment focuses on current target behaviors and their controlling conditions.

3. The behavioral assessment procedure leads to specification of the client's problematic behavior(s), its controlling antecedents and consequences, and formulation of behavioral change goals.

4. Five major elements of behavioral assessment are: problem area, problem selection, target behavior, response strength, and controlling conditions (antecedents and consequences).

5. A problem area is often manifested in the role or position in which the individual experiences difficulty.

6. Four criteria that can be considered in determining problem priorities for intervention are: (a) the most immediate concern of the client and/or significant others, (b) the problem that has severe negative consequences if not handled immediately, (c) the problem that can be corrected most quickly, and (d) the problem that requires handling before other problems can be treated.

7. Problematic behaviors refer to behavioral excesses, behavioral deficits, and faulty discriminations.

8. The strength of a target response is indicated by measures of frequency per time unit (rate), duration, latency, and/or intensity. Frequency per time unit is the most commonly used measure of response strength.

9. The controlling conditions of a target behavior refer to certain antecedents and consequences. Antecedents precede, signal, or trigger a specific behavior. Consequences follow a target behavior and influence the likelihood that it will be performed again.

10. Data related to the strength and controlling conditions of the target behavior should be recorded during assessment, intervention, and follow-up periods. These data can be obtained from client reports, reports of significant others, direct observations, and assessment checklists and questionnaires.

11. The practitioner's observations of the client's target behavior(s) can be validated by interviewing individuals associated with the client's problem.

SUGGESTED READINGS

BARLOW, D. H., (Ed.), *Behavorial Assessment of Adult Disorders* (New York: Guilford Press, 1981).

CAUTELA, J. R., and KASTENBAUM, R., "A Reinforcement Survey Schedule for Use in Therapy, Training, and Research," *Psychological Reports,* 1967, *20,* 1115–1130.

DAVIDSON, P. O., and DAVIDSON, S. M., *Behavioral Medicine: Changing Health Life-styles* (New York: Brunner/Mazel, 1980).

GAMBRILL, E., *Behavior Modification: A Handbook of Assessment, Intervention and Evaluation* (San Francisco: Jossey-Bass, 1977).

JOHNSON, S. M., and BOLSTAD, O. D., "Methodological Issues in Naturalistic Observation: Some Problems and Solutions for Field Research," L. A. Hammerlynck, L. C. Handy, and E. J. Mash (Eds.), *Behavior Change: Methodology, Concepts, and Practice.* (Champaign, Ill.: Research Press, 1973), pp. 7–67.

KAZDIN, A. E., *Behavior Modification in Applied Settings,* Revised edition (Homewood, Illinois: The Dorsey Press, 1980).

MAGER, R. F., *Preparing Instructional Objectives* (Palo Alto, Calif.: Fearon Publishers, 1975).

MARTIN, G., and PEAR, J., *Behavior Modification: What It Is and How to Do It* (Englewood Cliffs, N.J.: Prentice-Hall, Inc., 1978), pp. 282–304.

MASH, E. J. and TERDAL, L. G. (Eds.), *Behavioral Assessment of Childhood Disorders* (New York: Guilford Press, 1981).

SARBIN, T., "On the Futility of the Proposition that Some People Be Labeled Mentally Ill," *Journal of Consulting Psychology,* 1967, *31,* 447–453.

STUART, R. W., and STUART, F., *Marital Precounseling Inventory* (Champaign, Ill.: Research Press, 1973).

SUNDEL, M., and LAWRENCE, H., "Behavioral Group Treatment with Adults in a Family Service Agency," P. Glasser, R. Sarri, and R. Vinter (Eds.), *Individual Change through Small Groups* (New York: Free Press, 1974), pp. 325–347.

SUNDEL, S. S., and SUNDEL, M., *Be Assertive: A Practical Guide for Human Service Workers* (Beverly Hills, Calif.: Sage Publications, 1980).

THOMAS, E.J., *Marital Communication and Decision Making* (New York: The Free Press, 1977).

THOMAS, E. J., WALTER, C. L. and O'FLAHERTY, K., "A Verbal Problem Checklist for Use in Assessing Family Verbal Behavior," *Behavior Therapy,* 1974, *5,* 235–246.

WODARSKI, J. S., FELDMAN, R. A., and PEDI, S. J., "Effects of Different Observational Systems and Time Sequences Upon Non-Participant Observers' Behavioral Ratings," *Journal of Behavior Therapy and Experimental Psychiatry,* 1975, *6,* 275–278.

WOLPE, J., "Behavior Therapy versus Psychoanalysis: Therapeutic and Social Implications," *American Psychologist,* 1981, *36* (2), 159–164.

WOLPE, J., *The Practice of Behavior Therapy* (Elmsford, N.Y.: Pergamon Press, 1969), Chapter 3, 22–54.

WOLPE, J., and LANG, B. J., "A Fear Survey Schedule for Use in Behavior Therapy," *Behavior Research and Therapy,* 1964, *2,* 27–30.

WOLPE, J., and LAZARUS, A., "Life History Questionnaire," J. Wolpe and A. Lazarus, *Behavior Therapy Techniques* (Elmsford, N.Y.: Pergamon Press, 1966), Appendix 1, pp. 165–169.

POST-TEST QUESTIONS

(4) 1. Give two examples of behavioral deficits and two examples of behavioral excesses.

(4) 2. A caseworker tells her supervisor that a client is always late for his appointments.

a. Which of the following questions should the supervisor ask her in order to obtain baseline measures of the complaint?
(Circle the correct answer(s)).

1. Why do you think the client is always late?

2. How many minutes late is the client?

3. How many times has the client been late this month?

4. What do you think the client's lateness means?

b. Give one hypothetical answer to each question you chose above that would provide baseline data of the target behavior.

(3) 3. From the information given in the following paragraph, identify Shirley's target response, its antecedents, and its negative consequences.

Shirley's boss frequently asks her to work late. Last week, he made four such requests. When her boss makes these requests, Shirley holds her head down and says, "Okay." Shirley had unpleasant arguments with her husband twice over working late, and on another night they arrived late to a play.

(3) 4. From the information given in the paragraph below, identify the target response, its antecedent, and the probable positive reinforcer.

Children are talking in a group. No one is talking to Howard. When Howard tells jokes about himself, the other children gather around and laugh at him. The social worker observes that the other children rarely speak to Howard unless he is making fun of himself.

9

CONDUCTING A BEHAVIORAL ASSESSMENT

objectives

Given a case example, you should be able to:

1.   specify two antecedents related to the target response,
2.   state a negative consequence of the target response,
3.   state a probable reinforcer maintaining the target response, and
4.   formulate a behavioral change goal including a desired client response, a relevant antecedent, and a probable positive reinforcer.

Mr. Domino was showing a customer some furniture. The customer was difficult to please and complained about the cost of everything she saw. Mr. Domino became 'frustrated and angry.' He raised his voice, clenched his fists, frowned, and moved his arms rapidly up and down. Mr. Domino insulted the customer by telling her that she had bad taste in sofas, that she didn't know quality furniture when she saw it, that she would never find anything that suited her, and that no salesman in his right mind would put up with her fussiness. The customer became enraged. Her face turned red; she yelled back at him and said she would report him to the manager. The customer then turned on her heels and left the store.

Chapter 9

(1) 1. Which of the following statements best describes the purpose of behavioral assessment? (Circle the correct answer.)

    a. Reconstruct an individual's personality.

    b. Help a person learn to accept him or herself.

    c. Specify appropriate behaviors.

    d. Identify target behaviors and their controlling environmental conditions and formulate behavioral change goals.

(3) 2. Using the information from Case Study 7 (see Appendix 1), state (a) two of Stephen's target responses, (b) the probable positive reinforcer that maintained them, and (c) the antecedent to the target responses.

(1) 3. In order to determine controlling antecedents of the target behavior, an appropriate question to ask a client is (circle a or b):

    a. Where does this problem occur?

    b. Why do you continue to engage in this behavior?

(3) 4. Using the information from Case Study 5 (see pages 105–106) state an intermediate treatment goal for Mr. Lewis specifying (a) a desired response and (b) a relevant antecedent.

(1) 5. How is behavioral reenactment used in behavioral assessment?

In the last chapter we described a method for identifying problem areas and target behaviors, establishing problem priorities, and specifying antecedents and consequences. In this chapter we present a framework for assessing the problem selected by the individual and practitioner for treatment or intervention. The four major components of behavioral assessment are addressed: (1) target response(s), (2) antecedents, (3) consequences, and (4) response strength, **RAC-S,** an acronym for target Response, Antecedents Consequences, and response Strength, will be applied as an assessment framework for analysis of target responses and their controlling conditions.

The practitioner can use the following procedure to gather data for behavioral assessment. The client should be involved as much as possible at each step of this procedure.

1. List the client's problems, identified through interviews, observations, checklists, and/or questionnaires.
2. Select one problem for immediate attention, based on the criteria in Chapter 8.
3. Obtain examples of the problem, including a description of the following components: (a) target response(s); (b) controlling antecedents; (c) the negative consequences for the client and/or significant others; (d) possible reinforcers; and (e) response strength, including measures of frequency per time unit (rate), duration, intensity, and/or latency.
4. Specify measures of response strength to be recorded and design a plan for monitoring the response. Indicate who will observe and record the response.
5. Obtain measures of response strength.
6. Formulate terminal, intermediate, and initial behavioral change goals, specifying: (a) the desired response(s), (b) the antecedent(s), and (c) the positive reinforcer(s).

RAC-S

The RAC-S paradigm (Figure 9-1) provides a framework for examining: (1) the relationship between the target response and its possible controlling antecedents; (2) the relationship between the target response and its possible controlling consequences; and (3) the target response and its measures of frequency, intensity, latency, and/or duration. Sample questions relevant to each component are listed. These questions are suggested as guides for the practitioner to use in obtaining relevant information during observations and interviews.

In order to delineate the client's problem, the practitioner obtains examples of it, either by direct observation or by asking the client and/or significant others to describe a recent example of the problem. The client or significant other is asked to give an explicit account of this event. Using the examples provided, the practitioner attempts to specify the RAC-S information, including: (1) the target response(s), (2)

FIGURE 9-1 RAC-S paradigm

In the presence of

A
Antecedents

1. When is the target behavior performed?
2. Who is present
3. Where is the client?
4. What happens before the target response?
   a. What is said?
   b. Who says it?
   c. What nonverbal behavior is emitted?
   d. Who emits it?

S
Response Strength

1. How many times did the response occur during the past minute? Hour? Day? Week? Month?
2. How long does each occurrence of the behavior last (duration)?
3. How can the intensity of the behavior be described?
4. How quickly does the response occur after presentation of an antecedent stimulus?
5. How long has the behavior been a problem?

R ────────────────► **C**

Target Response(s)

1. What does the client say?
2. What nonverbal behavior does client emit?

Positive (C⁺) / Negative (C⁻) Consequences

C⁺ and/or C⁻

1. What happens after the target response?
2. Who responds to the client?
3. When does this consequence occur?
4. Who judges the client's behavior to be problematic?
5. What behaviors do others perform that could influence the client's behavior?

C⁺

1. What seems to maintain or support the response (possible reinforcers)?
2. What attention does the client receive?
3. What benefit does the client receive?
4. What happens that could influence the client to perform the behavior again?
5. What negative event is removed or avoided?

C⁻

1. What losses are sustained by the client?
2. What physical or verbal assault is inflicted on the client?
3. What losses are sustained by other individuals or society?

controlling antecedents, (3) negative consequences, (4) possible reinforcers, and (5) measures of response strength such as frequency per time unit (rate), duration, intensity, and/or latency. Questions similar to those listed in Figure 9-1 are asked to elicit details necessary to complete this initial assessment.

BEHAVIORAL REENACTMENT

It is sometimes difficult to accurately specify RAC-S data on the basis of examples provided by the client or others. For example, many people can describe another person's behaviors in the problematic situation but are unaware of their own behaviors influencing that situation.

Behavioral reenactment is a role-play technique used to obtain RAC-S information on the client's behaviors in the problematic situation (Lawrence & Sundel, 1972). In behavioral reenactment, the client role plays himself or herself in the problematic situation. The practitioner and/or group members (if the assessment is occurring in a group setting) role play the parts of significant others according to the client's descriptions. The practitioner observes the client's verbal and nonverbal behaviors during the role play and compares these observations with the client's previous descriptions. This technique is particularly useful in validating the accuracy of a client's verbal report of the target behavior and its controlling conditions.

For example, Mrs. Roark, a casework supervisor, complained that the executive director singled her out for criticism. She insisted that nothing she did or said was responsible for the criticism. Mrs. Roark reenacted a recent incident in which the executive director criticized her. During the role play, Mrs. Roark spoke in short, clipped phrases, sneered, and stood defiantly with her hands on her hips when the executive director asked about staff members on her unit. After the reenactment, the practitioner and group members pointed out discrepancies between Mrs. Roark's account of the incident and the responses they observed during the reenactment. Thus the behavioral reenactment provided a concrete example of Mrs. Roark's problematic responses and also helped to identify controlling antecedents and consequences.

COLLECTING ASSESSMENT INFORMATION

Measures of response strength (frequency, latency, intensity, and/or duration) should be obtained prior to suggesting a solution to the client or implementing the behavioral-change program. The behavior modifier assigns the client to record baseline data at home or outside the practice setting. The client reports these data at each interview. The client records the data on prepared forms such as the Assessment Form (Figure 9-2) and the Behavioral Recording Chart (Figure 9-3). The client can also carry a 3-inch by 5-inch card for conveniently recording target behaviors. Wrist counters and other devices are also available for this purpose.

Individuals other than the client, such as the practitioner or significant others, may be responsible for collecting and recording assessment data. The rationale for assigning the client to collect baseline data between treatment sessions is to obtain measures that accurately reflect the occurrence of target responses in the client's natural environment. The practitioner explains the recording assignment and then asks the client to restate it. The practitioner should answer all questions and clarify any ambiguities related to the assignment. Failure to confirm the client's ability to carry out the assignment can result in inaccurate or incomplete data collection.

Initially, the client may be assigned to record the target response(s) and measures of response strength. When the client demonstrates the ability to observe and record target behaviors accurately, the practitioner can also assign the client to record antecedents and/or consequences related to the target behavior(s). These RAC-S data are then used in formulating goals.

FIGURE 9-2 Assessment form

1. State the problem and give an example of its occurrence.

2. Specify the target response(s) to be observed in precise terms. Be sure that a stranger reading this description would know exactly what the client is *saying* or *doing*.

   Behavioral excesses:

   Behavioral deficits:

3. Describe the antecedents related to the target response(s).

   1.

   2.

4. Describe in specific terms the negative consequences of this problem.

   1.

   2.

5. State the possible reinforcers for the target response(s).

   1.

   2.

FIGURE 9-3 Behavioral recording chart

DAYS	DESCRIPTION OF RESPONSE	RESPONSE STRENGTH:[a]
Sun.		
Mon.		
Tues.		
Wed.		
Thurs.		
Fri.		
Sat.		
		Total:

[a]Specify measure of response strength to be used (frequency per time unit, duration, intensity, and/or latency).

APPLICATION OF RAC-S

Mr. Domino's *presenting problem* (the problem that he said brought him to seek help) was frequent arguments with his wife over financial matters. Information provided by the Problem Inventory and Problem Checklist indicated that Mr. Domino also had difficulty disciplining his teenage son and working with customers. After further discussion, Mr. Domino, a furniture salesman, indicated that his work situation was of most concern because his sales had dropped and he was in danger of losing his job. Mr. Domino had worked at his present job for six years. When asked for an example of his problem, Mr. Domino reported a recent incident in which his boss criticized him for being rude to customers. Mr. Domino also mentioned several occasions that month when he lost his temper and insulted customers, two incidents occurring within the past week. Although Mr. Domino feared that he would be fired if this pattern continued, he said he did not know how to make himself act differently. Mr. Domino had discussed this problem with his family physician who suggested counseling, since he was in good physical health.

Mr. Domino had difficulty specifying the circumstances of his last unpleasant encounter with a customer. The counselor arranged a behavioral reenactment to obtain concrete examples of Mr. Domino's behavior in the problematic situation. The counselor role played a customer and Mr. Domino role played himself in a simulation of a recent incident in which Mr. Domino lost his temper with a customer. Mr. Domino described the situation as follows: He was showing a customer some furniture. The customer was difficult to please and complained about the cost of everything she saw.

During the behavioral reenactment, the counselor observed that Mr. Domino raised his voice, clenched his fists, frowned, and moved his arms rapidly up and down. Mr. Domino insulted the customer by telling her she had bad taste in sofas, that she didn't know quality furniture when she saw it, that she would never find anything that suited her, and that no salesman in his right mind would put up with her fussiness. The customer became enraged. Her face turned red; she yelled back at him and said she would report him to the manager. The customer then turned on her heel and left the store. When questioned after the role play, Mr. Domino reported feeling "frustrated and angry." He said that he had behaved similarly in recent incidents at work.

In order to determine the controlling antecedents for Mr. Domino's inappropriate responses, he was asked questions similar to those on the RAC-S Paradigm shown in Figure 9-1. For example, where and when were the target behaviors performed? Who was present? What was said? Who said it? The target behaviors occurred when Mr. Domino was in the store with a customer, usually with another salesman nearby. Just before Mr. Domino became angry and insulted the customer, the customer said something about the price of the item in relation to a competitor. Mr. Domino said, "They [the customers] sometimes say that they have seen the same item for less money at National's [another furniture store in town]. That really makes me mad. We provide much better service for the price."

Mr. Domino stated the negative consequences of his target responses: his boss criticized him, he would lose his job if he continued to offend customers. Further

101

FIGURE 9-4   Assessment form filled out on Mr. Domino by practitioner

1. State the problem and give an example of its occurrence.

    Mr. Domino is afraid that he will be fired. A customer commented about the high prices of furniture in the store and he insulted her in a loud voice. His boss criticized him.

2. Specify the target response(s) to be observed in precise terms. Be sure that a stranger reading this description would know exactly what the client is *saying* or *doing*.

    Behavioral excesses: Raising his voice, clenching his fists, moving arms up and down rapidly, making insulting remarks ("You have terrible taste in sofas"; "No salesman in his right mind would put up with your fussiness").

    Behavioral deficits: Making too few sales. Failure to discuss furniture with customers in a calm pleasant manner.

3. Describe the antecedents related to the target response(s).

    1. A customer complains about prices related to a competitor's.

    2. Mr. Domino is in the store with a customer with other salesmen nearby.

4. Describe in specific terms the negative consequences of this problem.

    1. His boss criticizes him.

    2. He might lose his job.

5. State the possible reinforcers for the target response(s).

    1. Other employees show approval when he insults customers (they smile, praise him).

    2. Unpleasant customers leave the store.

interviewing or observation was necessary to discover the possible reinforcing consequences for Mr. Domino's target behaviors. Again, the RAC-S Paradigm (Figure 9-1) suggests questions that could be used to help identify possible reinforcers for his behaviors. For example, what maintains the responses? What attention or other benefits does the client receive? Mr. Domino stated that he did not like his present job, but was afraid that he would be unable to find another one that could support his family. He did not associate much with the other "dumb" employees, who were mostly younger. When he "told the customer off," however, the other employees expressed their approval. Further information about possible reinforcers was obtained through behavioral reenactments in which the counselor role played

FIGURE 9-5 Behavioral recording chart filled out by Mr. Domino

DAYS	DESCRIPTION OF RESPONSE	RESPONSE STRENGTH: DURATION, FREQUENCY PER DAY
Sun.	Off work	0
Mon.	Raised voice; insulted customers	5 min., 1/day
Tues.		0
Wed.	Insulted customers; clenched fists	2 min., 1/day
Thurs.	Scowled; insulted customers	5 min., 1/day
Fri.		0
Sat.		0
		Total: 3 times/week Range: 2-5 min.

Mr. Domino and Mr. Domino role played other employees telling him that they liked the way he told that lady "where to go."

Mr. Domino's Assessment Form is shown in Figure 9-4. After the Assessment Form was completed, Mr. Domino was instructed to record the frequency and duration of his target behaviors on the Behavioral Recording Chart. The Behavioral Recording Chart filled out by Mr. Domino is shown in Figure 9-5.

The Behavioral Recording Chart enables the practitioner to compare the client's subjective recall of the problematic situation with a record based on the client's actual performance. A written record also can be used to correct subjective estimates of response strength. Sometimes the activities of observing and recording RAC-S data produce a temporary change in the frequency of the target response(s).

FORMULATING BEHAVIORAL CHANGE GOALS

After the target response and its antecedents, consequences, and response strength are specified and collected as baseline measures, behavioral change goals can be formulated. The goals should specify the desired responses, and their antecedents and consequences. Whenever feasible, measures of response strength should be included. Initial and intermediate goals are established as approximations to terminal goals. Goals should include criteria for evaluating their attainment.

The terminal behavioral change goals for Mr. Domino, for example, were: (1) to decrease inappropriate verbal and nonverbal responses with complaining customers (lower his voice; stop clenching his fists and waving his arms; decrease his insulting remarks to customers who complain) and (2) to increase the frequency of appropriate responses with complaining customers (discuss furniture with customers in a calm and pleasant manner; increase sales). When problematic antecedents occur,

Mr. Domino will refrain from making inappropriate comments or gestures. Instead, appropriate responses would include speaking in a normal tone of voice and justifying the cost of the furniture in terms of the guarantee and services that accompany the purchase. The probable reinforcers under these circumstances could be the customer's responsiveness and subsequent purchase, as well as positive comments from his employer on his improved behavior and increased sales.

The practitioner should always encourage the client to actively participate in establishing behavioral change goals. The client's participation in goal setting is important because of its implications for making major changes in his or her life. For example, one possible goal for Mr. Domino could have been to obtain a different job. The decision to leave a problematic situation rather than attempt to modify the problematic behavior or conditions of that situation is ultimately the client's responsibility. The practitioner should point out alternative goals, however. After the counselor discussed alternative goals with Mr. Domino, he decided to work on modifying the target behaviors he had reported.

When a goal is established to decrease problematic behaviors, the practitioner should also specify the appropriate behaviors that should be performed in that situation, as indicated in Mr. Domino's terminal goals. For example, Mr. Domino recorded the number of times per week that he insulted customers; achievement of his behavioral goal should indicate a *decrease* in this measure. The response data also included the number of times per week that Mr. Domino responded appropriately to complaining customers; achievement of this treatment goal should be reflected by an *increase* in this measure. These data provide feedback to the client and practitioner on the extent to which behavioral change goals are being achieved and the client's problem ameliorated.

Sometimes clients or significant others find it easier to specify target behaviors they want decreased than to describe appropriate behaviors to be performed in the problematic situation. For example, a mother complained that her 3-year-old son started climbing on chairs when she talked on the phone. The mother stated the goal as "Johnny does *not* climb when I am talking on the phone." The practitioner asked the mother to specify what Johnny *should do* at that time—for example, play quietly with his toys, look at a book, or watch television.

Initial and intermediate goals should be established as successive approximations to the terminal goal[1]. Intermediate goals of increasing difficulty or complexity should be formulated that are attainable as the client progresses through the behavioral change program. Positive reinforcement should be arranged for the client as each approximation to the terminal goal is reached. The procedure of shaping with successive approximations applies a similar approach to develop a terminal behavior by positively reinforcing successive approximations that lead to it.

An initial goal for Mr. Domino was that he respond in a soft voice to critical questions the counselor asked him in role plays. An intermediate goal for Mr. Domino was for him to respond appropriately in role plays of situations involving complaining customers. Another intermediate goal was for Mr. Domino to speak softly to fussy customers.

Behavioral assessment requires a thoughtful and systematic plan for specifying target responses and their controlling conditions. Assigning the client an active role in behavioral assessment and goal-setting helps insure that the goals will accurately reflect the client's personal, social, and cultural values. The effort expended by the practitioner and client in carrying out a behavioral assessment provides the basis for formulating an intervention plan appropriate for the client. A successfully executed intervention plan ultimately depends on the adequacy of the behavioral assessment.

ETHICAL ISSUES IN GOAL SETTING

Although the client should actively participate with the practitioner in formulating behavioral change goals, the practitioner must assume major responsibility in certain situations. When the client commits acts that are illegal or detrimental to himself or herself, society, or significant others, there are legal and societal sanctions regarding the modification of such behaviors. If the practitioner disagrees with a client's goals, the practitioner should discuss the conflicting issues with the client. If the client's goal violates the practitioner's professional ethics, the practitioner should try to persuade the client to modify his or her goal. For example, a client may wish to attain a goal that would be exploitative of other individuals; the practitioner should dissuade the client from selecting such a goal. If the client's goal violates the practitioner's personal moral code, the practitioner should consider withdrawing from the case and assisting the client in obtaining professional assistance elsewhere. Goal setting involves consideration of personal, social, legal, and cultural factors necessary to make goals viable for the client in his or her environment.

CASE STUDY 5

Behavioral Assessment of Nonassertiveness

Mr. Lewis is a 30-year-old unmarried man who seeks assistance for his difficulty in establishing and maintaining satisfying relationships with women. He complains that women find him unpleasant to be around, and he never knows what to say in their presence. Of the last four women Mr. Lewis has taken out, all have refused a second date. Mr. Lewis only has one male friend.

Mr. Lewis is a bookkeeper for a clothing manufacturer. He has worked for the same firm for nine years. Although he was promised a promotion and raise two years ago, he still earns the same salary and is at the same position he was in when he first began with the company. He has never discussed his feelings about being treated unfairly with his boss, although other employees in similar circumstances have benefited from doing so.

The therapist asked Mr. Lewis to describe his experience on the last date he had. Mr. Lewis said that they were having coffee in a restaurant after seeing a movie, and he could not think of interesting things to say to his date. He concluded that he just "bored her to death" talking about his work. When the therapist asked Mr. Lewis to describe his date's conversation, Mr. Lewis said he couldn't remember much about what she said, since he was so concerned about making a good impression. On one occasion, Mr. Lewis said a young woman fell asleep while he was trying to explain a complicated bookkeeping procedure. The therapist observed that Mr. Lewis kept his head down during the interview, and often held his hand in front of his mouth when speaking so that his speech was difficult to understand. He sometimes drifted from one topic to another without waiting for the therapist's response to what he had said, and he frequently spoke in a monotone.

The therapist asked Mr. Lewis to describe his last conversation with his boss. Mr. Lewis was seated across the desk from his boss who asked him what he wanted. Mr. Lewis mumbled, looked down at the floor, and began to talk about his financial problems. When the boss responded by asking Mr. Lewis why he could not manage his finances properly, Mr. Lewis stammered and tried to defend his way of managing money. Finally, Mr. Lewis mumbled, "I'm sorry," and walked out, without raising the issues of his promotion and salary increase.

Upon further questioning, Mr. Lewis indicated that he often found himself being taken advantage of in situations in which he should have stated his opinions or defended his rights. Mr. Lewis said that he hoped to improve this situation through therapy and would cooperate with the therapist's recommendations. The therapist gave Mr. Lewis an assignment to record significant information about the situations in which he felt exploited.

SUMMARY

1. RAC-S is an acronym for target Response(s), Antecedents, Consequences, and response Strength, which is the behavioral assessment framework presented in this chapter.

2. The behavioral assessment procedure consists of the following steps: (a) list the client's problems; (b) select one problem for immediate attention; (c) obtain examples of the problem that specify the target response(s), antecedents, negative consequences, possible reinforcers, and response strength; (d) design a measurement plan, specifying measures of response strength to be recorded, (e) obtain measures of response strength, and (f) formulate terminal, intermediate, and initial behavioral change goals.

3. Behavioral reenactment is a role-play technique used to obtain specific data regarding the client's behavior(s) and its controlling antecedents and consequences in the problematic situation.

4. Measures of response strength should be obtained prior to establishing behavioral change goals. The client is given assignments to record RAC-S data between treatment sessions.

5. The Assessment Form and Behavioral Recording Chart are used to record relevant RAC-S data.

6. The RAC-S paradigm includes questions that the practitioner can use to elicit RAC-S data in interviews with clients.

7. Initial, intermediate, and terminal behavioral change goals are formulated with the active participation of the client. Initial and intermediate goals are established as a series of approximations to the terminal goal.

8. Issues related to goal setting include consideration of legal, cultural, social, moral, and personal factors.

SUGGESTED READINGS

GOLDIAMOND, I. "Justified and Unjustified Alarm over Behavioral Control," O. Milton (Ed.), *Behavior Disorders: Perspectives and Trends* (Philadelphia: Lippincott, 1965).

HAYNES, S. W., and WILSON, C. C., *Behavioral Assessment: Recent Advances in Methods, Concepts, and Applications* (San Francisco: Jossey-Bass, 1980).

LAWRENCE, H., and SUNDEL, M., "Behavior Modification in Adult Groups," *Social Work,* 1972, *17,* 34-43.

MEYER, V., and TURKAT, I. D., "Behavioral Analysis of Clinical Cases," *Journal of Behavioral Assessment,* 1979, *1,* 259-270.

ROGERS, C. R., and SKINNER, B. F., "Some Issues Concerning the Control of Human Behavior: A Symposium," *Science,* 1956, *124,* 1057-1066.

SCHAEFER, H. H., and MARTIN, P. L., *Behavioral Therapy,* 2nd ed. (New York: McGraw-Hill, 1975).

SUNDEL, S. S., and SUNDEL, M., *Be Assertive: A Practical Guide for Human Service Workers* (Beverly Hills, Calif.: Sage Publications, 1980).

SUNDEL, M., RADIN, N., and CHURCHILL, S. R., "Diagnosis in Group Work," in P. Glasser, R. Sarri, and R. Vinter (Eds.), *Individual Change through Small Groups* (New York: Free Press, 1974), pp. 105-125.

POST-TEST QUESTIONS

(4) 1. Using the information from Case Study 5, pages 105–106, state four of Mr. Lewis's target behaviors.

(1) 2. Specify one antecedent related to Mr. Lewis's conversation with his employer.

(2) 3. State two negative consequences of Mr. Lewis's nonassertive behaviors.

(1) 4. Now turn to pages 7–8 to see Case Study 1. Using the information from that case study, state a probable reinforcer maintaining Harold's drug use.

(3) 5. State an intermediate behavioral change goal for Mr. Lewis based again on the information from Case Study 5, specifying (1) a desired response, (2) a relevant antecedent, and (3) a possible positive reinforcer.

10
CONDITIONED POSITIVE REINFORCEMENT AND CHAINING

objectives

After completing this chapter, you should be able to:

1. describe a procedure you could use to establish something or someone as a generalized conditioned reinforcer,

2. state the advantage of using conditioned reinforcement over primary reinforcement in maintaining behavioral change in the client's environment,

3. describe a procedure that can be used to determine if an S^D has become a conditioned reinforcer, and

4. give an example of a problem that can be analyzed as a stimulus-response chain.

Mr. Clark, a patient in a mental hospital, was given money during a verbal conditioning study. He dropped one coin on the floor and left the rest of the coins he had earned on the table. The psychologist concluded that money did not function as a generalized conditioned reinforcer for Mr. Clark in the way that it does for most adults in our society.

Chapter 10

(2) 1. Which is usually more effective, a simple conditioned reinforcer or a generalized conditioned reinforcer? Support your answer.

(1) 2. What is the difference between an unconditioned reinforcer and a conditioned reinforcer?

(4) 3. Give two examples of generalized conditioned reinforcers and two examples of unconditioned reinforcers.

(1) 4. True or False. In order for a neutral stimulus to function as a conditioned reinforcer, a minimum of 100 pairings is necessary.

(3) 5. Identify the components of one unit of a stimulus-response chain.

CONDITIONED REINFORCEMENT

We have presented the elements of behavioral assessment and have described a procedure for conducting a behavioral assessment. We have shown how behavioral principles are applied in specifying target behaviors, antecedents, and consequences, and in formulating behavioral change goals. We now continue our presentation of behavioral principles with a focus in this chapter on conditioned reinforcement and chaining.

The principle of **conditioned reinforcement** is based on the finding that a neutral or nonreinforcing stimulus can become a reinforcer for a response through association with a reinforcing stimulus. For example, money is a conditioned reinforcer for most people because it has been paired or associated with other reinforcers such as food, drink, shelter, or entertainment. Similarly, social reinforcers such as approval, encouragement, and attention usually act as conditioned reinforcers because they have been associated with other reinforcers such as food and removal of physical discomfort.

Unconditioned or **primary reinforcers** such as food or beverages can be used to increase response strength and do not require prior association with other reinforcers; therefore, they are considered intrinsically or naturally reinforcing. Food, sex, sleep, water, warmth, and tactile stimulation are examples of unconditioned positive reinforcers. Some drugs can also act as unconditioned reinforcers.

Conditioned or **secondary reinforcers** are stimuli that acquire reinforcing properties through pairing or association with other reinforcers. Money, points, coupons, and attention are examples of conditioned positive reinforcers.

Conditioned reinforcement, as well as unconditioned reinforcement, can be positive or negative. Conditioned positive reinforcement is discussed in this chapter. Negative reinforcement, both unconditioned and conditioned, is covered in Chapter 13.

The paradigm for conditioned positive reinforcement is similar to that for unconditioned positive reinforcement:

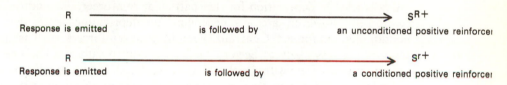

R ————————————————————————→ S^{R+}
Response is emitted   is followed by   an unconditioned positive reinforcer

R ————————————————————————→ S^{r+}
Response is emitted   is followed by   a conditioned positive reinforcer

Effect: The response, R, increases in strength and is more likely to be performed again.

The notation "r+" in "S^{r+}" signifies conditioned positive reinforcement; the notation "R+" in "S^{R+}" signifies unconditioned positive reinforcement. Until now we have used the symbol S^+ to denote a positive reinforcer. When the reinforcer is known, however, either S^{r+} or S^{R+} is used to indicate a conditioned or unconditioned positive reinforcer, respectively.

Factors that influence the effect of unconditioned reinforcers also apply to conditioned reinforcers. These include:

1. The conditioned reinforcer is most effective when it immediately follows the response.
2. The effectiveness of a conditioned reinforcer is affected by conditions of deprivation and satiation.
3. A response maintained on an intermittent schedule of conditioned reinforcement is more resistant to extinction than a response maintained on a continuous schedule of conditioned reinforcement.
4. When a conditioned reinforcer is withheld continuously from the response it has reinforced, the frequency of the response decreases as extinction takes place.

In order to remain effective, a conditioned reinforcer requires occasional pairing with an established reinforcer. For example, an individual must occasionally purchase something with the money he or she accumulates in order for money to continue to be effective as a conditioned reinforcer. Thus, a person will work for money only if the money has functioned as a conditioned reinforcer for purchasing various goods and services.

SIMPLE AND GENERALIZED CONDITIONED REINFORCERS

Conditioned reinforcers can be of two types: simple and generalized. **Simple conditioned reinforcers** have been paired with only one reinforcer and are associated only with that reinforcer. For example, a new restaurant gives out coupons that can be traded only for a soft drink; a retarded child solves math problems and receives tokens that can be exchanged only for bubble gum.

A **generalized conditioned reinforcer** has been paired with a variety of reinforcers. Money is probably the most common generalized conditioned reinforcer because of the many primary and conditioned reinforcers it can obtain.

The effectiveness of a simple conditioned reinforcer depends on the individual's level of deprivation for that particular reinforcer. Generalized conditioned reinforcers, however, are less dependent on deprivation levels than are simple conditioned reinforcers. Generalized conditioned reinforcers, such as money and attention, are less likely to become ineffective due to satiation because of the wide variety of reinforcers with which they are associated. If an individual is satiated with regard to one reinforcer, there are other reinforcers of which he or she is sufficiently deprived to insure the effectiveness of the generalized conditioned reinforcer.

For example, Carlos offered Max a token to run an errand. The token could be exchanged only for a chocolate bar. If Max had recently eaten two chocolate bars (low level of deprivation) it would be less likely that he would run the errand for a token than if Max had not eaten chocolate for several days (high level of deprivation). Carlos would be wise, therefore, to give Max a token that could be exchanged for either chocolate, gum, baseball cards, or a soft drink for running the errand. Using the generalized conditioned reinforcer increases the likelihood that Max would run the errand regardless of whether or not he had eaten chocolate recently, because it is unlikely that he would be satiated on all the items that he could obtain with the token.

ESTABLISHING A CONDITIONED REINFORCER

A stimulus that signals reinforcement for a response (S^D) can itself become reinforcing. As mentioned earlier, in order for a neutral stimulus to acquire reinforcing value, it must be associated or paired with an established reinforcer. Tokens, coupons, and gift certificates typically serve as conditioned reinforcers only after the individual learns that they can be exchanged for other goods.

In order to establish a neutral stimulus as a conditioned reinforcer, the neutral stimulus must be paired with an established reinforcer in a particular manner. The neutral stimulus must serve as an S^D for a response that produces the established reinforcer.

For example, a mother set up a token reinforcement program for her three children in which they could earn tokens for doing special jobs around the house. The tokens could then be exchanged for various privileges such as television, extra spending money, or additional desserts. The tokens did not serve as reinforcers for the children's performance of the jobs, however, until they were exchanged for the various reinforcers. The tokens were paired with a variety of established reinforcers and thus became generalized conditioned reinforcers. The neutral stimulus, in this example the token, served as an S^D indicating that the response of giving mother the token would be followed by delivery of one of the reinforcers, for example, extra spending money. In paradigm form, the example would look like this:

$$
\text{In the presence of} \left[\begin{array}{l} S^D \\ \text{Token} \\ R \end{array} \right. \longrightarrow S^{r+}
$$

Child gives mother the token   is followed by   extra spending mone

Effect: The response (giving mother the token) increases in frequency; the token is paired with S^{r+}, extra money.

Once the token has served as an S^D, it acquires reinforcing value because it has signalled delivery of the established reinforcer, extra spending money. A conditioned reinforcer, like an unconditioned reinforcer, increases the strength of a behavior it follows. Tokens, if they have become conditioned reinforcers, can be used by the mother to increase the strength of other behaviors, such as doing special jobs.

R ———————————————————→ S^{r+}
Child does a special job   is followed by   Tokens

Effect: Response of doing a special job increases in frequency, demonstrating that the tokens served as conditioned reinforcers. (They did not reinforce this response prior to pairing with the established reinforcer, money.)

REINFORCEMENT HISTORY

In establishing a neutral stimulus as a conditioned reinforcer, the practitioner should consider the individual's reinforcement history, that is, those stimuli that have served as reinforcers in the past and which may currently control the person's behaviors. Affection, attention, and approval are social reinforcers that are usually conditioned during infancy and early childhood. These stimuli are called social reinforcers because they become available through interaction with other persons. Social reinforcers (for example, smiles) are paired in childhood with the parents' ministering to the child's physical needs: for example, feeding, changing diapers, and relieving discomfort. The parents' social responses become conditioned reinforcers through pairing with the nurturant responses.

For example, the mother serves as an S^D in whose presence the infant eats. The mother (S^D) becomes associated with food and the relief of hunger, as well as with other care-giving responses such as cuddling, smiling, and speaking. She thereby becomes a social reinforcer for the child and has tremendous influence in establishing and strengthening the child's behaviors. Usually by the time a child reaches school age, parental approval, recognition, and praise can be used by the parents as reinforcers for many behaviors. The effectiveness of social reinforcers in influencing children's behaviors generalizes to other individuals, such as, teachers, neighbors, and relatives.

Some children rarely receive praise, affection, or attention contingent on appropriate behaviors. These children often emit disruptive or inappropriate behaviors that produce attention from parents, teachers, or other adults. The practitioner should teach these adults to provide social reinforcement for appropriate behaviors and to withhold it for inappropriate behaviors.

For some children, however, commonly used social reinforcers appear to be ineffective. With them, such stimuli do not help in conditioning or strengthening behaviors. Instead, it is necessary to establish praise, smiling, approval, and attention as conditioned reinforcers for such children by pairing these stimuli with known reinforcers.

ESTABLISHING RELATIONSHIPS WITH CLIENTS

In order to develop an effective working relationship with a client, the practitioner must be perceived by the client as a conditioned positive reinforcer. Practitioners commonly establish themselves as conditioned positive reinforcers for clients by listening to their problems and personal concerns and encouraging them to talk about themselves and their situations in a supportive, nonpunitive setting. The practitioner serves as an S^D in whose presence the client's talking about problems is followed by social reinforcers such as the practitioner's attention, problem analysis, encouragement, or advice. In this way, the practitioner is paired with delivery of established reinforcers and acquires the ability to influence a wide range of client behaviors as a generalized conditioned reinforcer.

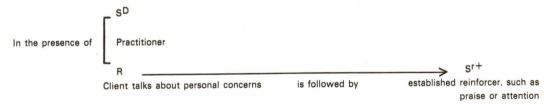

Effect: Client talks more frequently about personal concerns; practitioner becomes a conditioned reinforcer.

Socioeconomic, racial, or cultural factors can prevent clients from seeking help or participating in agency programs. Practitioners often have to bridge such barriers in order to provide services to clients. Sometimes coffee, tea, doughnuts, or other primary reinforcers, coupled with friendly conversation, are offered to the client by the practitioner without requiring the client's performance of any behaviors other than taking and consuming them. Practitioners can also pair themselves with reinforcers such as playing games or sports with children, or providing soft drinks and food to adolescents. Once the practitioner has become established as a conditioned positive reinforcer, he or she can selectively reinforce client responses by using approval, attention, and opinions to develop appropriate client behaviors. For example, once the practitioner serves as a conditioned reinforcer, he or she can strengthen a client's recording of assessment data:

R $\xrightarrow{\hspace{9cm}}$ S^{r+}

Client records assessment data   is followed by   practitioner's praise and feedback

Effect: Client continues to record assessment data.

FADING OUT PRIMARY REINFORCERS

Speech and appropriate interpersonal behaviors are typically maintained with social reinforcement. For some behaviors, however, conditioned reinforcers may prove to be ineffective. Primary reinforcers may be more effective in these situations. For example, food can be used to teach social skills to an autistic child or to increase speech in a chronic mental patient, as in Case Study 3 (see pp. 49–50). When establishing a behavior using an unconditioned or primary reinforcer, a conditioned reinforcer should be paired with the "back up" primary reinforcer so that the behavior can eventually be maintained by the conditioned reinforcer alone.

A social reinforcer, such as praise, should be presented along with or immediately after the primary reinforcer to promote shifting from primary to conditioned reinforcement. For example, in teaching a retarded child arithmetic, the special education teacher gives him a raisin for each problem he solves. When she gives him the raisin, she says, "very good." The delivery of the raisin is gradually shifted from a continuous to an intermittent schedule while the teacher continues to say "very good" after each correct solution. Soon the primary reinforcer (the raisin) is discontinued until only the social reinforcer ("very good") is presented after each response. The social reinforcer is then shifted to an intermittent schedule to approximate reinforcement availability in the child's environment. The child does not receive food in his classroom for every math problem he solves. He should receive approval or praise from the teacher and his parents when he completes his assignments, however; and he also earns grades for his work.

Shifting from food (primary reinforcement) to praise and approval (conditioned reinforcement) promotes the generalization and maintenance of the newly developed behaviors. Two advantages of using generalized conditioned reinforcers over primary reinforcers in behavioral change programs are: (1) the individual is less likely to satiate on a generalized conditioned reinforcer, and (2) generalized conditioned reinforcers are more abundantly available in our society contingent on appropriate behaviors. Using conditioned reinforcers promotes the generalization and maintenance of newly established, appropriate behaviors by increasing the likelihood that these behaviors will be reinforced in the client's environment.

TOKEN ECONOMY

The term **token economy** refers to a planned reinforcement program in which individuals earn tokens for performing desired behaviors. They can exchange these tokens for a variety of objects or privileges. The tokens serve as generalized conditioned reinforcers for appropriate behaviors and are given according to values assigned to performance of specific behaviors. For example, a hospitalized mental patient might receive one token each time he makes his bed, two tokens for brushing his teeth, and five tokens for participating in a therapy group. He can exchange these tokens for goods or privileges such as a candy bar (2 tokens), a pack of cigarettes (5 tokens), or a half-hour walk outside the ward (8 tokens). Similarly, when a teacher gives gold stars for performance of various academic and classroom behaviors, the gold stars can be exchanged by students for privileges such as extended play periods. Parents have also used conditioned reinforcers, such as points or stars, in home-based token economies to increase studying, performance of household tasks, and practicing musical instruments.

The token economy system has been implemented in institutions for mentally retarded individuals, mental patients, and juvenile offenders. Token economies tend to be most effective in institutional settings because the staff has greater control over the individual's reinforcement than is possible in the client's environment. The token economy provides incentives for individuals to acquire and perform behaviors that are necessary for functioning in the community. For an extended discussion of the token economy see Ayllon & Azrin (1968) and Kazdin (1977).

TESTING A NEUTRAL STIMULUS AS A CONDITIONED REINFORCER

As described earlier, the procedure for establishing a neutral stimulus as a conditioned reinforcer consists of pairing the stimulus with a known reinforcer. This procedure requires that the neutral stimulus be presented as an S^D for a response that is followed by reinforcement. This stimulus can subsequently be tested in two ways to determine if it has become a conditioned reinforcer (S^{r+}).

1. Present the S^D after a response other than the discriminated response. If the S^D increases the strength of the other response, it has become a conditioned reinforcer.
2. Withhold all reinforcers for the discriminated response until its response rate decreases. Then present the S^D after the response is performed. If the response increases, the S^D has become a conditioned reinforcer. *NOTE:* Using this procedure to determine if the S^D has become a conditioned reinforcer is usually more appropriate in a controlled experimental situation. In most applied settings it would be unethical to decrease the strength of an appropriate response in order to test the effectiveness of an S^D as a reinforcer.

For example, in Case Study 3 (pp. 49–50), the green light could be tested to determine if it had become a conditioned reinforcer for speaking. If presentation of the green light after any response other than speaking increased the strength of that other response, then the green light would be a conditioned reinforcer for that response. An alternative test would be for the psychologist to withhold the candy and praise until Mr. Clark's speaking decreased. Then the psychologist would present the green light immediately after Mr. Clark spoke. If Mr. Clark's speech increased, the green light would be a conditioned reinforcer. In this case, the second test is not recommended for ethical reasons. Since the goal of treatment was to increase Mr. Clark's speaking, any test that involved decreasing his speech would be of questionable value to him.

CHAINING

At first glance, some situations may appear too complex for behavioral analysis. In analyzing complex performances, however, we find that they often consist of **stimulus-response chains.** The principle of chaining is used by the practitioner: (1) to analyze behavior patterns, and (2) to develop sequences of behaviors to replace deviant performances and expand deficient behavior patterns. One unit of a stimulus-response chain consists of a discriminative stimulus (S^D), a response (R), and a conditioned reinforcer (S^{r+}). The entire chain is composed of a series of stimulus-response units that terminate with a primary or conditioned reinforcer (S^{R++}; S^{r++}). Each conditioned reinforcer in the chain also serves as the S^D for the next response, as shown below:

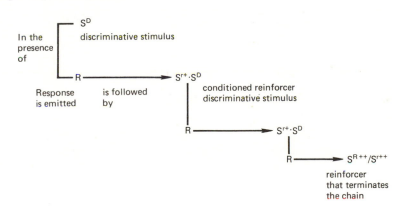

Effect: The term $S^{r+} \cdot S^D$ indicates that the S^{r+} for the preceding R is also the S^D for the following R. The chain runs to completion; each response is strengthened. When any one S^D is presented, the rest of the chain will follow.

Many everyday behaviors are controlled by stimulus-response chains. For example, eating between meals for an overweight person can be subjected to a stimulus-response chain analysis. The inappropriate eating behavior can be broken down into a series of stimulus-response units leading to a reinforcer that supports the entire chain. This stimulus-response chain might look like Figure 10-1.

FIGURE 10-1

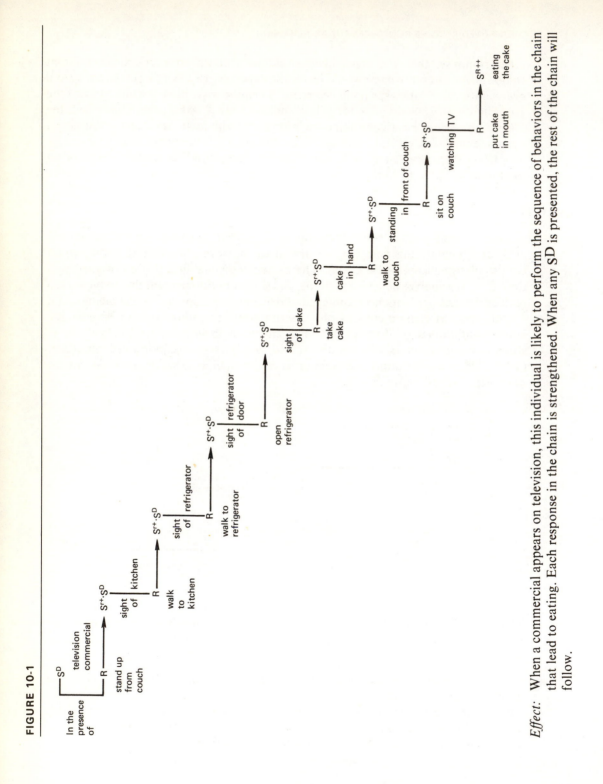

S^D television commercial

R stand up from couch

$S^{r+} \cdot S^D$ sight of kitchen

R walk to kitchen

$S^{r+} \cdot S^D$ sight of refrigerator

R walk to refrigerator

$S^{r+} \cdot S^D$ sight of refrigerator door

R open refrigerator

$S^{r+} \cdot S^D$ sight of cake

R take cake

$S^{r+} \cdot S^D$ cake in hand

R walk to couch

$S^{r+} \cdot S^D$ standing in front of couch

R sit on couch

$S^{r+} \cdot S^D$ watching TV

R put cake in mouth

S^{R++} eating the cake

In the presence of

Effect: When a commercial appears on television, this individual is likely to perform the sequence of behaviors in the chain that lead to eating. Each response in the chain is strengthened. When any SD is presented, the rest of the chain will follow.

118

Each response in the chain leads to a conditioned reinforcer that also serves as an S^D for the next response. In the above example, eating was associated with watching television, and television commercials acquired a discriminative function (S^D) for food-getting responses (R) that led to food consumption (S^{R++}). The intermediate behaviors of going to the kitchen, opening the refrigerator, and taking the cake became conditioned as part of the total stimulus-response chain.

In analyzing such sequences of behaviors, the practitioner should determine optimal points at which the chain could be broken to decrease undesired behaviors. In the inappropriate eating example, the stimulus-response chain could be interrupted at the final unit, when the individual sat on the couch putting the cake into his mouth. It is unlikely, however, that eating could have been interrupted easily at this point when the individual was under direct stimulus control of the cake.

The chain could be interrupted at an earlier point, for example, before the individual walks to the kitchen, so that the remaining units of the chain leading to eating can be prevented from occurring. The remaining units would not be extinguished, however, and they could be expected to recur upon reinstatement of any of the S^Ds currently maintaining the responses. The best place to break the chain is before it begins, in this example, before the person stands up from the couch. This could involve training the person to make alternative responses when a commercial is shown on television, such as reading the newspaper or writing a letter to a friend.

BACKWARD CHAINING

A backward stimulus-response chaining procedure can be used to develop appropriate response patterns as part of a client's behavioral change program. In **backward chaining** the last stimulus-response unit of the chain is established first and the other units are added in reverse order until the desired chain is complete. For example, a backward chaining procedure was used to teach a retarded child to put on a shirt and button it. The steps for this procedure consisted of:

1. The practitioner put the shirt on the child and buttoned it, except for one button that she left half buttoned. She showed the child how to push the button through the hole and asked him to repeat this response. The child pushed the button through the hole, and the practitioner gave him a piece of fruit and said "good."
2. In the second step the practitioner buttoned the child's shirt except for one button. The practitioner showed him how to grasp the button in one hand and the buttonhole in the other and push the button through the hole. When the child pushed the button through the hole by himself, the practitioner gave him a piece of fruit and said, "good job."
3. The third step consisted of the child wearing the shirt buttoned except for two buttons. The child buttoned the first button and then the second. The closed first button served as both a conditioned reinforcer for buttoning it and as the S^D for buttoning the second button.
4. The practitioner repeated this procedure until the child successively accomplished buttoning the entire shirt, putting his arms in each sleeve, and

taking the shirt out of the drawer. As each new response was added, the child performed it along with the remaining responses until the chain was completed and he received the fruit and praise.

When the final response of taking the shirt out of the drawer was added, the child took the shirt from the drawer, put each arm in the correct sleeve, and buttoned every button. At this stage, reinforcement was given only after the last response in the chain was performed. Each response produced a stimulus that served as: (1) a conditioned reinforcer for that response, and (2) an S$^\overline{D}$ for the next response in the chain. Thus, once a behavioral sequence is established, each response in the chain is maintained by the reinforcing stimulus it produces.

SUMMARY

1. A neutral or nonreinforcing stimulus can become a reinforcer for a response through association with an established or known reinforcer. A neutral stimulus that has become a reinforcer in this way is called a conditioned or secondary reinforcer. Conditioned reinforcers include social reinforcers such as approval, praise, and attention, as well as tangible items such as money, tokens, and coupons.

2. Unconditioned or primary reinforcers increase response strength and do not require prior association with established reinforcers. Primary reinforcers include food, water, and sex.

3. The same factors that influence the effectiveness of unconditioned positive reinforcement influence conditioned positive reinforcement. These include deprivation, satiation, schedules, and timing of delivery.

4. In order to remain effective, a conditioned reinforcer must occasionally be paired with an established reinforcer.

5. Conditioned reinforcers can be simple or generalized. Simple conditioned reinforcers are ones that have been paired with only a single reinforcer and are associated only with that reinforcer. Generalized conditioned reinforcers have been paired with a variety of reinforcers. The effectiveness of a simple conditioned reinforcer depends on the individual's level of deprivation of that particular reinforcer. Generalized conditioned reinforcers are less dependent on deprivation levels of specific reinforcers.

6. In order for a neutral stimulus to become a conditioned reinforcer, it must first serve as an S^D for a response that is followed by an established reinforcer.

7. Social reinforcers such as affection, attention, and approval are conditioned reinforcers for most people because these stimuli have served as S^{D}s for various responses that have been reinforced in the past.

8. Behavioral practitioners can become conditioned positive reinforcers for their clients.

9. When primary reinforcers are used to establish behaviors, conditioned reinforcers should be introduced to maintain the behaviors and the primary reinforcers should be faded out.

10. A token economy is a planned reinforcement program in which individuals can earn tokens for performing desired behaviors. The tokens can be exchanged for a variety of objects or privileges.

11. There are two ways to determine if an S^D has become a conditioned reinforcer: (1) Present the S^D after a response other than the discriminated response. If the response rate of that response increases, the S^D has become a conditioned reinforcer (S^{r+}); Or, (2) withhold all reinforcers for the discriminated response until the response rate decreases. Then present the S^D after the response is performed. If the response rate increases, the S^D also acts as a conditioned reinforcer. This procedure is usually inappropriate in applied settings because it would be unethical to decrease the strength of an appropriate response in order to test the S^D as a reinforcer.

12. The principle of chaining is used to analyze and develop sequences of behaviors. A stimulus-response chain consists of a series of stimulus-response units. Each unit consists of an S^D, a response, and a conditioned reinforcer (S^{r+}) that serves as an S^D for the next response. The chain terminates with a primary or conditioned reinforcer (S^{R++}; S^{r++}). Each response produces a stimulus that serves: (1) as a conditioned reinforcer for that response, and (2) as an S^D for the next response in the chain.

13. Stimulus-response chains are best broken before the first response is emitted because any S^D that occurs sets the occasion for the rest of the behaviors and stimuli of the chain to follow.

14. Backward chaining is used to develop appropriate behavioral patterns. In backward chaining, the last stimulus-response unit is established first, and the other units are added backwards until the entire chain is performed.

SUGGESTED READINGS

AYLLON, T., and AZRIN, N. H., *The Token Economy* (Englewood Cliffs, N.J.: Prentice-Hall, Inc., 1968).

FANTINO, E., "Conditioned Reinforcement: Choice and Information," in W. H. Honig and J.E.R. Staddon (Eds.), *Handbook of Operant Behavior* (Englewood Cliffs, N.J.: Prentice-Hall, 1977).

FRANKEL, A. J., "Beyond the Simple Functional Analysis—The Chain," *Behavior Therapy,* 1975, *6,* 254-260.

KAZDIN, A. E., *The Token Economy: A Review and Evaluation* (New York: Plenum, 1977).

KRASNER, L., "The Therapist as a Social Reinforcement Machine," in H. H. Strupp and L. Luborsky (Eds.), *Research in Psychotherapy* (Washington, D.C.: American Psychological Association, Inc., 1962), pp. 61-94.

MAYHEW, G. L. and ANDERSON, J., "Delayed and Immediate Reinforcement," *Behavior Modification, 4*(4), 527-546.

PHILLIPS, E. L., "Achievement Place: Token Reinforcement Procedures in a Home-style Rehabilitation Setting for 'Pre-delinquent' Boys," *Journal of Applied Behavior Analysis,* 1968, *1,* 213-223.

SCHOENFELD, W. N., ANTONITIS, J. J., and BERSCH, P. J., "A Preliminary Study of Training Conditions Necessary for Secondary Reinforcement," *Journal of Experimental Psychology,* 1950, *40,* 40-45.

VASTA, R., "On Token Rewards and Real Dangers," *Behavior Modification,* 1981, 5(1), 129-140.

WALLS, R. T., ZANE, T., and ELLIS, W. D., "Forward and Backward Chaining, and Whole Task Methods," *Behavior Modification,* 1981, 5(1), 61-74.

POST-TEST QUESTIONS

(2) 1. An institutionalized mental patient, Mr. Clark, was given money during a verbal conditioning study. He dropped one coin on the floor and left the rest of the coins he had earned on the table. The psychologist concluded that money did not function as a generalized conditioned reinforcer for Mr. Clark in the way that it does for most adults in our society. What could the psychologist do to establish money as a reinforcer for Mr. Clark?

(3) 2. You are a social worker in a community setting, and adolescents who have had one or two contacts with the police and juvenile authorities are referred to you. You station yourself in the low socioeconomic neighborhood where these youths live because you plan to engage a group of them in activities that will help them stay out of trouble with the law, improve their academic performance, interview for and successfully hold jobs, and solve various interpersonal and family difficulties. Give two examples that indicate what you could do to establish yourself as a generalized conditioned reinforcer.

(1) 3. Now turn to pages 49-50 to see Case Study 3. In this case study, the green light served as an S^D for Mr. Clark's speech. It was paired with candy and praise from the psychologist. How could the psychologist determine if the green light had become a conditioned reinforcer?

(2) 4. State two advantages of using conditioned reinforcement over primary reinforcement in maintaining behavioral change in a client's environment.

(4) 5.   Give an example of a problem that can be analyzed as a stimulus-response chain. Include at least two stimulus-response units, and label the appropriate components.

11

MODELING AND IMITATION

objectives

After completing this chapter you should be able to:

1. give an example that describes how the modeling plus reinforcement procedure is used to develop and strengthen a response,
2. give an example of modeling used to develop assertive behaviors in a group setting, and
3. describe the use of a modeling procedure with prompts, reinforcement, and fading, given a case example.

Neil has a hard time getting women to go out with him. He typically approaches them with statements such as, "You wouldn't like to go to the movies Saturday night, would you?" "I have two tickets to a play, if you wouldn't mind going." He speaks to them in a pleading, whining voice. These behaviors were observed by group members during a behavioral reenactment of Neil's last attempt to get a date. The therapist asked Nick, a group member, to model appropriate responses for Neil. Neil imitated the behaviors that Nick demonstrated and gradually learned to perform appropriate behaviors in a variety of role plays. Group members reinforced Neil with praise for appropriate imitation.

Chapter 11

(3) 1. Describe how a modeling-plus-reinforcement procedure can be used to develop a child's imitation of an adult using a fork correctly.

(3) 2. Indicate True (T) or False (F) beside each of the following statements:

   a. _____ If an individual does not perform a response after he or she has observed someone else perform it, the individual has not learned it.

   b. _____ It is more difficult to teach a song to a child who has no imitative skills than to a child who imitates excessively.

   c. _____ Imitated behavior cannot be conditioned through reinforcement when the client has no imitative skills as, for example, a severely retarded child.

(3) 3. Using the information from Case Study 6 below, how could modeling and reinforcement have been used to help Mr. Potts obtain a new job?

CASE STUDY 6

Developing Appropriate Behaviors in
Group Treatment

At a group therapy meeting, Mr. Potts complained of frequent "anxiety and depression." He had recently been laid off from his job, was bored, and had no outside interests. He spent most of his time sleeping or watching television.

In asking Mr. Potts to specify the behavioral components of his anxiety and depression, it was found that Mr. Potts felt "anxious" in situations where he was criticized by his wife or employer. He often felt "depressed" after these encounters. In a role play of these situations, Mr. Potts perspired heavily, his face turned red, his breathing became more rapid, and he rapped his knuckles against each other. His hands trembled and he made excuses as he replied to the criticism.

Mr. Potts and members of the group role played situations in which Mr. Potts was criticized by his employer and wife in order to assess his current behavior patterns. When Mr. Potts disagreed with the group members' analysis of his situation, role plays were conducted to allow Mr. Potts to observe someone else demonstrating his problematic behaviors and their effects on others.

In order to demonstrate appropriate repsonses to criticism, several group members played the part of Mr. Potts in role plays and responded appropriately to criticism. Afterwards, Mr. Potts played himself in role plays of the criticism situations. When Mr. Potts had difficulty imitating the appropriate behaviors, the therapist prompted him in making the appropriate responses. Mr. Potts practiced responding appropriately in role plays and received praise from the therapist and group members as soon as he demonstrated appropriate behaviors. Assignments were given to Mr. Potts to perform the behaviors practiced in the group in his natural environment.

Similar procedures were used to help Mr. Potts prepare for an interview for a new job. He soon completed a successful job interview and was hired as a bus driver.

To deal with Mr. Potts's "boredom," the group assigned him to pursue an outside interest or hobby. Mr. Potts decided to reestablish his interest in bowling. The therapist instructed Mr. Potts to go to a bowling alley, to observe people bowling, and to discuss his experience with two persons. Shortly thereafter, he and his wife joined a bowling league.

THE ROLE OF IMITATION IN THE ACQUISITION OF BEHAVIORS

Modeling and **imitation** play an important role in the acquisition of both appropriate and maladaptive behaviors. Children acquire many of their behavior patterns by observing and imitating their parents, teachers, friends, and others. Adults have also learned many responses through observation and imitation of the behaviors exhibited by influential individuals. Television, for example, provides a variety of models for people to imitate. Cereal, toothpaste, and beer commercials make frequent use of attractive, prestigious, and influential individuals to promote the purchase of these products by viewers. The message is that if you buy these products you will be handsome, influential, and popular like the models who sell them.

Maladaptive or deviant behavior can likewise be imitated. For example, Clem, who has never stolen anything, stole a pen from a drug store after observing his friend Hank, an admired athlete, take one.

A model is someone whose behavior is imitated. It is not necessary for imitated behavior to immediately follow the model's behavior in order to be performed at a future time. For example, a child watching television observes a prestigious actor throw his gum wrapper into a trash container and tell his audience to do the same. The child may *learn* this response, although she might not perform it immediately after observing the model's behavior. Imitation of the model's behavior might occur at some later time; for example, when chewing gum with friends, the child throws the wrapper in the trash can and encourages them to do the same.

MODELING VERSUS SHAPING

Modeling facilitates the acquisition of behaviors or sequences of behaviors that otherwise would be more difficult and take longer to develop. For example, when a shaping procedure is used to teach a retarded child to speak in sentences, the child typically emits many sounds before he emits an appropriate verbal response that can be reinforced. The behavior modifier initially reinforces behaviors that may only faintly resemble speaking in a complete sentence, the desired terminal verbal responses. The shaping procedure consists of developing one response class at a time (for example, forming a correct vowel with the lips). Even telling the child what to say with prompts and detailed instructions might not provide enough information for the child to perform all the nuances of the desired responses.

In contrast, modeling enables the child to observe the full range of responses involved in the behavioral sequence of speaking a complete sentence. Such complex behaviors are generally acquired more rapidly through modeling than through shaping, because in modeling the entire sequence of desired behaviors is demonstrated. The imitated response may consist of a small segment of a behavioral sequence such as saying the first letter of a word, or it may consist of a series of responses such as speaking a complete sentence. The process of acquiring a behavior through modeling is sometimes called *vicarious learning,* because the behavior is acquired by observing another individual.

THE MODELING PLUS POSITIVE REINFORCEMENT PROCEDURE

The **modeling procedure** consists of presenting a modeled stimulus (S^m) that is intended to influence performance of an imitated response. The imitated response is similar to the modeled stimulus.

The term **modeled stimulus** refers to the performance of the model that indicates the characteristics of the imitated response to be performed. The imitated response is physically similar to the modeled stimulus with regard to an observable dimension(s), such as position or movement. Although the imitated response might not be an exact reproduction of the modeled stimulus, it must share a common characteristic along a relevant dimension. If precise reproduction is the desired goal, however, the imitated response can be further differentiated by using differential reinforcement, shaping, prompting, and instructions in conjunction with modeling.

Positive reinforcement can be used to increase the strength of an imitated response. The **modeling plus positive reinforcement procedure** consists of presenting a modeled stimulus (S^m) which sets the occasion for an imitated response (R) that will be followed by a positive reinforcer. The modeling-plus-reinforcement paradigm is as follows:

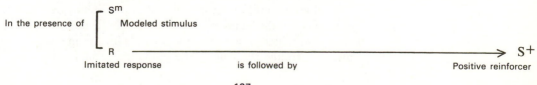

In the presence of S^m Modeled stimulus

R Imitated response   is followed by S^+ Positive reinforcer

Effect: Increased likelihood that the imitated response, R, will be performed again.

Now turn to pages 224–225 to see Case Study 1. In that study, Harold can complete more school assignments by saying "no" to his friends when they invite him to their homes before he has finished his homework. The social worker used the modeling-plus-reinforcement procedure to teach Harold how to respond appropriately to his friends' invitations. Using this procedure, the social worker modeled an appropriate way of saying, "No, I can't visit with you until I finish my assignments," with appropriate tone of voice, gestures, and facial expressions. Harold's imitated response was similar to the modeled stimulus. In paradigm form Harold's imitation would look like this:

In the presence of S^m
    Modeled stimulus
    Social worker modeled appropriate reply ("No I can't visit you until I've finished my assignment").

    R ————————————————————————————————→ $sr+$
    Imitated response   Positive reinforcer
    Harold said, "No, I can't visit you   Social worker praised Harold, "That was good.
    until I finish my assignment."   You were very convincing."

Effect: Harold is more likely to perform the imitated response (R) again.

In using the modeling-plus-reinforcement procedure, the model's performance serves as a modeled stimulus, S^m. The client observes the model, then imitates the S^m and receives a positive reinforcer for appropriate imitation.

The ability to imitate is not shared equally by all people. Some individuals exhibit limited or no imitation. For example, a severely retarded child may imitate motor behaviors but not verbal behaviors. An autistic child may not imitate motor or verbal behaviors. On the other hand, some autistic children imitate almost every sound or movement they observe. They constantly repeat certain words or bizarre actions. Thus, failure to imitate or excessive imitation can result in limited or inappropriate behavior patterns.

TEACHING COOPERATIVE PLAY
TO A CHILD WHO DOES NOT IMITATE

In teaching cooperative play to a child who does not imitate, the behavior modifier can begin by shaping a general class of imitative motor responses (for example, Baer, Peterson, & Sherman, 1967). The first goal is to teach the child how to imitate any modeled motor responses. In addition to modeling and reinforcement procedures, this method also involves shaping, verbal instructions, and prompting techniques. For example, the use of prompts like "Now you do what I do," "Follow me," or "Do this" often facilitates the child's imitation.

If the child still does not imitate the modeled stimulus, it may be necessary to physically guide her to perform the behavior. For instance, in teaching a child to roll a toy truck, the behavior modifier moves the child's hands for her in response to the model's demonstration of rolling the truck. The guidance or manipulation of the child's hands is gradually faded out as the child begins to roll the truck after presentation of the verbal prompt, "Do this, Veronica." The verbal prompt is faded out by progressively reducing the volume of the prompt until the child imitates rolling the truck after presentation of the modeled stimulus alone.

Modeling, prompting, and reinforcement are used to develop other motor responses until the child appropriately imitated any modeled motor responses. Once the child reliably imitates motor responses, the behaviors that comprise cooperative play are modeled. The child is positively reinforced for correctly imitating these modeled behaviors.

TEACHING COOPERATIVE PLAY
TO A CHILD WHO IMITATES EXCESSIVELY

Suppose you want to teach cooperative play to a child who exhibits excessive imitated motor and verbal responses. When you model a behavior, such as clapping your hands together and saying, "Do this," he will imitate your hand clapping. This child, however, not only claps his hands together but also continues to repeat your instructions, "Do this." In this case, it is necessary to: (1) extinguish the excessive imitated responses, (2) reinforce appropriately imitated responses, and (3) reinforce responses that are incompatible with the repetitive behaviors (for example, Risley & Wolf, 1967). Modeling, prompting, and reinforcement can be used to establish and strengthen appropriate imitated behaviors, while extinction is applied to weaken excessive imitated behaviors. Since this child does imitate, appropriate behaviors can be developed more readily than for a child who does not imitate at all.

APPLICATION OF MODELING

Verbal behaviors, as well as motor behaviors, can be developed with modeling, reinforcement, and prompting techniques (for example, Hingtgen, Coulter, & Churchill, 1967). For example, in teaching Mr. Clark (see Case Study 3, pages 225–226 to speak about slides he was shown, both visual and auditory stimuli were used. The following techniques were used. Mr. Clark was shown the slide of a boy and girl and asked, "What do you see in this slide?" He did not answer the question. The psychologist then modeled the appropriate response by saying, "It's a boy and girl." When Mr. Clark imitated the correct response, he received candy, points, and praise ("good") from the psychologist. The psychologist's prompts were faded out by saying them in a progressively softer voice until they were inaudible. The psychologist also faded out the prompts by omitting one word from the prompt each time it was given, beginning with the last word. If Mr. Clark answered before the prompt, he was reinforced immediately.

THE USE OF MODELING IN THE ACQUISITION OF
NOVEL BEHAVIORS

The modeling procedure facilitates the acquisition of novel behaviors and sequences of behaviors. Presentation of a positive reinforcer after an imitated response strengthens it and increases the likelihood that the response will be performed again. The client observes a model—the practitioner or a group member (if the client is participating in group treatment)—demonstrate appropriate behaviors in a role play of the client's problem. The client is then instructed to imitate the model's behaviors in a similar role play. The client is positively reinforced for appropriate imitation. In Case Study 6, pages 125–126, the therapist used this modeling and reinforcement technique to modify Mr. Potts's responses to criticism.

Imitation is influenced by the prestige or attractiveness of the model and the consequences of the model's behaviors (Bandura & Walters, 1963; Bandura, 1969; 1977). Individuals who are perceived as prestigious, influential, or physically attractive are often effective models, that is, their behaviors are imitated. Models are also more likely to be imitated when their behaviors are followed by positive reinforcers than when they are followed by neutral or punishing consequences (for example, Bandura, 1965; 1969). In a practice setting, the behavior modifier may at times model behaviors for clients to imitate. The client will more likely imitate such behaviors if the practitioner is seen as an attractive, successful person and if the modeled behaviors are reinforced.

ASSERTIVENESS TRAINING

Assertiveness training, also called **social skills training,** is a behavioral procedure in which an individual learns to express his or her opinions and rights without abusing the rights of others. Assertiveness training makes use of modeling procedures to improve deficient social or interpersonal skills. Such behavioral deficits are commonly referred to as nonassertive, unassertive, or underassertive behaviors. Many individuals with underassertive problems avoid eye contact with others, look at the floor or ceiling when conversing, mumble or speak in very soft voices, and agree with others rather than state divergent views or opinions. Rather than verbally express either positive or negative sentiments, such as pleasure or anger, these individuals typically remain silent. There are many times, however, when it would be both appropriate and desirable to express their rights and opinions. Failure to express themselves in these circumstances is detrimental for these individuals when followed by negative physical or social consequences. Assertiveness training can help to reduce the anxiety associated with deficient performances in interpersonal situations. Relaxation training can also be used in conjunction with assertiveness training to reduce such anxiety. Anxiety plays an important role in conditioning maladaptive behaviors, and will be discussed in Chapter 14.

Overassertive or aggressive behaviors may also lead to negative consequences, because these behaviors exceed appropriate expression of an individual's rights. Overassertive verbal and nonverbal responses often demean, humiliate, or physically harm others. Individuals with problems of overassertiveness often have difficulty making discriminations necessary to appropriately express their rights. For example, someone breaking in line might serve as an S^D for a person to shout an obscenity instead of to make an assertive response such as stating that the line forms at the rear. Individuals with problems of overassertiveness usually lack appropriate interpersonal skills. Furthermore, their overassertive or aggressive behaviors are often reinforced, so that they lack the incentive to act differently.

Sometimes when attempting to behave assertively, an individual with difficulties of underassertiveness may also perform overassertive behaviors such as interrupting someone who is speaking, shouting to get attention, glaring, or sneering. For example, while assertively stating his right to go out with a particular woman, Tom also sneered at his father who had forbidden him to see her. In this kind of situation, the practitioner can help the individual discriminate between appropriate and inappropriate attempts at assertiveness. Assertive training helps an individual develop both verbal and motor responses that are congruent with appropriate expressions of assertiveness in specific situations.

Some people are underassertive in almost every kind of social situation, while others behave overassertively. Most people, however, have assertive difficulties only with certain people or in certain situations.

Assertiveness includes both verbal and nonverbal behaviors that express legitimate rights of the individual. Some examples of the expression of these rights are: "Excuse me, the line ends over there"; "Mother, I prefer this dress"; "Waiter, this steak is well done and I ordered it medium"; or "Excuse me, but you charged me for two drinks and I only had one." We can all think of situations in which it is more appropriate to express one's rights and opinions than to remain silent.

Assertiveness and Human Service Workers

Assertiveness has become a widely discussed topic in the helping professions. Human service practitioners frequently encounter situations that call for assertive responses in their relationships with clients, superiors, colleagues, subordinates, and professionals from other disciplines (Sundel & Sundel, 1980). Practitioners should use their assertive skills in: (1) advocating for clients with community agencies; (2) communicating opinions and recommendations affecting clients to other professionals; (3) stating deficiencies in agency or institutional policies that adversely affect clients; and (4) discussing opinions and perspectives affecting clients with superiors, colleagues, and subordinates.

In addition to asserting themselves with clients, colleagues, and other professionals, practitioners can act assertively to influence news media, program sponsors, legislators, government officials, and others. Assertive behavior in these areas can communicate relevant knowledge and expertise necessary for effective planning, delivery, and evaluation of services.

Gretchen Learns Assertive Behaviors

Modeling, prompting, and reinforcement techniques are often used in assertive training. For example, every time Gretchen went shopping with her mother, she bought the clothes her mother selected. Gretchen, who was 22 years old, had purchased many dresses this way with her own money, but she rarely wore them. Although she sometimes told her mother which dress she liked and wanted to buy, she always wound up buying the dress her mother selected. Gretchen sometimes shopped alone secretly to return clothes her mother picked out and to buy the clothes she really wanted. Gretchen was dissatisfied with most of her wardrobe and with her failure to purchase the clothes she selected when shopping with her mother. She told the therapist, "I am a weak person because I can't even do a simple thing like tell my mother what I want to buy and buy it in front of her."

Role plays that involved behavioral reenactment of typical situations were arranged by the therapist, who played the part of Gretchen's mother. It was determined that Gretchen's underassertive behaviors consisted of turning her head away from her "mother," shuffling her feet, and mumbling, "Do you mind if I try this dress on?" When her "mother" criticized the clothes she selected, Gretchen usually said, "Whatever you say, Mother." Gretchen's underassertive behaviors led to negative consequences for Gretchen; she purchased clothes that she did not like and rarely wore. She also had very little money left over to buy the clothes she liked. Gretchen was angry with herself for not standing up to her mother, and this prevented her from discussing more pleasant topics with her mother.

A *hierarchy* of problematic assertive behaviors was constructed for Gretchen. The behaviors were ranked according to her difficulty in performing them (Wolpe, 1969; 1973). For example, Gretchen had the most difficulty buying clothes she selected in her mother's presence. This behavior was the highest item on her hierarchy. The item lowest on her hierarchy was stating her preference of a store in which to shop. A middle range item was telling her mother what color dress she wanted.

The therapist and Gretchen role played situations related to each behavior on the hierarchy, from least to most difficult, until Gretchen was able to perform the assertive behaviors. For example, Gretchen was instructed to tell her "mother" that since she was paying for her own wardrobe, she would buy the clothes she wanted. When Gretchen had difficulty behaving assertively in any of the role plays, the therapist modeled appropriate behaviors and then asked Gretchen to imitate her. Gretchen imitated assertive statements such as, "Mother, I earn the money for my clothes and I'd like to buy this dress." The therapist gave Gretchen feedback on the appropriateness of her tone of voice, eye contact, posture, facial expressions, and verbal content. Instructions, prompting, and reinforcement were included in Gretchen's assertiveness training program.

Gretchen practiced assertive statements in the therapist's office, correcting deficiencies in her verbal and nonverbal behaviors. The therapist gave Gretchen behavioral assignments to carry out between sessions, such as looking at her mother and speaking in a calm tone of voice while stating a preference. Gretchen reported her experiences in carrying out these assignments to the therapist. The therapist reinforced successful performances and provided additional instructions and training to help Gretchen perform more difficult assignments.

Assertiveness Training in Groups

Assertiveness training, modeling, reinforcement, prompting, and role-playing techniques also can be used in groups. Group members take part in observing and identifying underassertive and overassertive behaviors, in modeling assertive behaviors, in criticizing each other's performances, and in providing reinforcement for assertive behaviors. Group members participate in the assessment of each other's assertiveness difficulties, in the development of goals and intervention plans, and in the evaluation of their behavioral-change programs.

The practitioner's role as leader of an assertiveness-training group centers around the following activities: assessing assertiveness difficulties, establishing goals, planning and implementing behavioral-change programs, and evaluating progress. Each of these areas will be discussed below.

Assessment.   During assessment, the group leader's tasks are to: (1) help each group member identify his or her assertiveness difficulties and establish priorities, and (2) teach group members how to specify target behaviors and their controlling conditions. Assessment checklists and questionnaires can be used to accomplish these tasks (Sundel & Sundel, 1980). Behavioral reenactment can also be used to identify and clarify problem situations and target behaviors.

The leader assumes an active role in establishing and guiding group activities that lead to achievement of each member's goals (Lawrence & Sundel, 1972; Sundel & Lawrence, 1977). The leader models behaviors that are unfamiliar or difficult for group members to perform. These behaviors include praising members for recording pertinent assessment data and completing behavioral assignments, asking each other relevant questions, and discussing their problems in the group.

Goal formulation.   During goal formulation, the tasks of the group leader are to help each member: (1) specify desired assertive responses; (2) consider the positive consequences of acting assertively; and (3) evaluate the risks of behaving assertively. Group members should be encouraged to ask each other questions and to give each other feedback that will help in developing appropriate goals.

Feedback should focus on: (1) behaviors the individual performed assertively in role plays, and (2) suggestions on how to act differently next time. For example, "Your voice came through loud and clear. Next time stand up straighter and try to look at him when you speak." The group can also help members evaluate the risks of asserting themselves in problem situations and can help them weigh the advantages and disadvantages of remaining the same versus changing.

Planning and implementing an assertiveness-training program.   When planning and implementing an assertiveness-training program, the group leader sets up role plays, coaches individuals during the role plays, and models assertive responses. The leader also demonstrates for group members how to model and coach each other with prompts, cues, and instructions. Group members are actively involved in planning and implementing each other's assertiveness-training program by serving as: (1) models; (2) significant others, such as co-workers or family members, in role plays; (3) reinforcers; (4) feedback givers; and (5) evaluators.

Group members also help each other develop **behavioral assignments** or "homework" specifying behaviors to be performed between group sessions. Initially, the leader assumes major responsibility for giving behavioral assignments. As the members develop the necessary skills, however, they take a more active role in structuring their own assignments and those of others. In order to make it more likely that they can perform their assignments, members rehearse or practice the assertive responses in the group, getting feedback and suggestions for improvement.

Behavioral rehearsal is an important part of an assertiveness-training program. Behavioral rehearsal is a role-playing technique in which the client practices assertive behaviors that have been modeled by the therapist or group members. The inclusion of behavioral rehearsal in a behavioral-change program gives the client opportunities to practice assertive behaviors in a supportive environment, with corrective feedback, before attempting to perform them in the actual problematic situation.

Behavioral rehearsal was included in Gretchen's assertiveness-training program. She practiced assertive behaviors suggested or modeled by the therapist in the practice setting and received reinforcement, prompts, and other feedback from the therapist regarding her performance.

Evaluation. The tasks of the group leader in evaluation are: (1) to help each member evaluate goal progress on his or her assertiveness-training program, and (2) to identify additional difficulties of assertiveness. Group members use records of their behavioral assignments to aid in evaluating their progress. In addition, members can help each other evaluate changes in assertive performances they observed in role plays and interactions in the group.

SUMMARY

1. Many behaviors are learned through observation or vicarious learning. An individual observes someone demonstrate or model a behavior or sequence of behaviors. The individual then imitates the model's behavior.

2. A model is someone whose behavior is imitated. It is not necessary for imitated behavior to immediately follow the model's behavior in order to be performed at a future time.

3. The modeling procedure consists of presenting a modeled stimulus (S^m) that is intended to influence performance of an imitated response. The imitated response or sequence of responses is similar to the S^m. Modeling facilitates the acquisition of behaviors or behavior patterns that otherwise would be more difficult or take longer to develop.

4. Positive reinforcement can be used to increase the strength of an imitated response.

5. If an individual does not imitate at all, the practitioner can teach him or her to imitate a modeled stimulus by first shaping a general class of imitative responses. Prompts, instructions, and physical guidance can also be used with modeling to facilitate imitation.

6. If an individual imitates excessively, the practitioner can teach him or her appropriate imitation by: (a) extinguishing inappropriate imitated responses,

(b) reinforcing appropriate imitated responses, and (c) reinforcing responses that are incompatible with the undesired repetitive behaviors.

7.   Assertiveness training, or social skills training, is a behavioral-change procedure for improving deficient social or interpersonal skills. Modeling, instructions, prompts, reinforcement, shaping, relaxation training, and the use of response hierarchies are techniques used in assertiveness training. Deficits in assertive behavior are called nonassertive or underassertive behaviors. Excesses in assertiveness are called aggressive or overassertive behaviors.

8.   Assertive responses consist of speech, body gestures, and facial movements that convey the rights or opinions of an individual in a nonabusive manner.

9.   Assertiveness training can be used in groups. A variety of models are available in groups to demonstrate assertive behaviors. Group members provide feedback on the adequacy of assertive performances and offer suggestions for improvement.

SUGGESTED READINGS

ALBERTI, R. E. (Ed.),   *Assertiveness: Innovations, Applications, Issues.* (San Luis Obispo, Calif.: Impact Publishers, Inc., 1977).

BAER, D. M., PETERSON, R. F., and SHERMAN, J. A.,   "The Development of Imitation by Reinforcing Behavioral Similarity to a Model," *Journal of the Experimental Analysis of Behavior,* 1967, *10,* 405-416.

BANDURA, A.,   *Principles of Behavior Modification* (New York: Holt, Rinehart & Winston, 1969).

BANDURA, A.,   *Social Learning Theory* (Englewood Cliffs, N.J.: Prentice-Hall, Inc., 1977), Chapter 2, 15-55.

BANDURA, A.,   "Influence of Models' Reinforcement Contingencies on the Acquisition of Imitative Responses," *Journal of Personality and Social Psychology,* 1965, *1,* 589-595.

BANDURA, A., and WALTERS, R. H., *Social Learning and Personality Development* (New York: Holt, Rinehart & Winston, 1963).

CORSINI, R. J.,   *Roleplaying in Psychotherapy: A Manual* (Chicago: Aldine, 1966).

GLADSTONE, B. W., and SPENCER, C. J.,   "The Effects of Modeling on the Contingent Praise of Mental Retardation Counselors," *Journal of Applied Behavior Analysis,* 1977, *10,* 75-84.

HINGTGEN, J. N., COULTER, S. K., and CHURCHILL, D. W.,   "Intensive Reinforcement of Imitative Behavior in Mute Autistic Children," *Archives of General Psychiatry,* 1967, *17,* 36-43.

LANGE, A. J., and JAKUBOWSKI, P.,   *Responsible Assertive Behavior: Cognitive/Behavioral Procedures for Trainers* (Champaign, Ill.: Research Press, 1976).

LAWRENCE, H., and SUNDEL, M.,   "Behavior Modification in Adult Groups," *Social Work,* 1972, *17,* 34-43.

MALOTT, R., TILLEMA, M., and GLENN, S.,   *Behavior Analysis and Behavior Modification: An Introduction* (Kalamazoo, Mich.: Behaviordelia, Inc., 1978), Chapter 16.

RISLEY, T., and WOLF, M., "Establishing Functional Speech in Echolalic Children," *Behavior Research and Therapy,* 1967, *5,* 73-88.

SUNDEL, M., and LAWRENCE, H., "A Systematic Approach to Treatment Planning in Time-limited Behavioral Groups," *Journal of Behavior Therapy and Experimental Psychiatry,* 1977, *8,* 395-399.

SUNDEL, S. S., and SUNDEL, M., *Be Assertive: A Practical Guide for Human Service Workers* (Beverly Hills, Calif.: Sage Publications, 1980).

WOLPE, J., *The Practice of Behavior Therapy* (Elmsford, N.Y.: Pergamon Press, 1969, 1973), Chapter 5.

POST-TEST QUESTIONS

(3) 1. Give an example that describes how a modeling-plus-reinforcement procedure is used to develop and strengthen a response.

(4) 2. Give an example of the use of modeling in developing assertive behaviors in a group setting.

(4) 3. Describe the use of a modeling procedure with prompts, reinforcement, and fading, given the following information: A social worker is trying to teach a retarded child to answer questions about his family. When the social worker asks the child, "How many brothers do you have?" the child does not answer. The child can talk and can say all the words necessary to answer the question.

PUNISHMENT

objectives

After completing this chapter, you should be able to:

1. give an example of each of the two types of punishment procedures and the criterion for evaluating their effectiveness,
2. given a case example, identify the punishment procedure and label its relevant components,
3. give an example that contrasts extinction with response-contingent removal of a positive reinforcer,
4. given a case example, describe how the effectiveness of punishment can be maximized, and
5. give an example of punishment applied in a self-control contingency.

Mrs. Drake complained to a therapist at a community mental health center that she found it impossible to discipline her 9-year-old son, Stephen. He frequently hit his younger sister, Dianne, making her cry. Stephen also broke Dianne's toys during two recent incidents. On several occasions when Mrs. Drake intervened to stop Stephen from hitting Dianne, Stephen cursed and kicked Mrs. Drake. Verbal reprimands, threats, and attempts to physically punish Stephen failed to eliminate his undesirable behaviors.

Chapter 12

(2) 1. Name the two types of punishment procedures that can be used to suppress a response.

(1) 2. Briefly describe a time-out procedure.

(2) 3. Briefly describe two disadvantages of punishment procedures.

(4) 4. Mrs. Kelly asked Sharon to fold the laundry after it had been washed and dried. When Mrs. Kelly returned, Sharon was talking to her friend on the phone and the laundry had not been folded. What should Mrs. Kelly do to demonstrate her knowledge of the necessary conditions to maximize the effectiveness of punishment?

PUNISHMENT DEFINED

Up to now, we have covered several techniques for increasing the strength of behaviors. We have also presented two techniques for weakening or reducing the strength of a behavior—extinction and DRO. This chapter will address concepts and procedures of punishment, a topic that attracts controversy but is often misunderstood.

In common usage, the term punishment is associated with vengeance or retribution. In behavioral terms, however, **punishment** refers to procedures applied to suppress behaviors or decrease their strength, not to acts intended to inflict harm or injury on an individual. The punished behavior might not be eliminated, however, because it could be performed again when the individual who administered the punishment is not present. Thus, the term *suppress* is used to indicate that the punished response is not performed in the punished situation. In this chapter we discuss two punishment techniques: (1) **response-contingent presentation of a punisher**, and (2) **response-contingent removal of a positive reinforcer.**

AVERSIVE STIMULI AND PUNISHERS

The term **punisher** or **punishing stimulus** refers to a stimulus that suppresses or weakens a response it follows. Aversive stimulus is sometimes confused with the preceding term. An **aversive stimulus** is an event typically described by an individual as unpleasant, annoying, or painful. Electric shock, intense noise or light, physical attack (for example, hitting, pinching, kicking), traffic tickets, fines, and threats are common examples of aversive stimuli.

Aversive stimuli have been used as punishers; however, they do not always act to suppress behaviors. By definition, a punisher always acts to suppress a response or decrease its strength, whether or not the punisher is an aversive stimulus. For example, someone lights up a cigarette while conversing with you. Although smoking is pleasant and not aversive to this individual, it is unpleasant to you and the smoke acts as a punisher to decrease your talking to him. You terminate the conversation and walk away.

The distinction we are drawing between an aversive stimulus and a punisher is analogous to the comparison we made earlier between a reward and a positive reinforcer. You will recall that a reward is a reinforcer only if it acts to increase the strength of a response. Similarly, an aversive stimulus is a punisher only if it decreases the strength of a behavior.

Punishers, like reinforcers, can be primary (unconditioned) or conditioned stimuli. A primary punisher is intrinsically or naturally punishing; it does not require pairing with another punisher in order to suppress behavior. Shock, intense light or noise, and physical violence are common examples of unconditioned punishers. A conditioned punisher must first be paired or associated with an established punisher before it can act to suppress a behavior. Threats, fines, failing grades, and removal of privileges are common examples of conditioned punishers.

RESPONSE-CONTINGENT PRESENTATION OF A PUNISHER

The procedure for **response-contingent presentation of a punisher** consists of presenting a punishing stimulus immediately after the target response is performed. The punishment effect is a decrease in the strength of the target response and a decreased likelihood that the response will be performed again under similar conditions.

Baseline measures of the target response should be taken prior to initiating the punishment technique. The strength of the target response is measured again after the stimulus intended to serve as a punisher has been applied. If the stimulus acted as a punisher, the strength of the response will decrease in relation to its baseline measure(s). A stimulus is not a punisher unless it suppresses a response or decreases its strength. For example, loud disco music may serve as a punisher for some individuals' dancing but as a positive reinforcer for dancing for other individuals.

In paradigm form, the procedure for punishment by presentation of a punisher is as follows:

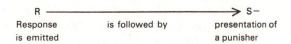

R ——————————————————→ S–
Response   is followed by   presentation of
is emitted   a punisher

Effect: Suppression of the response, R, and decreased likelihood of its performance.

The notation S⁻ in the above paradigm indicates a stimulus (S) whose presentation after a response decreases (⁻) the strength of that response. This form of punishment is found in a wide range of situations: for example, George tracks mud into the house and his mother shouts at him (Sʳ⁻); an autistic child bites herself and receives a slight electric shock (Sᴿ⁻); Martha volunteered to present extra cases at staff meetings, and was criticized for being a "brown nose" by her co-workers (Sʳ⁻). These examples in paradigm form would look like this:

R ⟶ Sʳ⁻
George tracks mud into the house   Mother shouts at him

Effect: George stops tracking mud into the house.

R ⟶ Sᴿ⁻
Child bites herself   Slight electric shock

Effect: Child stops biting herself.

R ⟶ Sʳ⁻
Martha volunteers to present extra cases   Colleagues call her a "brown nose"

Effect: Martha stops volunteering to present extra cases.

The decision to use response-contingent presentation of a punisher, particularly an unconditioned aversive stimulus such as shock, should be based on the following considerations:

1. the necessity for immediate effect, because of serious danger or injury to the individual or others;
2. the relative effectiveness of other techniques that are available, plus their advantages and disadvantages; and
3. the intermediate and long-term negative consequences for the individual or significant others if the behavior is not suppressed or weakened.

For example, consider the case of a severely retarded child whose body was covered with sores from self-mutilation. The child's hands and feet had to be tied to his bed so that he could not bite and scratch himself. Applying a small number of mild electric shocks to the child's legs immediately after he hit himself stopped the self-destructive behaviors. In similar cases, positive reinforcement of incompatible responses, social isolation, and extinction techniques proved to be less successful than electric shocks used as punishment (see, for example, Risley, 1968; Lovaas & Simmons, 1969).

When a young child who has been told repeatedly to play only in the yard runs into the street, the parents must apply a technique that will be effective immediately, preferably on the basis of a single administration. A hard slap on the rear end, accompanied by a stern reminder to "stay out of the street!" will usually stop the undesired, dangerous behaviors and establish the association of playing in the street with the slap and verbal admonition.

RESPONSE-CONTINGENT REMOVAL OF A POSITIVE REINFORCER

The second type of punishment technique is called **response-contingent removal of a positive reinforcer.** This technique consists of removing or withdrawing a positive reinforcer contingent on the occurrence of the target response. This is also called **response cost.** The punishment effect is a decrease in the strength of the target response and decreased likelihood that the response will be performed again under similar conditions. The paradigm for punishment by removal of a positive reinforcer is:

R ——————————————→ s⁺

Response   is followed by   removal of a
is emitted   positive reinforcer

Effect: Suppression of the response, R, and decreased likelihood of its performance.

The S+ in the above example indicates a stimulus (S) whose removal (+) decreases the strength of the target response. For example, making a mistake on an exam cost a student 5 points; when Sam got a part-time job, his family's welfare payment was reduced and he lost his medical benefits. In paradigm form, Sam's situation would look like this:

R ——————————————→ s⁺

Took a part-   was followed by   loss of medical
time job   benefits; less
                                        welfare money

Effect: Sam stopped working.

In using this type of punishment, the practitioner should attempt to discover which items and events are reinforcers for the client. These stimuli should be considered for use in a punishment procedure involving removal of a positive reinforcer. If the stimulus removed is not a positive reinforcer, its removal will be ineffective in decreasing response strength. When punishing undesired behaviors, the practitioner should also arrange for positive reinforcement to follow desired behaviors.

EXTINCTION AND PUNISHMENT

Extinction is sometimes confused with punishment by response-contingent removal of a positive reinforcer. In the extinction procedure, the reinforcer for the target response is withheld continuously; that is, each time the response occurs, the previously delivered positive reinforcer is withheld. In punishment by response-contingent removal of a positive reinforcer, a reinforcer *other than* the one maintaining the target response is withdrawn.

For example, when Beverly criticized the agency's executive director for his management practices, her co-workers listened and encouraged her. She failed to discuss her criticisms with the executive director, however, and continued to complain to her co-workers. They soon grew tired of her continuous complaints and extinguished this behavior by withholding their attention. When the executive director heard of her criticisms from other staff, he moved Beverly to a small windowless office away from her previous co-workers. His action removed several reinforcers from Beverly, including her previous large office with a big window, the status associated with this office, and proximity to the social reinforcers of her co-workers. Moving her office, however, acted as a punisher for Beverly's criticism of the executive director only if the strength (frequency, intensity, and/or duration) of her critical remarks decreased. Beverly might find other staff who are sympathetic to her position and reinforce her criticism. The extinction and punishment paradigms are shown below:

Extinction

R ——————————————→ s⁺
Response is emitted   is not followed by   positive reinforcer

Effect: Response decreases in strength and likelihood of occurrence.

R ——————————————→ s⁺
Beverly criticizes   is not followed by   co-workers listen
the executive director   and encourage her

Effect: Decrease in the frequency of Beverly's criticism of executive director's management practices.

Punishment

R ——————————————→ s⁺
Response   is followed by   removal of
is emitted   positive reinforcer

Effect: Decrease or suppression of the response and decrease in its likelihood of occurrence.

R ——————————————→ s⁺
Beverly criticizes   is followed by   executive director
executive director's   moves her to a small,
management practices   windowless office

Effect: Beverly stops criticizing the executive director or criticizes him less frequently.

In extinction, the response gradually decreases in strength; with punishment, cessation or decrease of the response is usually more immediate. For punishment to be effective, the positive reinforcer removed must exert greater control over the target response than does the reinforcer presently maintaining the target response. The removal of Beverly from her office must, therefore, exert greater control in decreasing her criticism of the executive director than the social reinforcement she receives from her co-workers for criticizing him. The punishment effect can be maximized by introducing an extinction procedure during punishment. Beverly's criticism might be more effectively reduced if both the extinction (termination of co-workers' social reinforcement) and punishment procedures described were implemented. This example illustrates how administrative authority can be used vindictively in stifling worker behaviors.

TIME-OUT

Time-out is a form of punishment by response-contingent removal of positive reinforcement. In time-out, the individual is removed from the problematic situation immediately after the target behavior is emitted and placed for a *brief period* in an environment with no or minimal availability of reinforcement. The time-out procedure involves removal of S^{D}s for the target response as well as removal of reinforcers. An example of this procedure can be found in Case Study 7 below. Mrs. Drake took Stephen to his room when he hit his sister. Taking Stephen to his room both prevented him from responding to S^{D}s (Dianne's teasing, making faces) in the problematic situation and removed positive reinforcement (mother's attention) for his inappropriate behaviors. The time-out room must be void of reinforcers that would lessen the effect of that environment as a punisher.

When using the time-out procedure, specific behavioral contingencies should be established. For example, the time-out period should be set for specified, brief periods. If the individual resists time-out by kicking, screaming, or cursing, a punishment contingency should be established in which such behaviors extend the time-out period, for example, by 5 to 10 minutes per incident. Release from time-out is made contingent on passage of the designated time and performance of appropriate behaviors in the time-out room. This time-out procedure, therefore, is markedly different from procedures used in some institutions where an individual is isolated for extended periods.

CASE STUDY 7

The Parent as a Behavior Modifier

Mrs. Drake complained to a therapist at a community mental health center that she found it impossible to discipline her 9-year-old son, Stephen. He frequently hit his younger sister Dianne, making her cry and inflicting bruises. He sometimes broke her toys during these incidents. When Mrs. Drake intervened to stop Stephen from hitting Dianne, Stephen cursed and kicked Mrs. Drake. Verbal reprimands, threats, and attempts to physically punish Stephen failed to eliminate his undesired behaviors.

The therapist instructed Mrs. Drake to monitor situations in which the hitting occurred. Mrs. Drake reported that Dianne often teased or made faces at Stephen prior to his hitting her. Mrs. Drake's report also indicated that she spent most of her time in the evenings trying to discipline Stephen.

Treatment consisted of Mrs. Drake telling Dianne to stop teasing and making faces at Stephen, with the contingency arranged that if she teased and made faces she would lose privileges such as watching television or having a bedtime snack. On two subsequent occasions, Dianne lost television privileges and a bedtime snack. After these two experiences, Dianne stopped teasing and making faces at Stephen.

Treatment further consisted of instructing Mrs. Drake to tell Stephen to go to his room when he hit Dianne. If he refused to obey, Mrs. Drake would physically carry or move Stephen to his room, where he was required to remain by himself for 15 minutes. If he kicked or cursed Mrs. Drake, the time was extended 5 minutes. If he screamed or made loud noises while in his room, the time was also extended 5 minutes.

The first time Mrs. Drake took Stephen to his room, he kicked and cursed. He also screamed while in the room. Stephen remained in his room for 25 minutes. The same thing happened the second time. The third time Mrs. Drake instituted the treatment procedure, Stephen stopped cursing and kicking her. The fourth time the procedure was applied, Stephen went to the room by himself and quietly remained there until his time was up. After the fifth time the procedure was employed, Stephen no longer hit his sister.

Mrs. Drake was also instructed to spend leisure time with Stephen in the evenings. Since Stephen liked to play cards with his mother, she was to play cards with him in the evening.

OVERCORRECTION

Overcorrection is a procedure used to decrease the strength of an individual's inappropriate behaviors, while at the same time providing S^Ds and reinforcers for performing appropriate behaviors (Azrin & Foxx, 1971). There are two components of overcorrection: restitutional overcorrection and positive practice overcorrection (Ollendick & Matson, 1978).

Restitutional overcorrection involves restoring the environment to the condition it was in before the inappropriate act was committed and then improving it even further. For example, in one instance the restitutional overcorrection procedure for stealing food required the individual to return the stolen item and then buy an identical item and give it to the victim (Azrin & Wesolowski, 1974). As another example, when Stan spit his gum on the gym floor, normally he might simply be required to pick it up and throw it in the trash. But with restitutional overcorrection Stan might be required to pick up litter from the entire first floor of the building and throw it in the trash.

Positive practice overcorrection involves repeating the correct behaviors that are incompatible with the inappropriate behaviors. For example, when students spoke out of turn or left their seats in class without permission, they were required to state the rule that was broken, state the correct procedure, raise their hands and wait to be called on by the teacher, and ask the teacher for permission to speak. The teacher reinforced correct practice with verbal praise. This procedure was repeated for 5 to 10 minutes during recess (Azrin & Powers, 1975). The positive practice overcorrection procedure for Stan involved having him chew a piece of gum for 15 seconds, then throw it in the trash. This was repeated for 5 to 10 minutes after each incident of his spitting gum on the gym floor. Positive practice can be used alone or in conjunction with restitutional overcorrection.

Overcorrection involves several behavioral principles:

1. Reinforcement for the inappropriate behavior is removed—for example, the stolen food item is returned.
2. Time-out is implemented for the inappropriate behavior. When the individual is engaged in overcorrection, he or she is removed from the reinforcing environment.
3. Positive reinforcement is given for correct practice.
4. The individual learns to perform appropriate behaviors in the presence of appropriate S^Ds.

MAXIMIZING THE EFFECTIVENESS OF PUNISHMENT

Conditions related to the effectiveness of punishment have been investigated. In order to maximize the effectiveness of the punishment procedure, the following conditions should be observed (see Azrin & Holz, 1966):

1. The punisher should immediately follow the target response.
2. The punisher should be administered each time the response is performed.
3. The punisher should be of sufficient intensity to suppress the target response.
4. Alternate appropriate behaviors should be specified.
5. Appropriate behaviors should be reinforced.
6. Reinforcement for inappropriate behaviors should be removed or reduced.
7. The punishment contingency should be arranged so that the individual cannot escape the punisher.

In both types of punishment, the punisher (that is, either the presentation of a punishing stimulus or the removal of a positive reinforcer) should occur *immediately after* the response. If punishment of the target response is delayed, the intended punisher could inadvertently suppress other behaviors that follow the target response. For example, a child disobeyed his grandmother who said "Wait until your father gets home; then you will get it!" Six hours later, the child was finally reprimanded by his father. Even though the father's punishment might be associated verbally with the undesired behavior, any behaviors occurring at the time punishment was delivered could be punished, such as greeting his father at the door.

Other factors influencing the effectiveness of punishment are the *intensity* and *frequency* of the punisher. The punishing stimulus should be sufficiently intense to suppress the undesired response. Similarly, the reinforcer removed should exert more control over the individual's behavior than the reinforcer maintaining it. The punisher should be delivered on a continuous schedule, that is, each time the target response is performed. Like different schedules of reinforcement, however, different schedules of punishment have been shown to generate characteristic patterns of responding (Azrin & Holz, 1966).

Four-year-old Billy climbed trees though his mother warned him to stay away. She found him in a tree with other children urging him to climb higher. To maximize the effects of punishment, she sent the other children away (removal of positive reinforcement); scolded Billy (presentation of an intense punishing stimulus); specified another activity that Billy could engage in; and reinforced him for playing at the appropriate activity.

In another example of punishment, a talkative client frequently drifted off the subject during interviews and rambled onto other topics. Each time the client began to ramble, the practitioner immediately said, "Stop! You are off the subject." The therapist then specified what the client should talk about in order to provide S^Ds for client responses that the practitioner could reinforce. The practitioner asked, for example, "What were you doing when the problem occurred?" If answered appropriately, the practitioner said, "That's getting at the problem. Please continue," thus reinforcing the client for staying on the topic. The effects of this procedure were to decrease the frequency of rambling and to increase the frequency of talking about relevant topics.

DISADVANTAGES OF PUNISHMENT

Several side effects or disadvantages of punishment can occur that limit the overall effectiveness of punishment as a behavioral control technique (see Azrin & Holz, 1966). These effects include the following:

1. The punished response may reappear in the absence of the punisher. Example: a group leader punished Stan, an adolescent, for spitting his gum out on the gym floor by having him pick up litter from the entire gym. Stan no longer spit his gum on the gym floor when that group leader was around. He might spit his gum in the hall, however, or in a classroom when the leader is not present, and Stan is not required to remove his gum from the floor.

2. Aggression may occur in the form of physical or verbal attacks against the individual administering the punishment. *Example:* When the group leader made Stan clean up the gym, Stan cursed him.

3. Aggression may be directed toward someone or something that is in no way responsible for the delivery of the punisher. *Example:* The boss criticized Harry for handing in his report late; when Harry arrived home, he criticized his son for the way he wore his hair.

4. Through association, the person who administers a punisher can become a conditioned punisher as well; the punished individual may then avoid him or her. *Examples:* Stan now avoids the group leader who punished him. Grandparents often reward their grandchildren and refrain from punishing them, to avoid this association.

5. A punisher could suppress appropriate behaviors as well as inappropriate behaviors performed when the punisher is delivered. This is especially likely if punishment is not delivered immediately after the inappropriate response. *Example:* A supervisor criticized a worker for turning in an incomplete case report. At the time she was criticized the worker was reviewing case records to determine client progress. The supervisor's delayed criticism could act as a punisher to weaken the worker's appropriate behaviors of reviewing case records.

6. The person administering the punishment might be imitated by observers. *Example:* Adam heard his Dad yell at him to clean up his room. Later Adam yelled at his sister to clean up her room in the same tone of voice.

7. The intended punisher might be ineffective. It could serve instead as an S^D for a response that is reinforced. The intended punisher could also act as a conditioned positive reinforcer that increases, rather than decreases, the strength of the target behavior. An intended punisher is a stimulus that is administered to decrease response strength but is ineffective in doing so. *Example:* Mrs. Gardino was busy cooking dinner, and her son, Tony, started playing with the telephone receiver. Although she told him several times to leave it alone, he persisted until she finally screamed at him. He began to cry, and she immediately ran over to him, talked to him soothingly, and played with him until he stopped crying. Tony might have learned from this experience that one way to get mother's attention is to play with the telephone receiver. Mother will yell, but if he cries, she will talk to him and play with him.

In paradigm form, the last example would look like this:

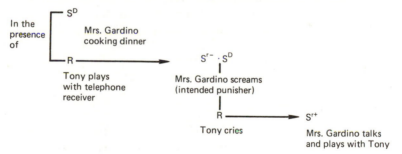

Effect: Tony's playing with the telephone when Mrs. Gardino is cooking dinner increased in strength and likelihood of occurrence.

The effect of this stimulus-response chain was that Mrs. Gardino's screaming (S^{r-}) became a conditioned positive reinforcer (S^{r+}) through association with the reinforcers of playing with and talking to Tony. Mrs. Gardino's screaming, therefore, increased the likelihood of Tony's playing with the telephone; her screaming also served as an S^D for crying. Furthermore, Mrs. Gardino's screaming can reinforce Tony's other inappropriate behaviors, such as watching TV at bedtime or running away from her at the shopping center.

For another example of an intended punisher serving as a conditioned positive reinforcer, consider a marital argument. When Mrs. Fitzhugh criticized her husband, he swore at her until she began to cry. After he apologized and comforted her, they made up and had sexual intercourse. The stimulus-response chain in paradigm form looks like this:

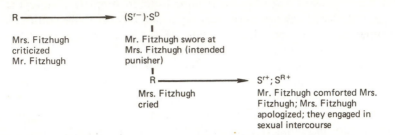

Effect: Mrs. Fitzhugh's criticism of Mr. Fitzhugh increased in strength and likelihood of occurrence.

Mr. Fitzhugh swore (S^{r-}) at Mrs. Fitzhugh, hoping to decrease her criticism. Instead, his swearing served as the S^D for her crying (R), which was followed by sex (S^{R+}). The swearing thus became a conditioned positive reinforcer (S^{r+}).

Arguments can become conditioned reinforcers if they have served as S^Ds for responses that lead to sexual reinforcement. In this case, the marriage counselor's assessment revealed the following pattern: When Mrs. Fitzhugh cried, her husband comforted her and they usually had sexual intercourse. Although the S^Ds for Mrs. Fitzhugh's crying varied, the reinforcers remained the same. In this way, Mrs. Fitzhugh's crying came under the stimulus control of many S^Ds, most of which were related to her husband's swearing at her or speaking to her in a loud voice. Thus, any behavior of Mrs. Fitzhugh's that resulted in her husband's swearing or shouting could set off the stimulus-response chain. In this way, Mrs. Fitzhugh's criticism or Mr. Fitzhugh's swearing could strengthen other argumentative behaviors because of their previous association with positive reinforcers.

PUNISHMENT AND SELF-CONTROL

Punishment can be self-administered to suppress undesired behavior. A punishment contingency can be established by an individual to control his or her own behavior. For example, a Republican social worker might establish the following contingency: "If I complete less than two case reports each day this week, I will send ten dollars for each incomplete report to the Democratic National Committee." Another individual might establish the following contingency: "Everytime I eat between meals, I will give away my ticket to the basketball game." A third example might be carrying a cigarette case that delivers a mild shock if opened at intervals of less than 30 minutes to decrease smoking.

Of course, to maximize punishment, self-administered reinforcement contingencies should be added: "For every report I complete this week, I will leave work 10 minutes early," "For each day I eat only during meal times, I will put one dollar away to buy a new record album." Although self-contingency management programs lack the control provided by an external behavior modifier, these self-control procedures have been used successfully to modify undesired behaviors (for example, Mahoney & Thoresen, 1974).

THE FUTURE OF PUNISHMENT

In spite of the disadvantages of punishment and the stringent requirements for insuring its effectiveness, punishment is still commonly used as a behavioral control technique. One reason for this is that it usually works immediately to suppress undesired behavior. The short-term consequences are reinforcing, therefore, for the individual who administers the punishment. For example, Mr. Hanes spanked his daughter, Terri, when she complained about eating her vegetables. Terri stopped complaining; thus, Mr. Hanes was reinforced for spanking her. Because an individual's behavior is frequently governed by short-term consequences, punishment will probably continue to be commonly used for decreasing undesired behaviors.

The public needs to be better educated in the effective use of reinforcement techniques to replace common punishment practices, especially the use of physical violence. Punishment with intense aversive stimuli should be used only rarely when the undesired behavior is detrimental or dangerous and its immediate cessation is necessary. It is important to recognize, however, that many of our behaviors are influenced by punishment contingencies. By analyzing problematic situations, practitioners can identify punishment contingencies used by individuals to control the behavior of others or which prevent an individual from performing desired behaviors.

SUMMARY

1. Punishment is a behavioral technique that suppresses a response or decreases its strength. A response weakened by punishment is less likely to be performed again under similar conditions.
2. There are two types of punishment techniques: (1) response-contingent presentation of a punisher, and (2) response-contingent removal of a positive reinforcer (response cost).
3. A punisher is a stimulus that suppresses a response or decreases its strength. Although a punisher suppresses a response, it may not eliminate it, since the response could occur in the absence of the punisher.
4. An aversive stimulus is an unpleasant, annoying, or painful event. An aversive stimulus acts as a punisher only if it suppresses a response or decreases the strength of a behavior.
5. Primary or unconditioned punishers include electric shock, intense light or noise, and physical attacks. Examples of conditioned punishers are fines, failing grades, and removal of privileges.
6. Response-contingent presentation of a punisher consists of presenting a punishing stimulus immediately after the target response. The punishment

effect is to suppress a target response or decrease its strength and to decrease the likelihood that the response will be performed again.

7. The following factors should be taken into account when deciding to use a punishment procedure: (1) necessity for immediate effect; (2) relative effectiveness of other techniques available; and (3) the negative consequences for the individual or significant others if the behavior is not decreased.

8. Punishment by response-contingent removal of a positive reinforcer involves removing or withdrawing a positive reinforcer contingent on performance of the target response. The punishment effect is to suppress a target response or decrease its strength.

9. The extinction and punishment procedures and effects are contrasted. Extinction involves withholding the positive reinforcer that maintains the response. The response decreases gradually. In punishment, a reinforcer *other* than the one that maintains the response is withdrawn. The response typically decreases immediately.

10. Time-out involves removing the individual from the problematic situation to a place with no or minimal availability of reinforcement contingent on performance of the undesired response. The time-out period is brief.

11. Factors that maximize the effectiveness of punishment include: (1) The punisher should follow immediately after the target response. (2) The punisher should be of sufficient intensity to suppress the undesired response. (3) The punisher should follow the target response each time it is performed, that is, on a continuous schedule. (4) Alternate appropriate behaviors should be specified. (5) Appropriate behaviors should be reinforced. (6) Reinforcement for inappropriate behaviors should be removed. (7) Arrangements should be made so that the individual cannot eascape from the punishing stimulus.

12. The disadvantages of punishment include: (1) The punished response may reappear in the absence of the punisher or the individual who administers it. (2) Aggression in the form of physical or verbal attacks against the individual administering punishment can occur. (3) Aggression may be directed toward someone or something that is not responsible for delivery of the punisher. (4) The person who administers a punisher can become a conditioned punisher through association with the punisher administered. (5) A punisher could suppress appropriate behaviors as well as inappropriate behaviors performed when punishment is delivered. (6) The person administering the punishment may be imitated by observers. (7) An intended punisher can serve as an S^D for an undesired reponse that is reinforced.

13. Punishment can be used by individuals in self-control contingencies to decrease the strength of undesired behaviors.

SUGGESTED READINGS

AZRIN, N. H., and FOXX, R. M.,   "A Rapid Method of Toilet Training the Institutionalized Retarded," *Journal of Applied Behavior Analysis,* 1971, *4,* 89–99.

AZRIN, N. H., and HOLZ, W. C. "Punishment," in W. K. Honig (Ed.), *Operant Behavior: Areas of Research and Application* (Englewood Cliffs, N.J.: Prentice-Hall, Inc., 1966), pp. 380–447.

AZRIN, N. H., and POWERS, M. A., "Eliminating Classroom Disturbances of Emotionally Disturbed Children by Positive Practice Procedures," *Behavior Therapy,* 1975, *6,* 525–534.

AZRIN, N. H., and WESOLOWSKI, M. D., "Theft Reversal: An Overcorrection Procedure for Eliminating Stealing by Retarded Persons," *Journal of Applied Behavior Analysis,* 1974, *7,* 577–581.

BAER, D. M., "Laboratory Control of Thumb Sucking by Withdrawal and Re-presentation of Reinforcement," *Journal of the Experimental Analysis of Behavior,* 1962, *5,* 525–528.

CASTRO, L., and RACHLIN, H., "Self-Reward, Self-Monitoring, and Self-Punishment as Feedback in Weight Control," *Behavior Therapy,* 1980, *11*(1), 38–48.

LICHSTEIN, K. L., and STALGAITIS, S. J., "Treatment of Cigarette Smoking in Couples by Reciprocal Aversion," *Behavior Therapy,* 1980, *11*(1), 104–108.

LOVAAS, O. I., and SIMMONS, J. Q., "Manipulation of Self-destruction in Three Retarded Children," *Journal of Applied Behavior Analysis,* 1969, *2,* 143–157. Reprinted in O. I. Lovaas and B. D. Bucher (Eds.), *Perspectives in Behavior Modification with Deviant Children* (Englewood Cliffs, N.J.: Prentice-Hall, 1974), pp. 465–487.

MAHONEY, M. J., and THORESEN, C. E., *Self-Control: Power to the Person* (Belmont, Calif.: Brooks/Cole, 1974).

OLLENDICK, T. H., and MATSON, J. L., "Overcorrection: An Overview," *Behavior Therapy,* 1978, *9,* 830–842.

RISLEY, T. R., "The Effects and Side Effects of Punishing the Autistic Behaviors of a Deviant Child," *Journal of Applied Behavior Analysis,* 1968, *1,* 21–34.

SOLOMON, R. L., "Punishment," *American Psychologist,* 1964, *19,* 239–253.

TYLER, V. O., and BROWN, G. D., "The Use of Swift, Brief Isolation as a Group Control Device for Institutionalized Delinquents," *Behavior Research and Therapy,* 1967, *5,* 1–10.

POST-TEST QUESTIONS

(3) 1. Give an example of the two types of punishment procedures and indicate how you would evaluate their effectiveness.

(2) 2. Give an example that contrasts extinction with punishment by response-contingent removal of a positive reinforcer.

(5) 3..   Give an example of how you could maximize the effectiveness of punishment with a highly talkative client who frequently gets off the subject during your interviews and rambles on other topics.

(3) 4.   Using the information from Case Study 7, pages 143–144, name the punishment procedure administered to Stephen by Mrs. Drake. Draw a paradigm of an incident that would lead her to use this procedure. Label the appropriate components.

(1) 5.   Give an example of punishment applied in a self-control contingency.

13
NEGATIVE REINFORCEMENT

objectives

After completing this chapter, you should be able to:

1. contrast the effects of punishment and negative reinforcement,
2. give an example of escape behavior developed by negative reinforcement,
3. describe social interactions in terms of positive and negative reinforcement, given a case example, and
4. describe avoidance behavior, given a case example.

Mrs. Munsen berated her husband for going out with his friends, refusing to help around the house, and spending little time with her and their children. When she criticized him, Mr. Munsen swore at her and told her to mind her own business. Mrs. Munsen became so upset during these arguments that she burst into tears, ran into the bedroom, and locked the door.

Chapter 13

(1) 1. What is a major advantage of avoidance conditioning in maintaining a response?

(3) 2. Give an example of the behavioral technique that produces escape behavior.

(4) 3. Give an example of the behavioral procedure that results in avoidance behavior.

(2) 4. Give an example of (a) a primary aversive stimulus that could be used as a negative reinforcer and (b) a conditioned aversive stimulus that could be used as a negative reinforcer.

NEGATIVE REINFORCERS, PUNISHERS, AND AVERSIVE STIMULI

In the example that opened this chapter, one way Mrs. Munsen could *escape* her husband's swearing and insults was to lock herself in the bedroom. The behavioral technique that produces escape behavior is called negative reinforcement. The **negative reinforcement procedure** or technique consists of presenting a stimulus that signals or sets the occasion for a response that terminates, removes, or reduces the effect of the stimulus. The removal of this stimulus, the negative reinforcer, *increases* the likelihood that the escape response will be performed again under similar conditions.

Negative reinforcers can be primary (unconditioned) or conditioned (secondary) stimuli, as is the case with positive reinforcers and punishers. Examples of **primary negative reinforcers** include shock, intense light, noise, foul odors, and physical violence. **Conditioned negative reinforcers** include threats, fines, bad grades, frowns, and insults.

Aversive stimuli can act as negative reinforcers when their removal *increases* response strength, or as punishers when their presentation *decreases* response strength. Aversive stimuli, like rewards, are influenced by individual, social, and cultural factors; a stimulus that is unpleasant, annoying, or painful to one individual may not be aversive to another. Although a stimulus may be aversive to an individual, he or she may not always make a response to terminate it. For example, a nonsmoker who finds smoke aversive may continue to converse with someone who is smoking and not make a response that could remove the smoke. In this case, the aversive stimulus has not acted as a negative reinforcer because an escape response was not made.

The terms punisher and negative reinforcer have sometimes been incorrectly used synonymously. The term punisher, however, refers to a stimulus whose *presentation decreases* response strength; the term negative reinforcer refers to a stimulus whose *removal increases* response strength.

ESCAPE BEHAVIOR

The term negative reinforcement is used because the reinforcement function is to increase response strength. The word negative indicates the removal or reduction of the effect of the stimulus. **A negative reinforcer** is a stimulus that signals or sets the occasion for an escape response. The stimulus is defined as a negative reinforcer if its termination or reduction increases the strength of the escape response.

In the **negative reinforcement procedure,** a negative reinforcer (S⁻) is presented that remains in effect until an escape response is emitted (R) that terminates or reduces the effect of the negative reinforcer (S̸). The S⁻ acts as a discriminative stimulus that signals or sets the occasion for the response to be reinforced, in this case, negatively reinforced. The negative reinforcement paradigm is as follows:

Effect: The escape response (R) increases in strength and likelihood of occurrence.

The $S̸$ in the above paradigm indicates a stimulus (S) whose removal (̸) increases response strength.

Examples of escape behavior can be found in a wide variety of situations. When your belt feels too tight around your waist (S^{R-}), you loosen it a notch or two (R). This response terminates the pressure around your waist (S^{R}̸). The likelihood is increased that you will perform this response on future occasions when your belt is tight.

John's wife, Karen, complained that he never took her anywhere (S^{r-}). John went to a neighborhood bar (R) to get away from (escape) Karen's complaints (S^{r}̸). The likelihood is increased that on future occasions when Karen complains, John will go to the neighborhood bar. In paradigm form, the above example would look like this:

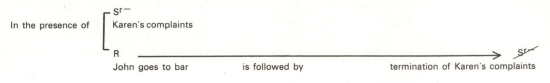

In the presence of

S^r-
Karen's complaints

R ————————————————————————————————→ S^r-
John goes to bar   is followed by   termination of Karen's complaints

Effect: John goes to the bar more frequently when Karen complains.

       In the above example, John's response of going to the bar was negatively reinforced. Removal of the negative reinforcer (complaints) also strengthens other responses that have the same or similar effect on the environment (removing the complaints) as the reinforced response (going to the bar). Thus, not only is a single response (going to the bar) reinforced, but a class of responses, each member of which could terminate his wife's complaining, is also strengthened. For example, driving to the bowling alley, bicycling to a friend's home, and walking around the block are all members of the response class that could terminate Karen's complaining. You will recall from Chapter 6 that when a response is positively reinforced, in fact, each member of the response class is also strengthened.

ESCAPE AND PUNISHMENT

       When a punishment procedure is applied, it is important that the individual not escape from the punishing situation. An escape response made during punishment will reduce the effectiveness of the punishment and increase the likelihood that the escape response will be performed again in a similar situation. For example, Fred was denied use of the car because he came home one hour past his curfew. Later that evening, Fred hot wired the car and drove it away. The escape responses of hot wiring the car and driving it were negatively reinforced by removal of the punishing effect of being without a car. Thus, the escape responses were strengthened and would be more likely to be performed again in similar situations.

       Although punishment and negative reinforcement techniques may involve similar stimuli, they have opposite effects on a behavior. Thus, aversive stimuli act as punishers when their presentation decreases response strength, and they act as negative reinforcers when their removal increases response strength. For example, a program evaluator requested data on client outcomes from treatment staff at a community mental health center. They told him that they were too busy to retrieve the data. The program evaluator stopped asking them for such data. His response was punished.

       The paradigm depicting this example is as follows:

R ————————————————————————————————→ S^r-
Program evaluator requested data   Staff said they were too busy

Effect: The program evaluator stopped asking for data. R was punished.

       Another program evaluator requested equivalent data from the same staff members and sent memos every day. The staff provided the data to satisfy the re-

FIGURE 13-1   Reinforcement and punishment paradigms

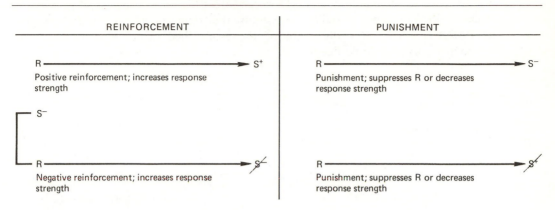

REINFORCEMENT	PUNISHMENT
R ————————————→ S⁺ Positive reinforcement; increases response strength	R ————————————→ S⁻ Punishment; suppresses R or decreases response strength
⌐ S⁻ └ R ————————————→ S⁄ Negative reinforcement; increases response strength	R ————————————→ S⁄ Punishment; suppresses R or decreases response strength

quests, thus terminating the requests and memos. The likelihood increased that the staff would comply with similar requests because providing the data was negatively reinforced by termination of the requests and memos.

In paradigm form the example would look like this:

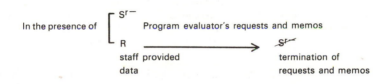

In the presence of ⌐ Sʳ⁻
                    │   Program evaluator's requests and memos
                    └ R ————————————→ Sʳ⁄
                      staff provided   termination of
                      data   requests and memos

Effect: Staff is more likely to comply with similar requests. R was negatively reinforced.

The reinforcement and punishment paradigms are shown in Figure 13-1.

AVOIDANCE BEHAVIOR

Negative reinforcement is also involved in **avoidance behavior.** An individual can avoid presentation of a negative reinforcer by performing a response that prevents its onset. A neutral stimulus is paired with a negative reinforcer so that it becomes a conditioned negative reinforcer (Sʳ⁻). The conditioned negative reinforcer is presented and acts as a discriminative stimulus or cue signaling that a second established negative reinforcer (S⁻) will follow unless a specific response (R) is made. This avoidance response is negatively reinforced by termination or reduction of the first negative reinforcer presented (Sʳ⁄). The avoidance response also prevents the onset of the established negative reinforcer. The first negative reinforcer (Sʳ⁻) serves as a discriminative stimulus to signal that an avoidance response will lead to negative reinforcement.

Thus, the avoidance paradigm consists of two steps: (1) the Escape Condition—pairing a neutral stimulus with a negative reinforcer that signals an escape response which is negatively reinforced; and (2) the Avoidance Condition—presentation of the conditioned negative reinforcer (formerly the neutral stimulus in Step 1 below) to signal an avoidance response that removes the conditioned negative reinforcer and prevents the onset of the established negative reinforcer. The avoidance paradigm looks like this:

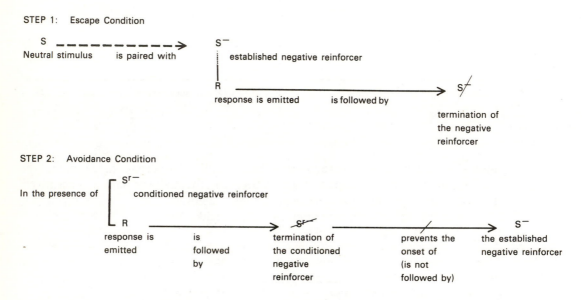

STEP 1: Escape Condition

S ——————————→ S⁻
Neutral stimulus   is paired with   established negative reinforcer

R ——————————————————→ S̷
response is emitted   is followed by
                        termination of
                        the negative
                        reinforcer

STEP 2: Avoidance Condition

Sʳ⁻
In the presence of   conditioned negative reinforcer

R ——————→ S̷ʳ ——————→ S⁻
response is   is   termination of   prevents the   the established
emitted   followed   the conditioned   onset of   negative reinforcer
            by   negative   (is not
                       reinforcer   followed by)

Effect: The avoidance response increases in strength and likelihood of occurrence; S⁻ is prevented.

For example, Jerry said to his father, "Buy me that toy or I'll scream right here in the store." Jerry's father, preoccupied with his shopping, ignored Jerry. Jerry started screaming until his father attended to him and bought him the toy. The father's response of buying Jerry a toy is strengthened and more likely to be performed in the future when Jerry threatens to scream. In paradigm form, the above example would look like this:

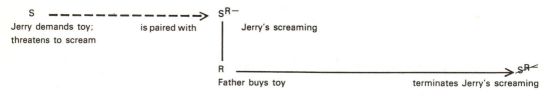

STEP 1: Escape Condition

S ——————————→ Sᴿ⁻
Jerry demands toy;   is paired with   Jerry's screaming
threatens to scream

R ——————————————————→ S̷ᴿ
Father buys toy   terminates Jerry's screaming

STEP 2: Avoidance Condition

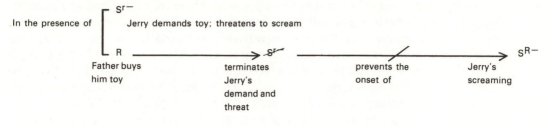

In the presence of
- S^{r-}
  Jerry demands toy; threatens to scream
- R ⟶ S^{r-} ⟶ S^{R-}
  Father buys him toy | terminates Jerry's demand and threat | prevents the onset of | Jerry's screaming

Effect: Likelihood is increased that father will buy Jerry a toy when he demands one.

Extinction of avoidance behaviors. In order to maintain avoidance behavior, occasional presentation of the established negative reinforcer is required. For example, if Jerry's father fails to perform the avoidance response of buying Jerry a toy, and if the negative reinforcer (screaming) does not occasionally follow, the avoidance response may extinguish. If Jerry's father fails to perform the avoidance response and Jerry screams, however, this single episode could reinstate and strengthen the father's avoidance response. An avoidance response that is intermittently reinforced is highly resistant to extinction and usually requires only occasional presentation of the second (established) negative reinforcer.

PHOBIAS AND NEGATIVE REINFORCEMENT

Certain problem behaviors, such as those related to phobic reactions, are avoidance responses that were established with intense traumatic stimuli. In a phobia, an aversive stimulus was paired with an intense negative reinforcer. This pairing increases the likelihood that the phobic individual will make an escape response in the presence of the negative reinforcer to avoid the feared stimulus. For example, Brad was terrified about going to the dentist. He never made an appointment unless he was in unbearable pain. When he approached the dentist's office, he usually turned around, drove back home, and cancelled his appointment. These escape and avoidance behaviors were probably associated with a previously experienced intense aversive stimulus. In all likelihood, Brad experienced great pain while a dentist was drilling his teeth, so that the sight of the dentist's office, perhaps even the thought of going to the dentist's office, became a conditioned negative reinforcer (S^{r-}). Any response that terminated the S^{r-} would also prevent the onset of pain (S^{R-}), and would, therefore, be negatively reinforced.

The avoidance behaviors are highly resistant to extinction, even on the basis of a single pairing of the dentist's office with pain. Brad is likely to avoid all contact with the dentist, even routine, nonpainful care. Brad might even avoid all buildings with dentists' offices in them.

159

Brad's fear has other components, such as sweaty palms, irregular heartbeats, panting, and elevated blood pressure. These are respondent or classically conditioned behaviors and will be covered in the next chapter.

A response that has been negatively reinforced in the presence of one stimulus can *generalize* to other similar stimuli. *Examples:* Brad turned away from all dentists' offices, not just the one in which he was negatively reinforced. Ted's excessive alcohol drinking was negatively reinforced by escape from his father's criticisms. His escape response generalized to other situations in which he was criticized by other individuals, including his mother and employer. The more similar the situation or person is to the original stimulus that signaled the escape response, the more likely that generalization will occur and the response will be performed in its presence.

In assessing problematic situations, the practitioner should try to determine if the client's target behavior is negatively reinforced by escape or avoidance behaviors. Fear of elevators, doctors, or dentists, for example, can prevent an individual from carrying out customary activities such as taking elevators at work or getting medical or dental examinations. When an individual spends considerable time in avoidance responding, he or she has less opportunity to perform behaviors that can be positively reinforced.

SUPERSTITIOUS BEHAVIOR AND NEGATIVE REINFORCEMENT

Escape behavior can also be involved in an accidental or superstitious contingency. In this case, a response is made and the effects of the stimulus are reduced or terminated. The response, however, is only accidentally or coincidentally associated with removal of the stimulus, and its removal is not contingent on performance of the escape response. For example, Mike was driving his car and suddenly the horn began to honk loudly (S^{R-}). He pushed and pulled various knobs on the dashboard and steering wheel, but the noise persisted. Finally he jiggled the turn signal (R) and the horn stopped honking (S^{R-}). The turn signal was not functionally connected to the horn, and termination of the honking was not contingent on jiggling the turn signal. Some other event, such as accidental shifting of contact wires under the hood, terminated the honking. Since Mike was negatively reinforced for jiggling the turn signal, it is likely that he will perform this behavior on similar occasions in the future.

Many people avoid walking under ladders, crossing in front of black cats, or stepping on sidewalk cracks. These behaviors are negatively reinforced because they reduce the fear associated with the possibility of ominous events, such as bad luck, a ladder falling, or "breaking your mother's back." Carrying good luck charms is believed by many to prevent the occurrence of unpleasant events. The charms also reduce fear and anxiety associated with a potential calamity.

Adam: Why are you carrying that plant around with you?
Jenny: To keep the monsters away.
Adam: There aren't any monsters here.
Jenny: See. It works!

NEGATIVE REINFORCEMENT AND INTERPERSONAL RELATIONSHIPS

Negative reinforcement can be observed in certain interpersonal relationships. For example, one person's behavior is positively reinforced while the other's behavior is negatively reinforced. In other situations, one individual's behavior is punished while the other's is negatively reinforced. In some relationships, both individuals give and receive negative reinforcement.

1. In the example of Jerry and his father, Jerry's demand for a toy and threats that he would scream were *positively reinforced* by his father's buying him the toy. His father's response of buying the toy was *negatively reinforced* by terminating Jerry's demand and threats.
2. Mr. Domino (see Chapter 9) attempted to *punish* his customers' complaints about furniture costs by raising his voice and insulting them. His insults and shouting were *negatively reinforced* by the customers leaving the store, thus terminating their complaints.
3. In Case Study 4, page 226–227, Mr. and Mrs. Munsen's behaviors were *negatively reinforced*. Mrs. Munsen locked herself in her room, which removed her from Mr. Munsen's insults. Mr. Munsen left the house, which removed him from the aversiveness of Mrs. Munsen's complaints.

In friendships and intimate relationships, it is desirable for each partner to receive an equitable amount of positive reinforcement from the other. This may involve increasing the frequency of desired behaviors, or increasing the frequency of positive reinforcement that is given for appropriate behaviors that already are performed. In marital counseling, the goals often involve increasing the frequency of positive reinforcement each partner gives and receives and decreasing the frequency of punishment and negative reinforcement. The method of behavior analysis allows the practitioner to study interpersonal behavior patterns and identify relevant positive reinforcers, negative reinforcers, and punishers. The practitioner's goal is to help couples improve their relationships by improving their exchange of positive reinforcers, and decrease their use of punishers and negative reinforcement.

Although negative reinforcement can be detrimental in social relationships, the escape or avoidance behaviors that are negatively reinforced can also be constructive. An escape response made in a dangerous situation will strengthen that response and enable the individual to respond appropriately to cues or warnings (S^{r-}) such as sirens, honking horns, and tornado warnings in order to avoid serious injury or disaster.

SUMMARY

1. Negative reinforcement is a technique to increase the strength of a response by terminating or reducing the effect of a stimulus called a negative reinforcer. A negative reinforcer is a stimulus that signals or sets the occasion for an escape response.

2. Aversive stimuli can act as punishers when their presentation decreases response strength, or as negative reinforcers when their removal increases response strength. Negative reinforcers can be primary (unconditioned) or conditioned.

3. Escape behavior terminates or reduces the effect of the negative reinforcer. The negative reinforcement procedure consists of presenting a negative reinforcer (S^-) that remains in effect until an escape response (R) is made that terminates or reduces the effect of the stimulus ($S^\leftarrow$).

4. Negative reinforcement is also involved in avoidance behavior. A conditioned negative reinforcer is presented that serves as a cue signaling that a second established negative reinforcer will follow unless an avoidance response is made. The response is negatively reinforced by terminating the conditioned negative reinforcer and preventing the onset of the second established negative reinforcer.

5. The avoidance paradigm consists of two steps: (1) the Escape Condition—pairing a neutral stimulus with a negative reinforcer that signals an escape response which is negatively reinforced; (2) the Avoidance Condition—presentation of the conditioned negative reinforcer (formerly the neutral stimulus in Step 1) to signal an avoidance response that terminates the conditioned negative reinforcer and prevents the onset of the established negative reinforcer.

6. Avoidance behaviors will extinguish unless the established negative reinforcer is occasionally presented.

7. Phobic reactions are related to avoidance behaviors that were established with intense traumatic stimuli. In a phobia, an aversive stimulus was paired with an intense negative reinforcer. This pairing increases the likelihood that the phobic individual will make an escape response in the presence of the negative reinforcer to avoid the feared stimulus.

8. Positive reinforcement, negative reinforcement, and punishment are all involved in analyzing interpersonal relationships. Although negative reinforcement can be detrimental to social relationships, escape and avoidance behaviors produced by negative reinforcement can be constructive in helping individuals respond appropriately to warnings and other signaling stimuli.

SUGGESTED READINGS

FICHTER, M. M., WALLACE, C. J., LIBERMAN, R. P., and DAVIS, J. R., "Improving Social Interaction in a Chronic Psychotic Using Discriminated Avoidance ("Nagging"): Experimental Analysis and Generalization," *Journal of Applied Behavior Analysis,* 1976, *9*(4), 377–386.

HECKEL, R. V., WIGGINS, S. L., and SALZBERG, H., "Conditioning Against Silence in Group Therapy," *Journal of Clinical Psychology,* 1962, *28,* 216–221.

LOVAAS, O. I., SCHAEFFER, B., and SIMMONS, J. Q., "Experimental Studies in Childhood Schizophrenia: Building Social Behavior in Autistic Children by Use of Electric Shock," *Journal of Experimental Research and Personality,* 1965, *1,* 99–109.

LOVIBOND, S. H., *Conditioning and Enuresis* (Elmsford, N.Y.: Pergamon Press, 1964).

MACCULLOCH, M. J., BRITLES, C. J., and FELDMAN, N. P., "Anticipatory Avoidance Learning for the Treatment of Homosexuality: Recent Developments and an Automatic Aversion Therapy System," *Behavior Therapy,* 1971, *2,* 151–169.

PATTERSON, G. R., and REID, J. B., "Reciprocity and Coercion: Two Facets of Social Systems," in C. Neuringer & J. Michael (Eds.), *Behavior Modification in Clinical Psychology* (Englewood Cliffs, N.J.: Prentice-Hall, Inc., 1970).

SOLOMON, R. L., and WYNNE, L. C., "Traumatic Avoidance Learning: The Principles of Anxiety Conservation and Partial Irreversibility," *Psychological Review,* 1954, *61,* 353–385.

POST-TEST QUESTIONS

(2) 1. Give an example contrasting the effects of punishment and negative reinforcement. Specify relevant responses and stimuli involved in each procedure.

(3) 2. Give an example of escape behavior developed by negative reinforcement. Label relevant responses and stimuli.

(2) 3. Now turn to page 225 to see Case Study 2. Describe the interaction between Carla and her mother in terms of positive and negative reinforcement, prior to the social worker's intervention.

(4) 4. Sylvia told Harold, "Buy me a new car or I'll leave you." Harold bought her a new car, and she stopped threatening to leave him. Draw a paradigm that describes the avoidance behavior, labeling relevant components.

14

RESPONDENT CONDITIONING

objectives

After completing this chapter, you should be able to:

1. draw a paradigm showing respondent conditioning of a phobia,
2. describe an operant procedure for treating both operant and respondent features of a phobia, and
3. identify operant and respondent behaviors, given case material.

Mr. Potts felt anxious when he was criticized by his wife or employer. He often became depressed after these encounters. In a role play of such situations, Mr. Potts perspired heavily, his face turned red, his breathing became more rapid, and he rapped his knuckles against each other. His hands trembled, and he made excuses in replying to the criticism.

(1) 1. Describe a procedure for extinguishing a classically conditioned response.

(8) 2. Given the following information, specify operant and respondent behaviors: A man gets in his car and drives home. As he walks in the door, the aroma of dinner cooking makes his mouth water. He runs to the kitchen, panting, kisses his wife, and sits down at the table.

(1) 3. Explain the persistence of emotional respondent behavior in the absence of identifiable reinforcing consequences for the individual.

(1) 4. How can a phobia be treated?

There are two broad classes of behavior: operant and respondent. Up to now we have focused on operant behavior. Operant behaviors are *emitted* or performed, and are controlled by their consequences. **Respondent** or **classically conditioned behavior** comprises the second class of behavior. Respondent behaviors are *elicited* by antecedent stimuli.

Respondent behaviors include physiological reflexes (for example, a knee jerk) and other responses mediated by smooth muscles, glands, or cardiac muscle of the autonomic nervous system. Tears caused by dirt in the eye, palms perspiring while taking a difficult exam, rapid breathing or gasping while riding a roller coaster, and pupillary constriction upon emerging into bright sunlight are all examples of respondent behaviors. Each of these responses is elicited or triggered by a preceding or antecedent stimulus.

RESPONDENT CONDITIONING

The term **respondent conditioning** refers to the development, learning, or establishment of a response based on the methods described by Ivan Pavlov and his followers (Pavlov, 1927; 1960). In the respondent conditioning paradigm, a neutral stimulus (S) acquires the ability to elicit a conditioned response (CR) through pairing with an unconditioned stimulus (US). The unconditioned stimulus (US) elicits an unconditioned response (UR) without requiring prior association of the US with another stimulus. The US automatically elicits the UR, with no prior conditioning required. For example, a freshly peeled onion elicits tears; food in the mouth elicits salivation; and a sudden, loud noise elicits a startle reaction or crying. Through repeated pairings with the unconditioned stimulus, a neutral stimulus (S) becomes capable of eliciting a conditioned response (CR) that is similar to the unconditioned response (UR). The neutral stimulus is then called a conditioned stimulus (CS).

In an early example of respondent conditioning, Watson and Rayner (1920) demonstrated how a neutral stimulus, a small white rat, became a CS capable of eliciting crying in a child, Albert. The rat was initially a neutral stimulus that did not elicit the UR, crying. Albert was given a white rat and played with it. A loud noise was produced behind the child by striking a steel bar with a hammer. The noise elicited a crying response (UR) from the child. The white rat and the loud noise were paired repeatedly. Then the child was given the rat alone. On this occasion the white rat elicited crying. It had become a CS through repeated pairing with the US. In paradigm form, the example would look like this:

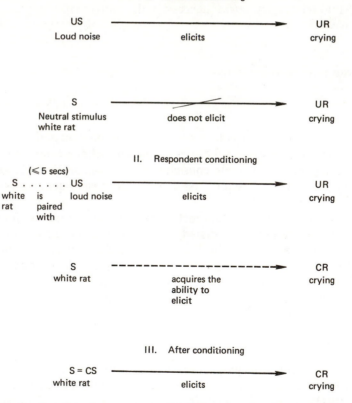

I.   Before conditioning

| US | | UR |
| Loud noise | elicits | crying |

| S | | UR |
| Neutral stimulus white rat | does not elicit | crying |

II.   Respondent conditioning

(≤ 5 secs)

| S . . . . . . US | | UR |
| white is loud noise rat paired with | elicits | crying |

| S | | CR |
| white rat | acquires the ability to elicit | crying |

III.   After conditioning

| S = CS | | CR |
| white rat | elicits | crying |

Effect: The neutral stimulus becomes a conditioned stimulus capable of eliciting a conditioned response, crying.

During conditioning, the neutral stimulus (S) is presented immediately prior to the US, optimally within 5 seconds, and overlapping it (Geis, Stebbins, & Lundin, 1965).

The strength of a conditioned response (CR) is measured by (1) the magnitude of the CR, and (2) the latency or interval between presentation of the CS and elicitation of the CR. The magnitude of a classically conditioned response is measured by contraction of a muscle or blood vessel, or secretion of a gland. For example, heart rate is measured by counting the pulse, muscle contraction is measured by the amount of electrical activity of the muscle, and salivation is measured by drops of saliva. Latency is measured by the amount of time that passes between presentation of the CS and elicitation of the CR. The shorter the latency, the stronger the response. The greater the magnitude, the stronger the response. The magnitude of the CR has been shown to be directly influenced by the number of pairings of the CS and US. Other variables affecting response magnitude and latency include the intensity of the US and the type or size of the US (see Pavlov, 1927; 1960).

Extinction of Respondent Behaviors

Classically conditioned responses, like operant responses, can be weakened by extinction. The CS must be paired occasionally with the US or the CR will extinguish. The **extinction procedure** consists of presenting the CS alone repeatedly until it fails to elicit the CR. Since the unconditioned stimulus no longer follows the conditioned stimulus, the conditioned response is weakened.

Generalization of Respondent Behaviors

The conditioned response is likely to be elicited by other stimuli similar to the CS along some dimension or characteristic. Stimuli most similar to the CS elicit the strongest CRs. As stimuli become less similar to the CS, they elicit weaker CRs. In the case of Albert described above, a rabbit, a seal coat, and a ball of cotton also elicited crying (CR). Other toys that were not similar to the white rat, such as wooden blocks, did not elicit crying. Thus, stimulus generalization occurs with respondent, as well as operant, behaviors.

EMOTIONAL BEHAVIOR

The respondent or classical conditioning paradigm is involved in the acquisition or conditioning of emotional behaviors. An emotional response is usually accompanied by physiological changes in heart rate, blood pressure, perspiration, and muscle tension. Various labels of emotional behavior, such as anger, joy, anxiety, or frustration are insufficient descriptions for behavioral analysis. Behavioral correlates of these labels should be delineated for an individual, so that others observing the behavior or reading a description of it could accurately identify the behavior.

People learn to identify their own feeling states early in life when a verbal label is associated with certain physiological changes by parents or significant others. For example, a child is shaking uncontrollably, breathing rapidly, with tears streaming down his flushed face. His mother asks him, "What's wrong? What are you *afraid* of?" The child replies that he was playing with a dog and it knocked him down. His mother says, "Don't be afraid of the dog." The operant and respondent behaviors of the child's encounter with the dog, therefore, become associated with the word "afraid." When experiencing similar physiological changes on future occasions, the child is likely to label them as "being afraid" or "fear." Many problem behaviors involve anxiety as a central component. Anxiety includes respondent behaviors such as changes in heart rate, blood pressure, muscle tension, and temperature.

RESPONDENT CONDITIONING OF PHOBIAS

When maladaptive anxiety or fear is attached to a specific object, it is called a **phobia.** In other words, the individual is afraid of something that objectively does not warrant anxiety. Phobias are acquired through a respondent conditioning paradigm in which a neutral stimulus acquires the ability to elicit anxiety through pairing with an aversive US. For example, a painful US, such as a dog bite, elicits anxiety URs such as increased heart rate and blood pressure, trembling, and shortness of breath. The US (bite) is paired with the sight of the dog who administered the bite (CS). The sight of the dog is initially a neutral stimulus (S), but it acquires the ability to elicit anxiety. During conditioning, the neutral stimulus (S) is presented immediately prior to the US. In paradigm form, the example would look like this:

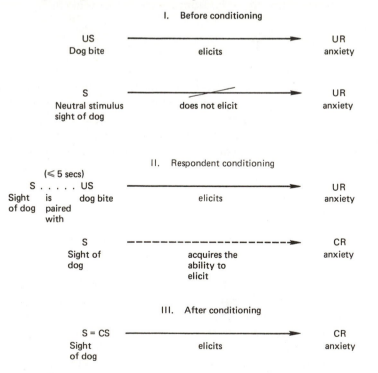

Effect: The sight of the dog, formerly a neutral stimulus, can now elicit anxiety.

ESCAPE, AVOIDANCE, AND RESPONDENT
CONDITIONING

Operant components of anxiety include escape and avoidance behaviors, such as making excuses, lying, rapid pacing, repetitive motor responses such as hand washing, and agitated speech patterns.

A phobic response may extinguish if the individual remains in the presence of the CS without making an escape or avoidance response. Phobias that are difficult to extinguish, however, usually have two major characteristics: (1) they were conditioned with a very intense US, and (2) they involve escape and avoidance responses that are negatively reinforced. In this situation, the CS also functions as an S^{r-}. The escape response terminates or removes the S^{r-}(CS). The US also functions as an S^{R-}. Avoidance behavior terminates the S^{r-}(CS) and prevents the individual from finding out that the S^{R-}(US) is no longer presented. The phobic individual is negatively reinforced for escaping from the S^{r-}(CS), and does not remain in its presence to test whether the S^{R-}(US) will be presented. A CR established by an intense US is highly resistant to extinction, even if paired only once with the CS.

In the example above, the dog-phobic individual will make the escape responses of running away or turning around as soon as she sees a dog at a distance. She will not wait for the dog to come close to her in order to find out that the dog is friendly and will not bite. In this case, the sight of the dog (CS) served as a conditioned negative reinforcer (S^{r-}) that set the occasion for an avoidance response (R) to be negatively reinforced by removal of the S^{r-}. The R also prevented the individual from finding out that the S^{R-}, pain of a dog bite, would not occur.

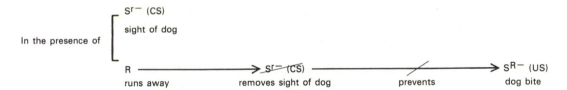

In the last chapter we discussed an individual's fear of the dentist's office in terms of escape and avoidance responses such as turning away from the dentist's office and from buildings where dentists had offices. During conditioning of this phobia, the dentist's office, originally a neutral stimulus (S), became capable of eliciting sweaty palms, irregular heartbeats, panting, and elevated blood pressure (anxiety CRs). The dentist's office was paired with the painful stimulus of drilling a cavity (US) which elicited the anxiety (UR). In this way, the sight of a dentist's office became capable of the CR (anxiety).

The CR is likely to generalize to other stimuli similar to the CS along some dimension or characteristic. For example, if the experience with the dog was extremely painful or frightening, other furry creatures or animals with four legs might elicit high anxiety for the phobic individual. Stimuli most similar to the CS will elicit the strongest CRs. As stimuli become less similar to the biting dog (CS), they will elicit weaker anxiety CRs.

Various stimuli in the conditioning environment can also become associated with anxiety, such as the place where the incident occurred, other individuals who were present, or the dog's bark. These stimuli also can become CSs that elicit anxiety CRs.

A stimulus can serve both as a CS and as a discriminative stimulus. For example, the CS of the dog's bark can also serve as a discriminative stimulus (S^{r-}) for the escape response of running into the house. When we eat in a restaurant the presence of meat on the tongue (US) elicits salivation (UR). Through previous conditioning, the sight of the waiter approaching (CS) or a picture of steak on the menu (CS) can elicit salivation (CR). These CSs can also serve as S^Ds for the operant responses of picking up a fork or ordering the steak from the menu.

It is sometimes difficult to determine if a behavior is under operant or respondent control. In order to do so, it is necessary to determine whether the response is elicited by a CS or US (antecedent) or controlled by a reinforcer or punisher (consequence). For example, crying can be operant or respondent. If Betsy's crying is elicited by an inoculation or a bruise, it is respondent crying. If, however, Betsy's crying is observed to increase as a result of reinforcing consequences (parents comply with Betsy's demands), her crying was operantly conditioned.

Many situations involve both operant and respondent behaviors. For example, in Case Study 6, page 228, Mr. Potts emitted the operant responses of rapping his knuckles together and making excuses when he was criticized. Criticism also elicited the following respondent behaviors: Mr. Potts perspired heavily, his hands trembled, his face turned red, and his breathing became more rapid. In assessing problematic situations, respondent as well as operant behaviors should be identified so that the intervention plan includes relevant techniques for modifying each type of behavior.

The RAC-S behavioral assessment framework presented in Chapters 8 and 9 can also be applied to problematic situations involving respondent behaviors. For assessment of respondent behaviors, the RAC-S schema focuses on the response (R), its eliciting antecedents (A), and response strength (S). The eliciting antecedents are the US and CS, and the target responses are the UR and CR. As mentioned earlier, the strength of respondent behavior is measured by magnitude and/or latency. The negative consequences of the problematic response (CR) for the individual or significant others are also examined.

MODIFYING PHOBIC BEHAVIORS

Both operant and respondent techniques can be used to modify phobic behaviors. These methods are used to develop behaviors incompatible with anxiety in the phobic situation. Successful treatment involves modification of operant escape and avoidance behaviors, as well as respondent (CR, UR) behaviors that constitute "anxiety" for the individual in the phobic environment.

Shaping

Shaping with successive approximations is an operant method for modifying phobic responses. This procedure consists of the following steps:

1. Identify the feared stimulus and target behaviors.
2. Identify the desired terminal behaviors.
3. Identify positive reinforcers that can be used to develop responses incompatible with escape and avoidance responses.
4. Establish a hierarchy of behaviors related to approaching the feared stimulus, and rank the responses from lowest to highest according to their ability to elicit anxiety.
5. Present the lowest response on the hierarchy (least anxiety producing), and reinforce the individual for responses incompatible with anxiety or avoidance.
6. Continue presenting items on the hierarchy and providing reinforcement for appropriate behaviors, until the individual performs the desired terminal behaviors without anxiety.
7. Reinforce the terminal behaviors when they are performed.

The following example describes how a practitioner treated a child's school phobia with shaping. The practitioner carried out the seven steps of the procedure outlined above, starting with the first step, identification of the feared stimulus and target behavior:

1. The practitioner observed that as soon as the child entered the school he trembled, began to stammer, his face turned white, and his body became tense and rigid. When the child approached the classroom, he quickly turned and ran away. The practitioner also observed that, as the child moved further away from the school, he became calmer and his physiological responses returned to normal. The feared stimulus was the classroom.
2. The desired terminal behaviors were: the child walks to school, enters the building and his classroom, and stays the whole day.
3. The practitioner used attention, comic books, and jelly beans as positive reinforcers.
4. The practitioner established a hierarchy of feared responses based on distance from the school and the child's classroom. The following intermediate goals, based on the hierarchy, were established for the child: talking about his friends and favorite events at school; walking toward the school from blocks away; walking toward the school from one block away; walking across the street from the school; crossing the street toward the school; standing in the school yard; walking up the steps into the school; walking in the halls of the school; entering the classroom; and sitting at his desk.
5. When the child talked about playing soccer wih his friends from school, the practitioner showed the child a comic book and they laughed at the characters.

6. When they walked in the direction of the school, the practitioner took the child to the drugstore and bought a bag of jelly beans, the child's favorite candy. The practitioner walked progressively closer to the school with the child, reinforcing his approach behaviors with jelly beans. The practitioner also began to talk about the various activities the child would be involved in at school, and how much fun he could have with his friends.

7. This procedure was continued until the child exhibited no anxiety when talking about school, walked directly to the school, went inside, entered the classroom, and remained at school for the entire day. The child was reinforced by his parents and teacher for performing the desired terminal behaviors.

The shaping procedure dealt with both operant and respondent features of the phobia. Through successive approximations, the child gradually was able to move closer to the feared stimulus without experiencing anxiety. Talking positively about specific school activities helped establish additional S^Ds for the child's school-approach behaviors that could be positively reinforced. Responses incompatible with anxiety and avoidance were positively reinforced. Escape and avoidance responses, therefore, were extinguished as the child remained in the feared situation without anxiety.

Respondent extinction was also involved in treating the school phobia. CSs that previously elicited anxiety CRs were no longer paired with the US and gradually lost their ability to elicit the CRs. In addition, the CSs elicited the CRs of eating candy and laughing; consequently, the CSs could elicit the pleasant, nonanxious responses associated with laughter and candy. One investigator (Lazarus, 1960) used a similar approach in treating a child who was afraid of riding in cars.

It is often advantageous to use more than one technique in treating a problem behavior. For example, a modeling technique could be combined with a shaping procedure to treat a child's school phobia. By using individuals whom the child admires to model and encourage the performance of school approach behaviors, the practitioner can facilitate performance of operant and respondent behaviors necessary to overcome the phobia.

Systematic Desensitization

Systematic desensitization is a respondent procedure for modifying phobic responses. It involves teaching the client deep muscle relaxation to suppress anxiety by pairing phobic or anxiety-eliciting stimuli with relaxation stimuli. The main premise of systematic desensitization is that an individual who is deeply relaxed cannot be anxious and tense at the same time. We will describe the basic features of the desensitization procedure and its applications. The desensitization procedure, which was developed by Joseph Wolpe, has been elaborately presented elsewhere (see Wolpe, 1958; 1969; 1973; Wolpe & Lazarus, 1966).

The first step in this procedure is to teach the client deep muscle relaxation. The client is given instructions in progressive relaxation procedures and is assigned relaxation exercises to practice at home (for example, Bernstein & Borkovec, 1973; Lazarus, 1971; Wenrich, Dawley & General, 1976; Wolpe, 1973). Relaxation instructions for desensitization are based on Jacobson's method of progressive relaxation (Jacobson, 1938). During relaxation training, the client is comfortably reclining in a quiet room. The client is taught to systematically tense and relax specific muscle groups one at a time. The individual learns to relax each muscle group to an increasingly greater extent until the entire body is deeply relaxed. Sometimes imagery is used to enhance the relaxation effect, for example, an individual imagines himself resting in a very peaceful setting.

Relaxation training consists of alternately tensing and relaxing all the muscle groups in the body. Muscle groups may be covered in the following order: arms, hands, forehead, eyes, nose, mouth, tongue, jaws, neck, shoulders, back, chest, stomach, buttocks, legs, calves, and feet. Relaxation instructions are given several times for each muscle group. The client is instructed to practice the relaxation exercises at home. The practitioner can also give the client the relaxation instructions on tape to use until he or she has memorized them and can relax without the aid of the tape.

The following excerpt is typical of the narrative used in relaxation training:

> Settle back as comfortably as you can. Let yourself relax to the best of your ability. . . . Now, as you relax like that, clench your right fist, just clench your fist tighter and tighter, and study the tension as you do so. Keep it clenched and feel the tension in your right fist, hand, forearm . . . and now relax. Let the fingers of your right hand become loose, and observe the contrast in your feelings. . . . Now, let yourself go and try to become more relaxed all over. . . . Once more, clench your right fist really tight . . . hold it, and notice the tension again. . . . Now let go, relax; your fingers straighten out, and you notice the difference once more. . . . Now repeat that with your left fist. (Wolpe & Lazarus, 1966, p. 177)

The second step in systematic desensitization is to construct a hierarchy of responses related to the feared stimulus. This can be done in conjunction with relaxation training. The hierarchy begins with the least anxiety-eliciting item and progresses to the most anxiety-producing event. Here is an example showing the items on a hierarchy developed with a female client who complained of an airplane phobia:

1. Calling an airline to make plane reservations.
2. Seeing a plane take off and land.
3. Riding in a taxi on the way to the airport.
4. Waiting in the lounge before boarding a plane.
5. Walking down the ramp to the plane.
6. Sitting in her seat on the plane, waiting for takeoff.
7. Hearing the landing gear lock into place for landing.
8. Sitting on the runway, waiting for takeoff.
9. Hearing the roar of the engines as the plane lifts off the ground.

Prior to treatment, the client had never actually gone past the third item on the hierarchy. She usually became so anxious that she canceled her reservation and took a train or drove her car.

In the desensitization procedure, the client imagines one item or scene at a time from the hierarchy while relaxed, beginning with the least anxiety-producing item. The client is instructed to imagine the scene presented by the practitioner—for example, calling to make airplane reservations. The client reports her subjective level of anxiety after each scene. If the client indicates anxiety, the practitioner instructs the person to relax again and then presents a weaker scene. When the client indicates no anxiety while imagining the weaker scene, the anxiety-arousing scene is presented. This scene is presented again and repeated until the client no longer experiences anxiety while imagining the scene. Subsequent items on the hierarchy are presented in the same manner, and the procedure is followed until the entire hierarchy is completed. This process usually lasts for approximately 20 to 30 minutes at each session.

The client is usually not treated in the actual problematic situation. The effects of relaxation in the presence of imagined anxiety-arousing stimuli have been found to transfer to the real situation, once the client has achieved relaxation capable of suppressing or inhibiting anxiety responses (CRs). Discovering the original conditioning stimulus (US) is usually not considered essential for successful treatment of phobias. Awareness or "insight" into the originally conditioned phobic situation usually is insufficient to reduce the client's anxiety or alter the client's avoidance of the feared stimulus.

Although phobias can be treated by operant or respondent procedures, the behavioral practitioner attempts to modify both operant and respondent behaviors related to the phobia. The operant procedure focuses on developing motor and verbal behaviors incompatible with escape and avoidance in the feared situation; the newly developed approach behaviors gradually lower the individual's anxiety to the feared stimulus. The respondent procedure focuses on conditioning physiological responses incompatible with anxiety in the phobic situation, while developing imagined approach responses that generalize to the actual situation.

Flooding

Flooding is a technique for treating phobias by extinction of avoidance responses. Flooding consists of exposing the individual directly, or in imagination, to the phobic stimulus (CS) for a prolonged period of time, while preventing any escape or avoidance responses. Instead of gradually working up a hierarchy of anxiety-eliciting stimuli as in systematic desensitization, the CS is presented continuously until it no longer elicits anxiety (CR). Reports of successful flooding typically involve in vivo exposure durations of 100 minutes or longer (Chaplin and Levine, 1981; Levis and Hare, 1977).

Recent literature and analysis of the results of flooding have been mostly positive (for example, Eysenck, 1979; Leitenberg, 1976; Shipley and Boudewyns, 1980), including assertions of its superiority to systematic desensitization. Flooding appears to be effective in treating phobias such as public speaking anxiety and agoraphobia. Successful results have also been reported in the treatment of obsessive and compulsive behavior patterns. However, questions have been raised regarding the possible negative effects of flooding, such as increased anxiety to the phobic stimulus when presented in full strength, and psychological discomfort to the client (Horne and Matson, 1977; Mikulas, 1978).

OPERANT-RESPONDENT OVERLAP

Until recently, operant and respondent behaviors were regarded as comprising two completely separate and distinct classes of behavior. Behavioral principles applicable to one class of behavior were not considered applicable to the other. Operant behaviors were restricted to the so-called voluntary or striated, skeletal muscles. Respondent behaviors were restricted to elicited, "automatic," or "involuntary" autonomic responses involving smooth muscles, glands, and reflexes. Current research has made such rigid distinctions between operant and respondent behaviors more difficult to uphold.

Biofeedback

Biofeedback is a process that allows an individual to monitor and influence his or her physiological responses using auditory, visual and other sensory feedback. Measures of physiological responses such as heart rate, muscle tension, brain waves, or skin temperature are displayed continuously on a monitor so that the individual can observe changes in physiological responses. Biofeedback has been used to operantly control autonomic functions. Biofeedback can be applied in conjunction with behavioral techniques to facilitate relaxation training and various self-control procedures. Behaviors categorized as respondents, previously thought to be exclusively under autonomic or involuntary control (for example, brain waves, blood pressure, and heart rate), have been operantly strengthened and weakened. Individuals have been taught to control physiological responses by manipulation of reinforcing consequences.

Practitioners in the growing field of behavioral medicine are applying biofeedback techniques in conjunction with behavioral techniques to treat health problems. Biofeedback technology has significant implications for the treatment of cardiac, visceral, and psychosomatic disorders previously considered to remain outside the individual's control. Biofeedback has been applied to a wide range of physiological dysfunctions including the treatment of insomnia, migraine, muscle reeducation, and psychosomatic complaints (for example, Blanchard & Epstein, 1978; Stoyva, 1978; Shapiro et al., 1980).

MODIFYING BEHAVIORAL EXCESSES

The treatment of behavioral excesses using respondent techniques is complex and requires a thorough knowledge and understanding of the basic behavioral principles as well as supervised experience in a treatment setting. The following behavioral procedures will be covered briefly, therefore, to familiarize you with their basic components and relate these to the respondent paradigms we have discussed in this chapter. Respondent conditioning techniques have included the use of aversive stimuli such as electric shock and nausea-inducing drugs (emetics) to treat behavioral excesses such as drug addiction, alcoholism, smoking, and sexual deviations (Russell, Armstrong, & Patel, 1976; Lemere & Voetglin, 1950; Callahan & Leitenberg, 1972).

Aversion Therapy

In aversion therapy a stimulus that elicits anxiety (US) is paired with a conditioned stimulus (CS) that elicits an inappropriate conditioned response (CR). For example, in treating a child molester, the picture of a naked child (CS) elicited sexual arousal (CR). Treatment consisted of pairing the picture with an electric shock (US), until the picture elicited anxiety (CR) instead of sexual arousal (CR). In paradigm form, the example would look like this:

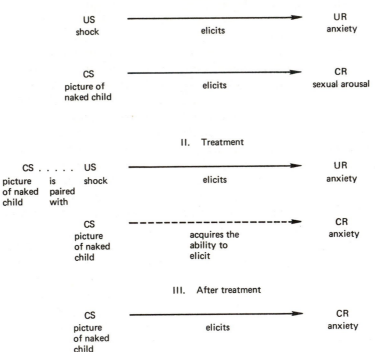

Aversion Relief

Aversion therapy techniques have been used in conjunction with avoidance conditioning so that the CS also serves a discriminative function (S^{r-}) for an avoidance response (for example, Feldman & MacCulloch, 1965). The therapist should specify an appropriate avoidance response for the client to make, such as turning from the child's picture to that of an adult female. In this way, the client can increase performance of responses incompatible with the maladaptive behavior.

Questions have been raised about the ethics of using painful stimuli such as emetics and electric shock to reduce maladaptive behaviors. Legal guidelines based on court decisions, as well as ethical considerations, dictate the proper use of aversive stimuli. In general, painful stimuli should not be used unless it is essential that the behavior be suppressed and other techniques have been tried without success. Positive reinforcement of incompatible behaviors, punishment using nonpainful stimuli, and covert techniques are examples of behavioral techniques that have been used to modify aberrant behaviors. If other procedures have been unsuccessful and the target behavior is harmful to the individual or others, the use of aversive stimuli by an experienced behavior therapist can be considered. Obtaining the consent of the individual or a close relative is advised (Martin, 1975).

In many situations it is inappropriate or inconvenient to use actual aversive stimuli, such as shock. Several covert techniques have been developed based on the finding that imagined aversive events can be effective in suppressing inappropriate behaviors (Cautela, 1966). The word *covert* refers to unobservable events and processes such as thoughts, perceptions, beliefs and related cognitive phenomena. Systematic desensitization involves covert stimuli imagined by the client.

Attempts have been made to incorporate and expand the application of covert or cognitive events and techniques in behavior modification practice (Cautela, 1966; Mahoney, 1974; Meichenbaum, 1977). The cognitive behavior modification approach focuses on decreasing destructive thought patterns and developing more appropriate ones as a basis for behavior change.

Covert Sensitization

Covert sensitization (Cautela, 1967) is an anxiety-eliciting technique employing imagined stimuli to decrease an undesired behavior. Instead of suppressing anxiety with relaxation as in systematic desensitization, covert sensitization utilizes stimuli that elicit anxiety for clients who exhibit behavioral excesses that are reinforced. This technique has been used in the treatment of stealing, overeating, sexual deviations, smoking, drug addiction, and alcoholism (Cautela, 1966; Harbert, Barlow, Hersen, & Austin, 1974; Janda & Rimm, 1972; Sipich, Russell, & Tobias, 1974).

In covert sensitization, the maladaptive behavior is described in great detail and paired—in the client's imagination—with highly aversive stimuli. A typical aversive scene used in covert sensitization includes a vivid description of nausea and vomiting induced by the individual's approach toward the attractive but inappropriate stimulus. The "pleasant" respondent behaviors associated with the maladaptive operant behavior are suppressed by the anxiety or nausea responses elicited by the imagined aversive stimuli.

In implementing covert sensitization, the therapist should instruct the client to make appropriate escape and avoidance responses that can be negatively reinforced by termination or reduction of the imagined aversive stimuli. The client is negatively reinforced when he or she has imagined performing appropriate responses and signals this. Practicing these appropriate responses in the treatment setting increases the likelihood that the client will perform them when the actual problematic situation arises.

In using covert sensitization to decrease alcohol abuse, the therapist instructs the client to imagine taking a drink at work, at home, and in the other places where he usually drinks. These drinking stimuli are then paired, also in the client's imagination, with highly aversive stimuli that elicit anxiety and nausea (CR), such as insects crawling all over the alcohol and glass. These two scenes—the pleasant drinking situations and the highly aversive insects crawling—are repeatedly paired until the alcohol-drinking scenes elicit the nausea CRs previously associated with the insects.

Other covert procedures have been applied in treating client behaviors. Various techniques have been described in the literature, including covert positive reinforcement (Cautela, 1970b), covert negative reinforcement (Cautela, 1970a), covert extinction (Cautela, 1971), and covert modeling (Cautela, 1970b; Kazdin, 1975; 1978). The primary advantage of the covert procedures is that the individual does not have to perform the undesired behaviors but simply imagines them. In addition, a physically painful or aversive stimulus is not administered. Covert techniques are convenient to use in the practice setting, because they do not require any special equipment or materials. The use of covert techniques, however, raises questions about the practicality of measuring and controlling unobservable events and scientifically evaluating their effects.

Thought Stopping

Thought stopping is a covert technique used to treat recurring negative or self-defeating thoughts. Thoughts of death, losing control, low self-worth, overeating, and unrequited love are among the problems that have been treated with this technique (Campbell, 1973; Gambrill, 1977; Phillips, 1978; Rimm & Masters, 1979; Wolpe, 1958; 1969). Thought stopping typically progresses from overt to covert control. For example, the procedure begins with the client describing to the therapist the obsessive or negative thoughts. When the client starts to verbalize a negative thought (for example, "I can't do anything right."), the therapist shouts "Stop!" The purpose is to block the undesired thought and redirect the client's attention. The therapist's shouting is gradually faded out, as the client takes over telling herself "Stop!" first out loud and then to herself. The procedure is repeated until the client reports that all problematic thoughts have been blocked. Thought stopping is most effective when followed by redirection of thoughts to positive, assertive, or self-reinforcing statements (Hays & Waddell, 1976; Rimm & Masters, 1979). These positive self-statements are said covertly by the client.

SUMMARY

1. Respondent behavior is elicited by an antecedent stimulus and includes physiological reflexes (for example, knee jerk) and other responses mediated

by smooth muscles, glands, or cardiac muscle of the autonomic nervous system.

2. In the respondent conditioning paradigm, a neutral stimulus (S) acquires the ability to elicit a conditioned response (CR) through pairing with an unconditioned stimulus (US). The unconditioned stimulus (US) elicits an unconditioned response (UR) without requiring prior association of the US with another stimulus. To establish a conditioned response, the neutral stimulus is optimally presented immediately prior to the US (within 5 seconds) and overlapping it.

3. The strength of a CR is measured by: (1) its magnitude and (2) its latency, the interval between presentation of the CS and elicitation of the CR.

4. The CS must be occasionally paired with the US or the CR will extinguish.

5. Anxiety is a central component of many problem behaviors. Anxiety includes respondent behaviors such as changes in heart rate, blood pressure, glandular secretions, perspiration, muscle tension, and temperature.

6. A phobia involves maladaptive anxiety or fear attached to a specific object (for example, snakes, elevators).

7. A phobia is acquired through respondent conditioning in which a neutral stimulus acquires the ability to elicit anxiety through pairing with an aversive US that elicits the UR.

8. Operant components of anxiety include escape or avoidance behaviors that are negatively reinforced by removal of the S^{r-} or reduction of its effects.

9. A stimulus can act both as a CS, eliciting a respondent behavior, and as an S^D, signaling an operant behavior that will be reinforced. Both the operant and respondent features of a problem situation are considered by the practitioner.

10. Shaping with successive approximations is an operant method for modifying phobic responses.

11. Systematic desensitization is a respondent method for treating phobic behaviors. This method involves systematic and gradual pairing of relaxation stimuli with phobic stimuli until the phobic stimuli no longer elicits anxiety.

12. Behaviors categorized as respondent, previously thought to be exclusively under involuntary control, have been operantly strengthened and weakened (for example, heart rate, skin temperature).

13. Biofeedback techniques use auditory, visual, and/or other sensory feedback to measure changes in physiological or respondent behaviors such as heart rate, muscle tension, and blood pressure.

14. Aversion therapy has been used to treat behavioral excesses, such as drug addiction, alcoholism, and sexual deviations. The purpose of aversion therapy is to elicit anxiety responses that suppress pleasant responses associated with the undesired stimulus.

15. Aversion relief therapy reinforces an avoidance response made in the presence of an inappropriate stimulus. The client learns to perform responses incompatible with maladaptive responses to the stimuli.

16.   Covert sensitization is a technique pairing imagined stimuli related to an un-desired behavior with imagined anxiety-eliciting stimuli. This technique is used to reduce behavioral excesses such as stealing, overeating, and sexual deviations. Imagined escape and avoidance responses are reinforced by removal of the anxiety-producing stimulus.

17.   Thought stopping is a covert technique for treating negative or self-defeating thoughts. The word "Stop!" said first out loud and then subvocally, is used to block out the undesired thoughts and redirect the client's attention.

SUGGESTED READINGS

BELLACK, A. S., and HERSEN, M.,   *Behavior Modification: An Introductory Textbook* (Baltimore: Williams & Wilkins, 1977).

BERNSTEIN, D. A., and BORKOVEC, T. D.,   *Progressive Relaxation Training: A Manual for the Helping Professions* (Champaign, Ill.: Research Press, 1973).

BLANCHARD, E. B., and EPSTEIN, L. H.,   *A Biofeedback Primer* (Reading, Mass.: Addison-Wesley, 1978).

CALLAHAN, E. J., and LEITENBERG, H.,   "Aversion Therapy for Sexual Deviation: Contingent Shock and Covert Sensitization," *Journal of Abnormal Psychology,* 1972, *81,* 60–73.

CAMPBELL, L. M.,   "A Variation of Thought Stopping in a Twelve-Year-Old Boy: A Case Report," *Journal of Behavior Therapy and Experimental Psychiatry,* 1973, *4,* 69–70.

CAUTELA, J. R.,   "Treatment of Compulsive Behavior by Covert Sensitization," *Psychological Record,* 1966, *16,* 33–41.

CAUTELA, J. R.,   "Covert Sensitization" *Psychological Reports,* 1967, *20,* 459–468.

CAUTELA, J. R.,   "Covert Negative Reinforcement," *Journal of Behavior Therapy and Experimental Psychiatry,* 1970a, *1,* 273–278.

CAUTELA, J. R.,   "Covert Reinforcement," *Behavior Therapy,* 1970b, *1,* 33–50.

CAUTELA, J. R.,   "Covert Extinction," *Behavior Therapy,* 1971, *2,* 191–200.

CAUTELA, J. R.,   "The Present Status of Covert Modeling," *Journal of Behavior Therapy and Experimental Psychiatry,* 1976, *7,* 323–326.

CHAPLIN, E. W., and LEVINE, B. A.,   "The Effects of Total Exposure Duration and Interrupted Versus Continuous Exposure in Flooding Therapy," *Behavior Therapy,* 1981, *12*(3), 360–368.

DAVIDSON, P. O., and DAVIDSON, S. M.,   *Behavioral Medicine: Changing Health Life-styles* (New York: Brunner/Mazel, Inc., 1980).

EYSENCK, H. J.,   *You and Neurosis* (Beverly Hills, Calif.: Sage Publications, Inc., 1979).

FELDMAN, M. P., and MACCULLOCH, M. J.,   "The Application of Anticipatory Avoidance Learning to the Treatment of Homosexuality," *Behavior Research and Therapy,* 1965, *2,* 165–183.

FISCHER, J. and GOCHROS, H.,   *A Handbook of Behavior Therapy with Sexual Problems* (Elmsford, N.Y.: Pergamon Press, 1977).

GAMBRILL, E. D., *Behavior Modification: Handbook of Assessment, Intervention, and Evaluation* (San Francisco: Jossey-Bass, 1977).

GEIS, G. L., STEBBINS, W. C., and LUNDIN, R. W., *Reflex and Operant Conditioning,* vol. 1 (Englewood Cliffs, N.J.: Prentice-Hall, Inc., 1965).

HARBERT, T. L., BARLOW, D. H., HERSEN, M., and AUSTIN, J. B., "Measurement and Modification of Incestuous Behavior: A Case Study," *Psychological Reports,* 1974, *34,* 79–86.

HAYS, V., and WADDELL, K. J., "A Self-reinforcing Procedure for Thought Stopping," *Behavior Therapy,* 1976, *7,* 559.

HOMME, L. E., "Perspectives in Psychology: XXIV. Control of Coverants, the Operants of the Mind," *Psychological Record,* 1965, *15,* 501–511.

HORNE, A. M., and MATSON, J. L., "A Comparison of Modeling, Desensitization, Flooding, Study Skills, and Control Groups for Reducing Test Anxiety," *Behavior Therapy,* 1977, *8*(1), 1–8.

JACOBSON, E., *Progressive Relaxation* (Chicago: University of Chicago Press, 1938).

JANDA, L. H., and RIMM, D. C., "Covert Sensitization in the Treatment of Obesity," *Journal of Abnormal Psychology,* 1972, *80,* 37–42.

JONES, M. C., "The Elimination of Children's Fears," *Journal of Experimental Psychology,* 1924, *7,* 383–390.

KAZDIN, A. E., "Covert Modeling, Imagery Assessment and Assertive Behavior," *Journal of Consulting and Clinical Psychology,* 1975, *43,* 716–724.

KAZDIN, A. E., "Covert Modeling: The Therapeutic Application of Imagined Rehearsal," in J. L. Singer and K. Pope (Eds.), *The Power of Human Imagination: New Techniques of Psychotherapy* (New York: Plenum, 1978).

LAZARUS, A. A. *Behavior Therapy and Beyond* (New York: McGraw-Hill, 1971).

LAZARUS, A. A., "The Elimination of Children's Phobias by Deconditioning." H. J. Eysenck (Ed.), *Behaviour Therapy and the Neuroses* (Oxford: Pergamon Press, 1960).

LEITENBERG, H., "Behavioral Approaches to Treatment of Neuroses." H. Leitenberg (Ed.), *Handbook of Behavior Modification and Behavior Therapy* (Englewood Cliffs, N.J.: Prentice-Hall, 1976).

LEMERE, F., and VOETGLIN, W., "An Evaluation of the Aversion Treatment of Alcoholism," *Quarterly Journal of Studies on Alcohol,* 1950, *11,* 199–204.

LEVIS, D. J., and HARE, N., "A Review of the Theoretical Rationale and Empirical Support for the Extinction Approach of Implosive (Flooding) Therapy." M. Hersen, R. M. Eisler, and P. M. Miller (Eds.), *Progress in Behavior Modification* (New York: Academic Press, 1977).

MAHONEY, M. J., *Cognition and Behavior Modification* (Cambridge, Mass.: Ballinger, 1974).

MARTIN, R., *Legal Challenges to Behavior Modification: Trends in Schools, Corrections, and Mental Health* (Champaign, Ill.: Research Press, 1975).

MEICHENBAUM, D. H., *Cognitive Behavior Modification: An Integrative Approach* (New York: Plenum Press, 1977).

MIKULAS, W., *Behavior Modification* (New York: Harper & Row, 1978).

PAVLOV, I. P., *Conditioned Reflexes: An Investigation of the Physiological Activity of the Cerebral Cortex,* trans. G. V. Anrep (London: Oxford University Press, 1927). Also published in 1960 by Dover Publications, in association with Oxford University Press.

PHILLIPS, D., *How to Fall Out of Love* (New York: Fawcett Popular Library, 1978).

RESCORLA, R. A., and SOLOMON, R. L., "Two-process Learning Theories: Relationship between Pavlovian Conditioning and Instrumental Learning," *Psychological Review,* 1967, *74,* 151–182.

RIMM, D. C., and MASTERS, J. C., *Behavior Therapy: Techniques and Empirical Findings, 2nd ed.,* (New York: Academic Press, 1979).

RUSSELL, M.A.H., ARMSTRONG, E., and PATEL, U. A., "Temporal Contiguity in Electric Aversion Therapy for Cigarette Smoking," *Behavior Research and Therapy,* 1976, *14,* 103–124.

SHAPIRO, D., BARBER, T. X., KAMAYA, J., MILLER, N. E., STOYVA, J., and SCHWARTZ, G. (Eds.), *Biofeedback and Behavioral Medicine. Therapeutic Applications and Experimental Foundations, 1979/80* (Chicago: Aldine, 1980).

SHIPLEY, R. H. and BOUDEWYNS, P. A., "Flooding and Implosive Therapy: Are They Harmful?", *Behavior Therapy,* 1980, *11*(4), 503–508.

SIPICH, J. F., RUSSELL, R. K., and TOBIAS, L. L., "A Comparison of Covert Sensitization and 'Nonspecific' Treatment in the Modification of Smoking Behavior," *Journal of Behavior Therapy and Experimental Psychiatry,* 1974, *5,* 201–203.

STOYVA, J. (Ed.), *Biofeedback and Self-control: 1977/78* (Chicago: Aldine, 1978).

WATSON, J. B., and RAYNER, R., "Conditioned Emotional Reactions," *Journal of Experimental Psychology,* 1920, *3,* 1–14.

WENRICH, W. W., DAWLEY, H. H., and GENERAL, D. A., *Self-directed Systematic Desensitization* (Kalamazoo, Mich.: Behaviordelia, 1976).

WOLPE, J., *Psychotherapy by Reciprocal Inhibition* (Stanford, Calif.: Stanford University Press, 1958).

WOLPE, J., *The Practice of Behavior Therapy,* (Elmsford, N.Y.: Pergamon Press, 1969; 1973).

WOLPE, J., and LANG, B. J., "A Fear Survey Schedule for Use in Behavior Modification," *Behavior Research and Therapy,* 1964, *2,* 27–30.

WOLPE, J., and LAZARUS, A., *Behavior Therapy Techniques: A Guide to the Treatment of Neuroses* (Elmsford, N.Y.: Pergamon Press, 1966).

POST-TEST QUESTIONS

(3) 1. Turn to pages 226–227 to see Case Study 4. Using the information from that case, state one operant behavior and two possible respondent behaviors involved in Mrs. Munsen's "being upset."

(7) 2. The following examples include operant and respondent behaviors. Place an 0 in the space of those italicized behaviors that are operant, and an R for those that are respondent.

    a. 1. _____ A teenager in a treatment group *swears* at another boy.
          2. _____ The second boy's face *turns* red.

    b. 1. _____ You *ask* a client a question about his brother; you observe that his
          2. _____ breathing *quickens* and perspiration
          3. _____ *appears* on his forehead.

    c. 1. _____ You *give* Janet a piece of candy for completing her assignment.
          2. _____ Carol observes this and *starts whining*.

(2) 3. Draw a paradigm showing respondent conditioning of the following phobia: A child is afraid of dentists. When he approaches a dentist's office he begins to tremble, turns pale, breathes rapidly, then turns and runs away. This child has dental problems that must be taken care of soon, or he may lose many of his teeth.

(2) 4. Describe an operant procedure for treating both operant and respondent features of the phobia described in Problem 3.

TRANSFER OF CHANGE

objectives

After completing this chapter, you should be able to:

1. state three obstacles to generalization of desired responses from the practice setting to the client's environment,

2. state three ways to maximize successful generalization of desired responses from the practice setting to the client's environment,

3. describe how behavioral rehearsal can be used to develop desired behaviors, given a case example,

4. describe the use of behavioral assignments in a practice setting, given a case example, and

5. state the rationale for using behavioral rehearsal and behavioral assignments.

Dr. Field, a psychologist, has been treating Dr. Alphonse, an alcoholic client. As part of the treatment to decrease drinking, Dr. Field suggested several nondrinking behaviors appropriate in the social situation where Dr. Alphonse usually drank. These behaviors were new to Dr. Alphonse, but he agreed to try them out. What can Dr. Field do to promote successful maintenance of the nondrinking behaviors?

PRETEST QUESTIONS

Chapter 15

(2) 1. a. You are treating an alcoholic client. As part of the treatment program to decrease his drinking, you suggest several nondrinking behaviors appropriate in the social situations where he usually drinks. These behaviors are new to him, but he agrees to try them out. What is the most likely obstacle to success for this part of therapy?

     b. What can you do to counteract this effect or to plan for this problem?

(1) 2. Using the information from Case Study 6, page 228, describe how behavioral rehearsal was used with Mr. Potts to facilitate generalization of appropriate responses to criticism.

(1) 3. Behavioral assignments are given (circle the correct answer(s)):

     a. to structure the client's activities between therapy sessions.

     b. to help the client apply in her natural environment what she has learned in treatment.

     c. so the client can receive feedback from the therapist based on a specific task he has attempted to accomplish.

     d. all of the above.

(1) 4. True or False: It is usually more difficult for a desired behavior to generalize beyond the practice setting when more than one therapist is involved in developing the behavior.

(3) 5. Turn to pages 225–226 to see Case Study 3. State three ways you could maximize successful generalization of Mr. Clark's speech.

Transfer of change refers to the generalization or transfer of behavioral change from the practice setting to the client's natural environment. The **natural environment** refers to the physical and social surroundings in which the target behaviors were developed and in which behavioral changes are designed to be performed and maintained. Frequently, however, treatment takes place in another environment, such as a social agency or institution. The individual may perform the desired behaviors in the practice setting but not in the natural environment.

OBSTACLES TO TRANSFER OF CHANGE

Four obstacles to the transfer of behavioral change are: (1) insufficient reinforcement for desired responses in the client's natural environment; (2) reinforcement for inappropriate, maladaptive responses in the client's natural environment; (3) lack of similarity between the practice setting and the client's natural environment; and (4) insufficient development of desired responses in the practice setting. The practitioner should anticipate these potential obstacles in formulating a plan with the client for maximizing generalization and maintenance of desired behaviors.

One major obstacle to transferring behavioral change is insufficient reinforcement for desired responses in the client's natural environment. If appropriate behaviors are not reinforced, they will undergo extinction. For example, in the treatment setting, an alcoholic learned alternative responses he could make in typical drinking situations. When he performed the alternative responses in those situations, however, he was not reinforced. His friends did not support his non-alcohol-drinking behaviors; consequently, those behaviors extinguished rapidly.

A second obstacle involves reinforcement of the client's inappropriate, maladaptive responses in the natural environment. In some situations, the client is reinforced for performing undesired responses and not for appropriate behaviors. For example, the practitioner extinguished Debbie's tantrum behaviors (kicking, whining, and banging her head on the floor) and established quiet, solitary play behaviors in his office. At home, however, Debbie's mother was preoccupied with her painting and did not pay attention to Debbie when she played quietly. When Debbie started whining and tugging at her mother's pants, her mother scolded or pleaded with her. This attention reinforced the tugging and whining and increased the likelihood that Debbie's tantrum behaviors would be reinstated, because positive reinforcement was given only after undesired, disruptive behaviors.

A third obstacle to successful transfer of behavioral change involves lack of similarity between the practice environment and the client's natural environment. Antecedent stimuli in the client's environment must be similar enough to stimuli in the practice environment to serve as cues for the performance of desired behaviors. The practitioner develops appropriate client responses in the presence of certain stimuli (S^Ds and CSs) in the practice setting, such as office, group meeting room, or other agency or institutional environment. The practitioner should attempt to identify stimuli in the client's environment that are similar to the S^Ds and CSs in the practice setting that can signal desired responses to be reinforced and elicit appropriate responses. For example, the sight of a neon sign saying "BAR" served as an

S^D for Dr. Alphonse to enter the bar and order a drink. The neon sign might also have acted as a CS that elicited the CRs of salivation or pleasant emotional responses associated with drinking alcoholic beverages.

A therapist conditioning heterosexual behaviors in an adult male—for example, eye contact with women and conversational behaviors—must determine if appropriate women are available in the client's environment to set the occasion for these desired behaviors to be performed. If the client does not have opportunities to meet women during his normal activities, the practitioner should consider ways of modifying the client's environment so that the desired behaviors can be performed and reinforced. Similarly, a drug addict may perform and practice alternative behaviors to drug taking and procuring in the therapist's office. The situation on the street could be so different from the treatment setting, however, that it fails to provide S^Ds that would set the occasion for performance of the newly developed behaviors. The desired behaviors, therefore, would have a low probability of being performed in the client's natural environment.

A fourth obstacle to transfer of change exists when desired responses have not been sufficiently developed in the practice setting. Although appropriate stimuli (S^Ds, CSs) are present, the desired responses are not performed in the natural environment because these responses have not been practiced sufficiently in the treatment setting. For example, a client was instructed by his counselor to state his opinions to a colleague instead of remaining silent when he disagreed on an issue. Although the client said that he understood the counselor's instructions, when an issue arose the next day he did not perform the appropriate opinion-giving behaviors. The client had not rehearsed these behaviors adequately in the practice setting.

STRATEGIES FOR PROMOTING TRANSFER OF CHANGE

The transfer of desired behaviors can be promoted by identifying likely obstacles and designing an intervention plan that takes them into consideration. The following actions can be taken to promote transfer of change:

1. Involve significant individuals, such as family and friends, in the behavioral-change program.
2. Provide intermittent reinforcement for desired behaviors in the practice setting.
3. Develop and reinforce the desired behaviors in the client's natural environment instead of, or in addition to, the practice setting.
4. Use behavioral rehearsal to give the client opportunities to practice appropriate behaviors until the desired performance level is demonstrated.
5. Give the client behavioral assignments to perform behaviors in the natural environment that were rehearsed in the practice setting.

Significant individuals, such as family and friends, can also be involved in the client's behavioral-change program. These individuals can provide S^Ds and reinforcers for desired behaviors. In order to increase the likelihood that desired behaviors will generalize to the natural environment, significant others must learn to (1) establish and carry out reinforcement contingencies involving the client, and (2) act consistently in reinforcing desired behaviors and withholding reinforcement from undesired behaviors. Often the newly performed appropriate behaviors of the client will serve as reinforcers for their participation in transfer of change efforts.

In order to strengthen desired behaviors, the practitioner can shift from continuous to intermittent reinforcement in the practice setting after the response is developed. As described earlier, intermittent reinforcement can be employed to generate consistent response rates that are more resistant to extinction than continuous reinforcement (see Chapters 4 and 5). Usually, intermittent reinforcement more closely approximates the reinforcement schedules characteristic of the client's natural environment than does continuous reinforcement. The practitioner determines the appropriate type of reinforcement schedule for maintenance of the client's behavior. Significant others in the client's environment can also be given instructions to reinforce the desired behaviors on an intermittent schedule.

Lack of similarity between antecedent stimuli in the practice setting and those in the client's natural environment is an obstacle to transfer of behavioral change. The practitioner can eliminate this obstacle by developing desired behaviors in the client's natural environment rather than in the practice setting. In this way, the client learns to perform alternative appropriate behaviors under the actual environmental conditions that had signaled, elicited, and reinforced the maladaptive responses. If working in the natural environment is not feasible, various elements of the client's environment could be introduced into the practice setting, such as involving friends or relatives in the development of desired behaviors.

It may be necessary at times to remove the client from the natural environment so that appropriate behaviors can be established in a controlled situation. People who exhibit certain extreme kinds of behaviors are often presumed better treated in an institution or setting other than their natural environment. For example, individuals who attempt suicide, talk about hearing strange voices, refuse to eat or talk to anyone, or claim to be someone they are not are often removed from their homes and placed in closed settings. In these cases, the natural environment provides reinforcement for the maladaptive behaviors, does not provide reinforcement for desired behaviors, and/or does not provide S^Ds for appropriate behaviors that can be reinforced. It is important to work with significant individuals in the environment to which the client will return so that positive changes in client behaviors will be maintained. The use of more than one therapist to develop desired behaviors can also help to maximize transfer of desired behavioral changes by allowing the client to practice behaviors and perform them appropriately in the presence of more than one individual (Goldstein, Sechrest, and Heller, 1966).

Behavioral rehearsal is a technique to promote generalization of behavior change by providing a structured situation in which the client practices desired behaviors. Advice or suggestions for behaving appropriately is often insufficient to enable a client to perform desired behaviors. For example, clients may be told by friends, relatives, or authorities to "shape up" and change their behavior; such exhortative methods are usually ineffective in helping clients change undesired behaviors.

Clients can often identify their inappropriate behaviors and may also be able to specify their desired behaviors. They have difficulty in performing appropriate responses, however, because of anxiety, inexperience, poor interpersonal skills, or lack of reinforcement.

Behavioral rehearsal can strengthen a client's performance of desired behaviors by giving the client an opportunity to practice the behaviors in a supportive environment with corrective feedback, before attempting to perform them in the actual problematic situation. The client is given explicit instructions on behaviors to perform in role plays that simulate the problematic situation. The client practices or rehearses the desired behaviors that have been suggested and modeled by the practitioner or group members. During the role play the client may require additional instructions, prompts, coaching, and reinforcement in order to perform the behaviors appropriately. As the client gains proficiency and self-confidence through these rehearsals, it becomes more likely that the desired behaviors will be performed appropriately in the natural environment. Behavioral rehearsal continues until the client achieves the criterion performance specified in the behavioral change plan. Additional practice or training sessions conducted after the client has demonstrated the desired behaviors may further help to promote their transfer to the client's natural environment. In Case Study 8, behavioral rehearsal was used to facilitate the transfer of change of appropriate speech to Mrs. Gomez's and Mr. Terry's natural environment.

CASE STUDY 8

Developing Appropriate Conversation

Mrs. Gomez and Mr. Terry were elderly participants in an outpatient treatment group for discharged mental patients. In social situations they often asked questions and made comments that were unrelated to the topic being discussed. For example, when several group members were discussing a recent film, Mr. Terry asked the person speaking if he was going grocery shopping that afternoon. In addition, Mrs. Gomez and Mr. Terry were frequently observed talking continuously for five minutes or more without pausing for responses from others. These speech patterns resulted in their being ridiculed and excluded from many conversations held by other group members.

The psychiatric nurse devised a conversational exercise to be played by the six members of a group in which Mrs. Gomez and Mr. Terry participated. The nurse began the exercise by making a statement, and each of the other group members added a statement to her introduction. Each statement was required to bear logical connection to the previous statement.

At first Mrs. Gomez and Mr. Terry both added inappropriate statements to the previous ones. On these occasions they were stopped by the nurse or group members, who required them to make appropriate statements and complimented or praised them for doing so. Group members prompted Mrs. Gomez and Mr. Terry, offering hints and suggestions for correct statements. As they practiced the exercise on subsequent occasions, both Mrs. Gomez and Mr. Terry made fewer inappropriate remarks and increasingly more appropriate ones. The frequency of their appropriate remarks during conversations outside the group was also observed to increase. Appropriate speech was reinforced by staff and relatives.

The client is given **behavioral assignments** to perform desired behaviors in the natural environment. Performance of behavioral assignments facilitates the generalization of desired behaviors from the practice setting to the client's environment. They give the client an opportunity to try out behaviors that are discussed and rehearsed in the practice setting. At each meeting, the client is usually given a behavioral assignment that specifies a task to be performed in the natural environment. The assignments provide continuity to the behavioral change program by directing the client's activities between meetings toward performance of desired behaviors and achievement of behavioral change goals.

Behavioral assignments should be realistic. In order for the client to carry them out in the natural environment, the assignments should consist of behaviors that have been rehearsed in the practice setting. If the client has difficulty in carrying out an assignment, the practitioner can create a role play in which the client is required to demonstrate the behaviors involved in the assignment. The practitioner (and group members if applicable) identifies the client's appropriate and inappropriate responses demonstrated in the role play. The client's difficulties in performing desired behaviors are discussed. Deficient performances are rehearsed with additional instructions, prompts, and feedback provided to the client until he or she correctly performs the desired behaviors. The client may then be given the same or a modified assignment, depending on the difficulty experienced in performing the previous assignment and the current level of proficiency.

Behavioral rehearsal and behavioral assignments were used in the assertive training program with Gretchen (see Chapter 11). Gretchen practiced appropriate verbal and nonverbal behaviors in the therapist's office. She was also given behavioral assignments to carry out in her natural environment, such as looking at her mother and speaking in a calm tone of voice while stating her opinions. Gretchen reported her experiences in carrying out these assignments to the therapist. The therapist reinforced successful performances and provided additional instructions and training to help Gretchen perform difficult assignments.

Behaviors rehearsed in the practice setting should be those that can be reinforced in the community. In assessing the fit between community resources and client difficulties, practitioners may find that clients are not given the opportunity to perform newly-acquired behaviors in the community. For example, in conjunction with a program to teach job-interviewing skills to clients, the practitioner may have to work with businesses, community groups, and other professionals to develop job opportunities so that clients can perform newly-learned behaviors and be reinforced. Active involvement of practitioners in the community is necessary if major problems experienced by significant numbers of individuals are to be substantively addressed.

Collaboration with significant others in the client's community is often indicated to ensure that reinforcers are available for appropriate behaviors and unavailable for inappropriate behaviors, and that proper S^{D}s will be in place to facilitate the performance of appropriate client behaviors. Cooperative relationships are particularly important in providing assistance to low income, multi-problem families who have concerns about food, housing, and jobs as well as behavioral difficulties. This may involve working with families, peer groups, and other human service workers as well as institutions and agencies significant to the client, such as schools, employment agencies, housing authorities, and employers.

SUMMARY

1. Transfer of behavioral change refers to the generalization of behavioral change from the practice setting to the client's natural environment. The natural environment refers to the physical and social surroundings in which the target behavior was developed and in which behavioral changes are designed to be performed and maintained.

2. Four obstacles to the transfer of behavioral change are: (a) insufficient reinforcement for desired responses in the client's natural environment; (b) reinforcement of the client's inappropriate, maladaptive responses in the natural environment; (c) lack of similarity between the practice setting and the client's natural environment; and (d) the desired responses have not been sufficiently developed in the practice setting.

3. Transfer and maintenance of behavioral change can be promoted by the following strategies: (a) involve significant individuals, such as family or friends, in the client's behavioral change program; (b) provide intermittent reinforcement for desired behaviors in the practice setting; (c) work with the client in the natural environment to develop desired behaviors; (d) use behavioral rehearsal in the role plays that help the client develop and practice desired behaviors; (e) give behavioral assignments to the client that specify tasks to be performed in the natural environment between meetings with the practitioner.

SUGGESTED READINGS

DANGEL, R. F. and POLSTER, R. A. (Eds.), *Parent Training: Foundations of Research and Practice* (New York: Guilford Press, 1982).

GOLDSTEIN, A. P., SECHREST, L. B., and HELLER, K., *Psychotherapy and the Psychology of Behavior Change* (New York: Wiley, 1966).

HAWKINS, R. P., PETERSON, R. F., SCHWEID, E., and BIJOU, S. W., "Behavior Therapy in the Home: Amelioration of Problem Parent-Child Relations with the Parent in the Therapeutic Role," *Journal of Experimental Child Psychology*, 1966, *4*, 99–107.

LOVAAS, O. I., KOEGEL, R., SIMMONS, J. Q., and LONG, J. S., "Some Generalization and Follow-up Measures on Autistic Children in Behavior Therapy," *Journal of Applied Behavior Analysis*, 1973, *6*, 131–165.

MARTIN, G. L., and OSBORNE, J. G. (Eds.), *Helping in the Community: Behavioral Applications* (New York: Plenum Press, 1980).

MATSON, J., and EARNHART, T., "Programming Treatment Effects to the Natural Environment," *Behavior Modification,* 1981, *5*(1), 27–38.

McFALL, R. M., and LILLESAND, D. B., "Behavior Rehearsal with Modeling and Coaching in Assertion Training," *Journal of Abnormal Psychology*, 1971, *77*, 313–323.

MEYERS, A. W., MEYERS, H. H., and CRAIGHEAD, W. E., "Community Behavior Change," *Behavior Modification, 5*(2), 1981, 147–170.

PATTERSON, G. R., McNEAL, S., HAWKINS, N., and PHELPS, R., "Reprogramming the Social Environment," *Journal of Child Psychology and Psychiatry*, 1967, *8*, 181–195.

ROSE, S. D., SUNDEL, M., DeLANGE, J., CORWIN, L., and PALUMBO, A., "The Hartwig Project: A Behavioral Approach to the Treatment of Juvenile Offenders." R. Ulrich, T. Stachnik, and J. Mabry (Eds.), *Control of Human Behavior,* volume 2 (Glenview, Illinois: Scott, Foresman & Co., 1970).

SMITH, J. M., and SMITH, D. E. P., *Child Management: A Program for Parents and Teachers* (Champaign, Illinois: Research Press, 1976).

STEIN, T. J. and GAMBRILL, E. D., "Behavioral Techniques in Foster Care." *Social Work,* 1976, *21*(1), 34–39.

POST-TEST QUESTIONS

(3) 1.   List three obstacles to generalization of desired responses from the practice setting to the client's natural environment.

(1) 2.   Turn to pages 225–226 to see Case Study 3. Mr. Clark's speech was developed in a laboratorylike situation. State one reason his speech might not generalize from the treatment setting to the ward.

(2) 3.   State two ways you could maximize successful generalization of Mr. Clark's speech.

(2) 4.   Turn to pages 225–227 and review Case Study 4. State two behavioral assignments the marriage counselor gave Mrs. Munsen in that study.

(2) 5.   State two reasons for using behavioral assignments in implementing a behavioral change program.

(1) 6.   Refer to Case Study 8 on pages 189–190. How was behavioral rehearsal used to help Mrs. Gomez and Mr. Terry converse appropriately with their peers?

(1) 7.   What is the rationale for using behavioral rehearsal?

TREATMENT PLANNING AND EVALUATION

objectives

After completing this chapter, you should be able to:

1. identify environmental and client resources and barriers to goal attainment,
2. formulate an intervention plan, specifying the behavioral techniques and the procedures for implementing them,
3. state three criteria you could use in evaluating the effectiveness of a behavioral change program, and
4. describe a method for evaluating the results of a behavioral-change program.

Mr. Wallenta was a patient in a mental hospital. He spent most of his time sitting alone with his arms folded, in a corner, unshaven and unkempt. Behavioral change goals for Mr. Wallenta included development of self-care skills such as washing, brushing his teeth, combing his hair, and shaving. The intervention plan for developing these self-care skills involved the following behavioral techniques: modeling, shaping, and positive reinforcement.

Baseline measures were obtained for use in evaluating the effectiveness of Mr. Wallenta's intervention plan. Behavioral changes on these measures indicated movement toward attainment of his goals.

PRETEST QUESTIONS

Chapter 16

(1) 1. What does informed consent in a behavioral-change program refer to?

(1) 2. An intervention plan for teaching a hospitalized mental patient self-care skills could include: (circle one)

    a. covert sensitization and modeling

    b. positive reinforcement and systematic desensitization

    c. positive reinforcement, shaping, and chaining

    d. none of the above

(3) 3. State three ways in which a client's progress can be evaluated.

(2) 4. What is the purpose of a treatment contract?

In this final chapter we show how the behavioral principles and techniques can be conceptualized within a comprehensive assessment-intervention-evaluation framework. This builds on the RAC-S approach to behavioral assessment covered in Chapters 8 and 9.

Treatment planning involves developing and structuring interventions based on the assessment of an individual's problem and the goals that have been established. It includes the design of the treatment or intervention plan, and selection of behavioral techniques and the procedures for implementing them. The treatment plan should be prepared and implemented in a manner that allows for systematic evaluation. **Evaluation** refers to methods of measuring changes in the client's target behaviors to determine progress towards goal achievement or problem resolution over the course of treatment.

BEHAVIORAL ASSESSMENT, TREATMENT
PLANNING, IMPLEMENTATION, AND EVALUATION

The four major phases of service delivery using a behavioral approach are: (1) Behavioral Assessment, (2) Treatment Planning, (3) Implementation of Behavioral Change Program, and (4) Evaluation. The following outline covers the phases involved in providing client services using a behavior modification approach. Figure 16-1 is a flow chart of the Behavioral Assessment, Treatment Planning, Implementation, and Evaluation Procedure.

I. Behavioral Assessment
    A. List all client problems identified through assessment sources:
        1. interviews
        2. observations
        3. checklists and questionnaires
        4. referral sources
        5. reports of significant others
        6. physiological measures (for example, biofeedback)
    B. Rank order the problems according to their priorities for service. Select one problem for immediate attention, using the following criteria:
        1. the problem that is of immediate expressed concern to the client or significant others
        2. the problem that has severe negative consequences for the client, significant others, or society if not handled immediately
        3. the problem that can be corrected most quickly, considering resources and obstacles
        4. the problem that requires handling before other problems can be treated
    C. Obtain concrete examples of the problem. Specify target (*r*esponse(s), controlling *a*ntecedent(s), negative and positive *c*onsequences, and response *s*trength—frequency, intensity, duration, latency, and/or magnitude. Examples can be obtained from the following sources:
        1. behavioral reenactment
        2. observation of client in role plays or in natural environment
        3. client reports
        4. reports from referral source
        5. reports of significant others
        6. physiological measures (for example, biofeedback)
    D. Specify measures of response strength to be recorded and design a measurement plan. Indicate who will observe and record the response.
    E. Obtain measures of response strength.
    F. Formulate terminal, intermediate, and initial behavioral change goals; specify desired responses, antecedents, and reinforcers. Evaluate potential barriers to goal attainment.
II. Treatment Planning
    A. Identify client and environmental resources:
        1. identify available reinforcers
        2. identify individuals who control the delivery of reinforcers and punishers to clients
        3. identify relevant client assets and liabilities
        4. indicate how the behavioral change program relates to other services rendered to the client (for example, legal, medical, financial)
    B. Formulate the intervention plan
        1. specify the behavioral techniques and the steps for implementing them
        2. specify individual(s) to be involved
        3. describe plan for generalization and maintenance of treatment gains in the client's natural environment
        4. set approximate target date for achievement of each goal

III. Implementation of behavioral change program:
   A. Carry out procedures prescribed in intervention plan
   B. Monitor measures of response strength as stated in I, D
IV. Evaluation
   A. Compare strength of target response(s) before, during, and after implementation of behavioral change program
   B. Evaluate level of goal attainment, using the criteria stated in the behavioral change goals.
   C. When intermediate and terminal goals have been achieved, select the problem of next highest priority. Repeat the sequence from I, C. When all goals are achieved, make arrangements for follow-up contact.

FIGURE 16-1   Flow chart of behavioral assessment, treatment planning, implementation, and evaluation procedure

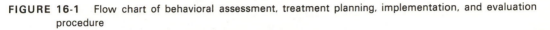

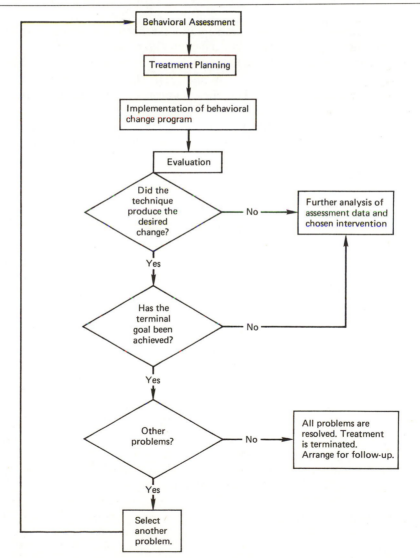

D. If the terminal goal has not been achieved, reassess the target behavior; the original assessment may be inaccurate. If the assessment is accurate, select and implement another intervention technique(s) and repeat the sequence from II.

TREATMENT CONTRACTS

The purpose of the **treatment contract** is to make explicit the client's expectations for service and the practitioner's assessment of what is required of the client and significant others. The client's commitment to solving his or her problem through a behavioral-change program is essential to achieving a successful outcome. The term treatment contract denotes the commitment of both the client and practitioner to carry out specific tasks that can lead to resolution of the client's problem. The contract also helps to ensure client involvement and participation in the treatment process.

The treatment contract specifies the behaviors required of the client and practitioner in problem selection, assessment, and goal formulation. In other words, the practitioner conducts a behavioral assessment of the client's problem(s) and formulates appropriate goals with the client. The client agrees to participate in relevant data-gathering procedures. The client agrees to carry out behavioral assignments given by the practitioner and regularly report their outcomes. The practitioner agrees to provide the guidance that will help the client attain his or her goals. Sometimes the treatment contract is a verbal agreement between the client and the practitioner. In other instances, however, a more formal agreement is written and signed by all parties concerned.

CLASSIFICATION OF BEHAVIORAL TECHNIQUES

Behavioral techniques can be classified according to their effects in altering response strength, that is, the four intervention outcomes or directions in which a target behavior can be modified. Behavioral techniques can be applied so that a response is (1) acquired or established, (2) increased in strength, (3) maintained at a particular strength or pattern of occurrence, or (4) decreased in strength (see Table 16-1). Behavioral techniques are applied as *interventions* to influence the frequency, intensity, duration, latency, and/or magnitude of target behaviors. Selection of a specific technique should be based on the directional requirements of the immediate, intermediate, or terminal goal(s). For example, if the behavioral change goal states that a behavior is to be decreased in strength, the relevant technique can be selected from among those in Table 16-1 in the column "Decrease Response Strength."

Table 16-1 is a chart of behavioral techniques classified according to their applicability in modifying response strength in a particular direction. Some of these techniques can be combined to form treatment packages. For example, assertiveness training might include positive reinforcement, model presentation, behavioral rehearsal, and differential reinforcement. Covert sensitization includes negative reinforcement and respondent conditioning techniques.

In selecting a behavioral technique, certain factors should be considered. These include cost (expense involved), efficiency (time), client and environmental

TABLE 16-1 A classification of behavioral techniques

ACQUIRE OR ESTABLISH A RESPONSE	INCREASE RESPONSE STRENGTH	MAINTAIN RESPONSE STRENGTH	DECREASE RESPONS STRENGTH
1. Shaping with successive approximations—Chapter 6	1. Positive reinforcement—Chapter 2	1. Schedules of reinforcement—Chapter 5	1. Satiation—Chapte
2. Stimulus fading—Chapter 7	2. Deprivation—Chapter 2	2. Differential reinforcement—Chapter 6	2. Operant extinction Chapter 3
3. Backward chaining—Chapter 10	3. Differential reinforcement—Chapter 6	3. Stimulus control—Chapter 7	3. DRO procedure—Chapter 6
4. Model presentation—Chapter 11	4. Stimulus control—Chapter 7	4. Behavioral assignments—Chapters 11, 15	4. Stimulus control—Chapter 7
5. Assertiveness training—Chapter 11	5. Negative reinforcement—Chapter 13	5. Negative reinforcement—Chapter 13	5. Punishment—Chapter 12
6. Negative reinforcement—Chapter 13	6. Behavioral rehearsal—Chapters 11, 15		6. Overcorrection—Chapter 12
7. Respondent conditioning—Chapter 14			7. Aversion therapies Chapter 14
			8. Systematic desens tion—Chapter 14
			9. Covert sensitizatio Chapter 14
			10. Thought-stopping-Chapter 14
			11. Respondent extinc Chapter 14
			12. Flooding—Chapter 14

resources and barriers, relative effectiveness of available techniques, comfort to the client, and ethical considerations. For example, although a punishment technique using aversive stimuli may be more immediately effective and efficient, a positive reinforcement and shaping procedure may have greater long-term effectiveness and fewer detrimental side effects. In addition, the use of positive reinforcement techniques may encounter less objections from the community than techniques involving aversive stimuli.

ETHICAL CONSIDERATIONS

Behavioral techniques should be used in accordance with the ethical codes and values of the human service professions. Like other therapeutic modalities, behavior modification programs should be implemented with the informed consent of the client. **Informed consent** means that the client understands the proposed interventions and voluntarily agrees to participate. If the client does not have the capacity to understand the proposed treatment, consent should be obtained from a relative or legal guardian.

If the client volunteers for treatment but subsequently resists the practitioner's efforts to establish or direct him or her toward achieving treatment goals, the basis for service should be reassessed. The practitioner should review the initial and current basis for treatment with the client, and point out the negative consequences, for the client or significant others, of the client's failure to modify the target behavior.

In providing services to children and to institutionalized populations such as the mentally retarded, delinquents, prisoners, and mental patients, special care should be exercised to ensure that individuals are not subjected to cruel or harsh interventions. Interventions that cause substantial discomfort to the client should be employed rarely, and only by experienced professional behavior therapists. In such cases, the benefits of these interventions must clearly outweigh the aversive consequences to the client or significant others of not using them.

FORMULATING THE INTERVENTION PLAN

After a systematic assessment is made of the client's situation, the practitioner should formulate an intervention plan. The plan is based on the behavioral change goals that are mutually established by the practitioner and the client. One or more behavioral techniques may be included in the intervention plan as part of a treatment package. The intervention plan provides a framework for systematically carrying out the behavioral change program to attain the client's goals.

Without an explicit plan, application of an isolated behavioral technique could be ineffective in achieving a client's goals. For example, positive reinforcement could be applied to increase the frequency of a motor response such as arm raising in an institutionalized mental patient, Mr. Wallenta, who spends most of his time sitting in a chair with his arms folded in a corner by himself, unshaven and unkempt. Although positive reinforcement would increase the frequency of arm raising, this activity in itself might not be beneficial for Mr. Wallenta if developed outside the context of a treatment plan. Since the behavioral change goals for Mr. Wallenta include development of self-care skills such as shaving, washing, brushing his teeth, and combing his hair, the practitioner's plan to increase arm raising would be an intermediate goal. The intervention plan for developing self-care skills might include the following behavioral techniques: modeling, shaping, and positive reinforcement. Modeling can be used to demonstrate the appropriate self-care behaviors; positive reinforcement is used to increase and maintain the strength of desired behaviors after they are performed; and shaping is used to develop successive approximations to the terminal goals.

IMPLEMENTING THE INTERVENTION PLAN

Prior to implementing the intervention plan, baseline measures of Mr. Wallenta's self-care skills were obtained. Mr. Wallenta was given an electric shaver every morning and the ward nurse observed him daily over a one-week period to record his frequency of shaving. He recorded the following data: (1) the number of days Mr. Wallenta appeared clean shaven, and (2) the number of times Mr. Wallenta attempted to shave. For example, Mr. Wallenta might pick up the shaver and put it to his face without enough pressure to remove the hairs. Baseline measures were also obtained for other self-care behaviors, including hair combing, washing, and brushing his teeth.

The intervention plan for Mr. Wallenta involved modeling, shaping, and positive reinforcement. The male nurse brought the electric shaver to Mr. Wallenta and demonstrated the correct way to shave. After showing Mr. Wallenta how he shaved himself, the nurse told Mr. Wallenta to "Shave yourself the way I just did." Mr. Wallenta took the shaver and held it up to his face. The nurse immediately reinforced him with a jelly bean and verbal praise. The nurse had determined prior to implementing the intervention plan that Mr. Wallenta was very fond of jelly beans. Mr. Wallenta normally had no way of getting jelly beans, so the nurse decided to use them as possible positive reinforcers in the initial stages of treatment.

The nurse continued to model each step involved in shaving, asking Mr. Wallenta to imitate the behaviors that were demonstrated. Correct imitations were immediately followed by jelly beans and praise. The nurse gradually raised the requirements for reinforcement to include a greater proportion of the behaviors resulting in a cleanly shaven face. In this manner, Mr. Wallenta learned to cleanly shave his entire face when given a shaver.

EVALUATING THE EFFECTIVENESS OF THE INTERVENTION PLAN

In the above example, the criterion for attainment of the shaving goal indicated that Mr. Wallenta be clean shaven at least five times a week. Achievement of this goal, therefore, required that Mr. Wallenta appropriately shave five out of seven days each week. When observed during the initial weeks of treatment, Mr. Wallenta shaved part of his face once or twice a week. Further along in treatment, Mr. Wallenta appeared clean shaven three or four times a week. By the end of treatment, the shaving goal was achieved so that Mr. Wallenta appropriately shaved himself five times or more a week.

If the target behavior (shaving) had not changed from its baseline rate after the interventions were employed for a reasonable amount of time (for example, two weeks), the target behavior would be reassessed. In many organizations, a case review date is set for supervisory or team review of client progress towards goal achievement. The practitioner should continually monitor and record the client's progress, however, regardless of case review dates.

Performance of desired behaviors should be evaluated in both the practice setting and the client's environment. The success of treatment, however, depends upon the client's ability to perform these behaviors in the actual problematic situation.

The Treatment Evaluation Form can be given to the client during the final session, to obtain his or her evaluation of the behavioral-change program. Figure 16-2 is a Treatment Evaluation Form used with a client. The form includes a statement of the client's problems and goals filled in by the practitioner. If the client lacks the skills required to fill out the form, it can be completed by significant others such as parents, teachers, or relatives. This form can also be sent to the client at periodic intervals following termination, such as three months, six months, or one year. The practitioner can also schedule periodic interviews with the client either at the practitioner's office or the client's home to evaluate the extent to which treatment gains have been maintained. Arrangements for follow-up contacts should be made prior to termination of treatment.

FIGURE 16-2   Treatment evaluation form[1]

The following are the problems you worked on and the goals you wanted to achieve. Please make any corrections you think are necessary to make them accurate. If the statements are correct, please initial your O.K.

Problems and goals worked on:

PROBLEMS	GOALS
1. You and your wife were constantly quarreling. She usually slept in the children's room. *D.g.*	1. Decrease number and severity of arguments with wife. Increase number of nights wife slept with you. *D.g.*
2. You remained silent at staff meetings, even when you disagreed with your co-workers. *D.g.*	2. Increase the number of times you state your disagreements with co-workers. *D.g.*

To what extent are the above listed problems solved?

	MUCH WORSE	WORSE	SAME	BETTER	MUCH BETTER	COMPLETELY SOLVED
Problem 1				✓		
Problem 2						✓
Problem 3						

To what extent were the above listed goals achieved?

	NOT AT ALL ACHIEVED	SMALL GAIN	MODERATE GAIN	MOSTLY ACHIEVED	GOAL ACHIEVED
Goal 1			✓		
Goal 2					✓
Goal 3					

[1]Adapted from Problem Checklist #2 from, "Behavioral Group Treatment with Adults in a Family Service Agency," by Martin Sundel and Harry Lawrence in *Individual Change Through Small Groups* by P. Glasser, R. Sarri, and R. Vinter (Eds.). Reprinted with permission of The Free Press, a Division of Macmillan Publishing Co., Inc., copyright 1974.

1.   How satisfied are you with your behaviors in the problematic situation?

Problem 1:   _____ Very dissatisfied   Problem 2:   _____ Very dissatisfied

             _____ Dissatisfied   _____ Dissatisfied

             ___✓___ Satisfied   _____ Satisfied

             _____ Very satisfied   ___✓___ Very satisfied

Comments:

2.   Overall, how satisfied are you with the results of treatment?

Problem 1:   _____ Very dissatisfied   Problem 2:   _____ Very dissatisfied

             _____ Dissatisfied   _____ Dissatisfied

             ___✓___ Satisfied   _____ Satisfied

             _____ Very satisfied   ___✓___ Very satisfied

Comments:

BEHAVIORALLY ORIENTED RECORD KEEPING

In order to determine the effectiveness of an intervention plan, a systematic procedure for planning and recording the client's treatment is essential. The practitioner should establish and follow a systematic record keeping plan that (1) delineates the client's problems and goals, (2) describes the interventions that have been employed, and (3) charts the client's progress towards treatment goals. Each problem should be listed separately along with specification of the target response(s), controlling antecedents and consequences, and a corresponding behavioral change goal(s). Relevant client and environmental resources and barriers should be described in relation to each goal. The intervention plan in the client's record should identify behavioral techniques appropriate for achieving the client's goals and the steps to be used in implementing them. Progress toward each goal should be recorded by date. The effects of the various interventions employed should be stated. When the client's goals are reached, follow-up contacts should be recorded including information on the client's current situation.

The following are excerpts from a sample record based on the information in Case Study 5, which can be reviewed on pages 227–228.

1.   *Problem:* Mr. Lewis said that he feels exploited at work. He was promised a raise and promotion two years ago, but he is in the same position, earning the same salary. Mr. Lewis has not discussed this problem with his boss.

Typical example: Mr. Lewis went in to ask his boss about a promotion and raise. When his boss asked what he wanted, Mr. Lewis told him about his financial problems. He left the office without discussing the promotion or raise.

Target responses: Mr. Lewis looks at the floor, mumbles, and leaves without discussing the promotion or raise.

Controlling conditions: Antecedent: in boss's office; boss asks him what he wants.

Consequences: Negative (Potential Punishers)—Mr. Lewis does not get raise or promotion; remains in same position at same salary; is dissatisfied with his behavior in this situation.

Positive (Potential Positive and/or Negative Reinforcers)—avoids possible conflict with boss.

Response strength: every interaction with employer—3 to 5 times/week.

2. *Goals:* Terminal—Mr. Lewis goes in to his boss's office and assertively asks for a raise and promotion.

   Possible risks: Boss could say, "no."

   Possible reinforcers: Boss acknowledges legitimacy of his request; boss agrees to his request

   Target date: three months

   Case review: 8 weeks

   Intermediate—makes legitimate request of his boss, maintaining eye contact and speaking clearly.

   Initial—decrease mumbling, decrease talking with hand over mouth; increase eye contact; increase the volume of voice and vary the pitch in conversation.

3. *Resources and barriers:* Resources—Mr. Lewis's stated cooperation and desire to improve his situation; his work record is good; he earns a steady income and is self-supporting; he has marketable job skills.

   Barriers—Mr. Lewis has had several unpleasant encounters with his boss.

4. *Intervention plan for initial goal:* verbal instructions, modeling, positive reinforcement, and behavioral rehearsal will be used (1) to decrease Mr. Lewis's mumbling and speaking with his hand over his mouth, and (2) to increase the amount of time he maintains eye contact while conversing with someone.

5. *Implementing the intervention plan:* Mr. Lewis will be given instructions on how to speak clearly and maintain eye contact. The practitioner will model clear speech and eye contact and will provide social reinforcement for approximations to desired speech. Behavioral rehearsal will be used to allow the client to practice the desired behaviors in the presence of the therapist. The client will be assigned various speaking exercises to practice into a tape recorder at home and to bring the tapes to the sessions for review with the practitioner.

   Practitioner's signature _____ Date_____

6. Sample progress note

    Date: 2/11, 3rd session Mr. Lewis's mumbling has decreased in role plays with me. He no longer places his hand in front of his mouth while talking. Mr. Lewis reported having a pleasant conversation with his boss about a complicated bookkeeping technique that he was able to explain. Mr. Lewis continues to speak in a monotone although the volume of his voice has increased when speaking into the tape recorder. He still has difficulty maintaining eye contact for more than several seconds.

    Plan for next contact—Mr. Lewis was given an assignment to continue practicing speaking exercises on his tape recorder. Mr. Lewis will role play a conversation with his boss at the next session.

CLIENT SATISFACTION

In evaluating the success of a behavioral-change program, the practitioner should consider the client's personal evaluation of the program's success (see Figure 16-2), as well as the evaluation of significant others such as family, friends, and referral source. Ideally, measures of the client's satisfaction with services should be consistent with his or her attainment of the treatment goals. Measures of satisfaction from clients and significant others obtained after intervention should be compared with their assessment of the target behaviors prior to implementation of the behavioral-change plan, to determine their perceptions of the extent of change and the benefits of services received.

The practitioner should discuss objective measures of progress toward goal achievement with the client and relate these measures to the client's personal satisfaction with behavioral change. Measures of client satisfaction should be obtained throughout the behavioral change program, so that both objective measures of goal progress and the client's perceptions of improvement can be compared. If the client's goals are achieved but the client feels dissatisfied, this may indicate a failure to have established goals that are considered significant by the client. It might also mean that other problem areas need to be considered in the client's behavioral-change program.

On the other hand, a client who has difficulty achieving behavioral-change goals may report satisfaction with the behavioral-change program. This individual may be deriving sufficient reinforcement from the relationship with the practitioner to compensate for lack of goal progress. The practitioner should help the client to realistically evaluate progress toward attainment of treatment goals and separate this evaluation from the client's satisfaction with his or her relationship with the practitioner.

A hallmark of the behavioral approach has been its emphasis on evaluating the effects of intervention programs. Most practitioner evaluations are based on case analysis using single subject designs. Although single case analysis typically does not involve statistical manipulation, more sophisticated evaluation designs and data analysis have also been used.

Rigorous methods have been applied in evaluating behavioral techniques and programs and comparing their effects with other intervention modalities (for example, Paul, 1967; Paul & Lentz, 1977; Sloane, 1975). Behavioral interventions have been particularly effective and found superior to other treatment modalities in the treatment of social skills deficits, fears, and nervous habits (see Kazdin and Wilson, 1978). In the treatment of autistic and hyperactive children and the mentally retarded, behavioral techniques have demonstrated efficacy beyond that shown by conventional psychotherapy (see Kazdin and Hersen, 1980). Behavioral researchers and practitioners are currently focusing their efforts on developing intervention modalities that demonstrate lasting generalization and maintenance of behavioral change in the client's natural environment.

Behavior modification appears to be moving toward increasing concern with societal and environmental problems. Public housing, energy conservation, waste management, organizational development and programming, and self-help strategies are areas of recent inquiry (for example, Martin & Osborne, 1980). Undoubtedly, there will be an exciting future for the field of behavior modification as its practitioners continue to develop and test innovative approaches to improve the quality of individual and community life.

SUMMARY

1. An outline of the behavioral assessment, treatment planning, implementation and evaluation framework was presented.
2. A treatment contract specifies the tasks to be performed by the client and the practitioner in working towards resolving the client's difficulties.
3. Behavioral techniques can be classified according to the change they produce in any of four outcomes or directions: acquire or establish, increase, maintain, or decrease the strength of a response.
4. A behavioral change program should be carried out only with the informed consent of the client, significant others, or legal guardian.
5. The intervention plan is formulated with the client, whenever feasible, and includes specification of behavioral techniques and the steps to be followed that can lead to goal attainment for the client.
6. Evaluation of the effectiveness of a behavioral change program is based on comparing the strength of the client's target responses before, during, and after intervention. Measures of response strength are monitored continuously so that the client and practitioner can determine the direction and extent of desired change.
7. Client satisfaction is a measure of the effectiveness of the practitioner's services as evaluated by the client. The practitioner should discuss measures indicating the client's progress toward goal achievement and relate this to the client's satisfaction with behavioral change.
8. A client's record should include reporting on the following components: problem(s), goals, resources and barriers to goal achievement, intervention plan, how the plan is implemented, and evaluation of progress.

The following journals are of interest to behavioral practitioners:

Behavioral Assessment
Behavioral Counseling Quarterly
Behavior Modification
Behavioural Psychotherapy
Behaviour Research and Therapy
Behavior Therapy
Child Behavior Therapy
International Journal of Behavioral Social Work and Abstracts
Journal of Applied Behavior Analysis
Journal of Behavioral Assessment
Journal of Behavior Therapy and Experimental Psychiatry
Journal of Behavioral Medicine
Journal of Child Behavior Therapy
Journal of the Experimental Analysis of Behavior

For information about membership, behavior modification conferences, and programs, write to:

Association for the Advancement of Behavior Therapy
420 Lexington Avenue
New York, New York 10017

Social Work Group for the Study of Behavioral Methods
c/o Dr. Elsie Pinkston, President
University of Chicago
School of Social Service Administration
969 E. 60th St.
Chicago, Illinois 60637

Society of Behavioral Medicine
Suite 2547
420 Lexington Avenue
New York, New York 10017

SUGGESTED READINGS

BUTTERFIELD, W. H. and WERKING, J.,   "Behavioral Methods in Primary Health Care." S. P. Schinke (Ed.), *Behavioral Methods in Social Welfare* (Hawthorne, N.Y.: Aldine, 1981).

KANFER, F. H., and GRIMM, L. G.,   "Managing Clinical Change: A Process Model of Therapy," *Behavior Modification,* 1980, *4,* 419–444.

KAZDIN, A. E., and HERSEN, M.,   "The Current Status of Behavior Therapy," *Behavior Modification*, 1980, *4*(3), 283–302.

KAZDIN, A. E., and WILSON, G. T., *Evaluation of Behavior Therapy: Issues, Evidence, and Research Strategies* (Cambridge, Mass.: Ballinger, 1978).

KRATOCHWILL, T. R. (ED.), *Single-Subject Research: Strategies for Evaluating Change* (New York: Academic Press, 1978).

KURAN, J. P., CORRIVEAU, D. P., MONTI, P. M., and HAGERMAN, S. B., "Social Skill and Social Anxiety: Self-report Measurement in a Psychiatric Population," *Behavior Modification*, 1980, *4*, 493–512.

MARTIN, G. L., and OSBORNE, J. G. (EDS.), *Helping in the Community: Behavioral Applications* (New York: Plenum Press, 1980).

PAUL, G. L., "Insight vs. Desensitization in Psychotherapy Two Years after Termination," *Journal of Consulting Psychology*, 1967, *31,* 333–348.

PAUL, G. L., and LENTZ, R. J., *Psychosocial Treatment of Chronic Mental Patients: Milieu versus Social Learning Programs* (Cambridge, Mass.: Harvard University Press, 1977).

SEIDNER, M. L., and KIRSCHENBAUM, D. S., "Behavioral Contracts: Effects of Pretreatment Information and Intention Statements," *Behavior Therapy,* 1980, *11*, 689–698.

SLOANE, R. B. ET AL., *Psychotherapy versus Behavior Therapy* (Cambridge, Mass.: Harvard University Press, 1975).

SUNDEL, M., and LAWRENCE, H., "A Systematic Approach to Treatment Planning in Time-Limited Behavioral Groups," *Journal of Behavior Therapy and Experimental Psychiatry,* 1977, *8*(4), 395–399.

SUNDEL, M. and LAWRENCE, H., "Behavioral Group Treatment with Adults in a Family Service Agency," in P. Glasser, R. Sarri, and R. Vinter (Eds.), *Individual Change Through Small Groups* (New York: The Free Press, 1974).

SUNDEL, S. S., and SUNDEL, M., *Be Assertive: A Practical Guide for Human Service Workers* (Beverly Hills, California: Sage Publications, Inc., 1980).

TURKAT, I. D., and FOREHAND, R., "Critical Issues in Behavior Therapy," *Behavior Modification*, 1980, *4*, 445–464.

WOLF, M. M., "Social Validity: The Case for Subjective Measurement or How Applied Behavior Analysis Is Finding Its Heart," *Journal of Applied Behavior Analysis*, 1978, *11*, 203–214.

YATES, B., *Improving Effectiveness and Reducing Costs in Mental Health* (Springfield, Illinois: Charles C. Thomas, 1980).

POST-TEST QUESTIONS

(2) 1. Turn to pages 227–228 to see Case Study 5. Now state one possible resource and one possible barrier to goal attainment, given the following behavioral change goal for Mr. Lewis: Mr. Lewis assertively asks his employer for a salary increase.

(4) 2. Develop an intervention plan for teaching Mr. Wallenta (see page 200) how to brush his teeth. He has never been observed to brush his teeth. Include two behavioral techniques and outline the procedure you would follow to achieve the goal.

(2) 3. Describe a method for evaluating the effectiveness of an assertiveness-training procedure that could be used with Mr. Lewis.

(2) 3. Describe a method for evaluating the effectiveness of an assertiveness-training procedure that could be used with Mr. Lewis.

COURSE POST-TEST

QUESTIONS FOR CASE STUDY 1

(3) 1. Specify three antecedents to Harold's drug taking.

(2) 2. State two negative consequences related to Harold's drug taking.

(4) 3. State four negative consequences of Harold's failing grades.

(2) 4. Specify two measures that could be used to evaluate movement toward treatment goals.

(3) 5. State three possible reinforcers (positive or negative) maintaining Harold's drug taking.

QUESTIONS FOR CASE STUDY 2

(2) 1. Specify the two measures used to determine movement toward treatment goals.

(4) 2. Describe the interaction between Carla and her mother in terms of positive and negative reinforcement. Draw a paradigm and label relevant components.

(2) 3. Name the operant procedure used to decrease Carla's screaming when she was asked to put her toys away. Describe how it was implemented; that is, to which of Mrs. Hernandez's actions does the procedure refer?

(1) 4. What was the social worker's rationale for instructing Mrs. Hernandez to praise Carla for putting her toys away?

QUESTIONS FOR CASE STUDY 3

(2) 1. In the case study, no goal is explicitly stated for treatment. State a possible treatment goal for Mr. Clark and specify a measure that could be used to determine whether it was achieved.

(1) 2. What data should be collected before implementing the treatment described in the case study?

(3) 3. Describe the function of the green light. Name and briefly state the purpose of the operant procedure involving the green light.

(2) 4. Apply the concept of conditioned reinforcement to explain how Mr. Clark's speech could have generalized to the ward from the treatment setting even though the unconditioned reinforcer, candy, was not given to him on the ward. What specifically did the psychologist do to promote the transfer of Mr. Clark's speech to the ward?

(3) 5. Describe how the psychologist could use a DRO procedure to determine if it was the candy and points that served as reinforcers for Mr. Clark's increased speech, and not the attention he received in the treatment situation.

QUESTIONS FOR CASE STUDY 4

(4) 1. State four possible desired behaviors that could be included in treatment goals for Mrs. Munsen. Indicate measures that could be used to evaluate movement toward those goals.

(2) 2. In behavioral terms, describe the rationale for the procedure involved in Mrs. Munsen's drawing up two lists of topics.

(2) 3. State two measures that could be used to evaluate the effectiveness of the discrimination training procedure employed by the counselor.

(1) 4.   How was Mr. Munsen's leaving the house negatively reinforced?

QUESTIONS FOR CASE STUDY 5

(2) 1.   State two desired behaviors that could be included in treatment goals appropriate to Mr. Lewis's problem of nonassertion.

(2) 2.   Describe two role-playing techniques that could be used as part of Mr. Lewis's treatment if he were participating in group therapy.

(2) 3.   Describe a procedure that Mr. Lewis could use to establish himself as a conditioned reinforcer for his dates.

QUESTIONS FOR CASE STUDY 6

(2) 1.   State the inappropriate behaviors emitted by Mr. Potts during criticism.

(3) 2.   How could a modeling-plus-reinforcement procedure have been used to help Mr. Potts obtain a new job?

(2) 3. What reinforcement was arranged for Mr. Potts in the treatment situation, and what were the conditions for its delivery?

(4) 4. List Mr. Potts's respondent behaviors elicited by criticism.

(2) 5. Identify the behavioral procedures that were used to promote generalization of desired behavior change from the group treatment setting to Mr. Potts's natural environment.

QUESTIONS FOR CASE STUDY 7

(5) 1. List five contingencies Mrs. Drake carried out with Stephen and Dianne.

(3) 2. Name the behavioral principle that was the basis for the punishment administered to Stephen and Dianne. Name the reinforcers involved for Stephen and Dianne.

(2) 3. The therapist told Mrs. Drake to spend time with Stephen in the evenings, and to play cards with him. The goal was to increase social behaviors performed by mother and son that would be positively reinforced by each other. Describe two possible situations that would indicate that this goal was being achieved.

(6) 4. Describe a shaping procedure Mrs. Drake could have used to establish cooperative play behaviors between Stephen and Dianne.

QUESTIONS FOR CASE STUDY 8

(4) 1. Specify the target behaviors and their negative consequences for Mrs. Gomez and Mr. Terry.

(3) 2. State three measurable goals of the procedure carried out by the psychiatric nurse.

(2) 3. Describe two behavioral techniques the psychiatric nurse could use to help Mrs. Gomez and Mr. Terry generalize appropriate verbal behavior outside the group.

(2) 4. Describe (a) a reinforcer that was given in the group to Mrs. Gomez and Mr. Terry contingent on appropriate speech and (b) a possible reinforcer that could maintain their appropriate speech outside the group.

COURSE POST-TEST ANSWERS

ANSWERS FOR CASE STUDY 1

(3) 1. Specify three antecedents to Harold's drug taking.

Answers: The antecedents to Harold's drug taking are: (1) Friends invite him over to listen to music and smoke marijuana. (2) Harold is with his girlfriend at her home. (3) Harold is home alone, looks in his notebook, and reads his class assignments. (Chapters 8 and 9.)[1]

(2) 2. State two negative consequences related to Harold's drug taking.

Answers: The negative consequences related to Harold's drug taking are: (1) He fails to complete class assignments. (2) He is unprepared for class, having completed only part or none of his assignment. (3) He receives failing grades. (Chapter 8.)

(4) 3. State four negative consequences of Harold's failing grades.

Answers: The negative consequences of Harold's failing grades are: (1) He is grounded by his parents. (2) His parents nag him. (3) He is denied certain privileges such as watching television and going out with his friends. (4) His allowance is withheld. (Chapters 8 and 9.)

(2) 4. Specify two measures that could be used to evaluate movement toward treatment goals.

Answers:

1. Harold turns in an increased number of complete assignments.

2. Harold decreases the frequency and amount of his drug taking. (Chapter 9.)

(3) 5. State three possible reinforcers (positive or negative) maintaining Harold's drug taking.

Answers: Possible reinforcers maintaining Harold's drug taking include: (1) He spends time with his girlfriend. (2) He avoids doing his homework. (3) He escapes the nagging of his parents. (4) He listens to records and spends time with his friends. (Chapters 9 and 13.)

[1] The chapter number in parentheses indicates the chapter where this material is covered.

(2) 1. Specify the two measures used to determine movement toward treatment goals.

Answers: The measures used to determine movement toward the treatment goals were (1) the decrease in frequency of Carla's screaming when told to put her toys away and (2) the increase in frequency of Carla's putting her toys away. (Chapter 16.)

(4) 2. Describe the interaction between Carla and her mother in terms of positive and negative reinforcement. Draw a paradigm and label relevant components.

Answers: Carla's screaming was positively reinforced by her mother's putting the toys away and promising to buy her new clothes. Mrs. Hernandez's responses of putting the toys away and promising to buy Carla new clothes were negatively reinforced in that they terminated Carla's screaming. (Chapters 2 and 13.)

R $\longrightarrow$ s^{r+}

Carla screamed   Mrs. Hernandez promised to buy new clothes; put toys away herself

S^{R-} Carla screamed

R $\longrightarrow$ S^{R-}

Mrs. Hernandez put toys away; promised new clothes   terminated Carla's screaming

(2) 3. Name the operant procedure used to decrease Carla's screaming when she was asked to put her toys away. Describe how it was implemented; that is, to which of Mrs. Hernandez's actions does the procedure refer?

Answers: Mrs. Hernandez used an extinction procedure to decrease Carla's screaming. When Carla screamed about putting her toys away, Mrs. Hernandez walked away from her. Mrs. Hernandez also refrained from making promises to buy Carla new clothes and from putting Carla's toys away herself. (Chapter 3.)

(1) 4. What was the social worker's rationale for instructing Mrs. Hernandez to praise Carla for putting her toys away?

Answer: In situations where undesired behaviors are decreased, it is important to establish and increase desired behaviors incompatible with the undesired behaviors. The social worker, therefore, instructed Mrs. Hernandez to praise and reinforce Carla when she put her toys away. (Chapter 3.)

(2) 1. In the case study, no goal is explicitly stated for treatment. State a possible treatment goal for Mr. Clark and specify a measure that could be used to determine whether it was achieved.

Criterion for correct answer: The goal should indicate that Mr. Clark speaks according to some observable, specific criterion.

Sample answers: The goal for treatment could be stated as: (1) Mr. Clark speaks five complete sentences during a thirty-minute treatment session. (2) Mr. Clark responds to five out of six questions asked of him by the psychologist during a twenty-minute treatment session. (Chapter 9.)

(1) 2. What data should be collected before implementing the treatment described in the case study?

Answer: Before implementing the treatment described, a baseline indicating the rate of Mr. Clark's speech in the treatment setting as well as on the ward should be obtained. (Chapter 2.)

(3) 3. Describe the function of the green light. Name and briefly state the purpose of the operant procedure involving the green light.

Answers: When illuminated, the green light served as an S^D for verbal responses that would be reinforced. When the green light was off, it served as an S^Δ during which time speech was not reinforced. The discrimination training procedure was used to teach Mr. Clark to speak only when the green light was on. (Chapter 7.)

(2) 4. Apply the concept of conditioned reinforcement to explain how Mr. Clark's speech could have generalized to the ward from the treatment setting even though the unconditioned reinforcer, candy, was not given to him on the ward. What specifically did the psychologist do to promote the transfer of Mr. Clark's speech to the ward?

Answers: His speech was probably maintained by conditioned reinforcers on the ward, such as people responding to his speech, staff praising him for speaking, and other patients commenting favorably on his speech. The psychologist, by saying "Good," was using a conditioned reinforcer, praise, with the primary reinforcer, candy, to promote the shifting from unconditioned to conditioned reinforcers more readily available on the ward. (Chapter 10.)

(3) 5. Describe how the psychologist could use a DRO procedure to determine if it was candy and points that served as reinforcers for Mr. Clark's increased speech, and not the attention he received in the treatment situation.

Answer: The psychologist could have used a DRO procedure in which Mr. Clark would be given candy and points for behaviors other than speaking. If Mr. Clark's speech decreased, the candy and points were positive reinforcers for Mr. Clark's speech. The psychologist could further demonstrate the effectiveness of the candy and points as reinforcers by reconditioning Mr. Clark's speech using these reinforcers. (Chapter 6.)

(4) 1. State four possible desired behaviors that could be included in treatment goals for Mrs. Munsen. Indicate measures that could be used to evaluate movement toward those goals.

Answers: The following are possible desired behaviors that could be included in treatment goals with their measures for evaluating movement toward the goals: (1) Increase in frequency of Mrs. Munsen's making breakfast for Mr. Munsen. (2) Decrease in frequency of Mr. Munsen's going out drinking with friends in the evenings. (3) Increase in frequency of Mr. and Mrs. Munsen's going to movies or other entertainment together. (4) Increase in frequency of Mr. Munsen's accompanying Mrs. Munsen on shopping trips. (5) Decrease in intensity and frequency of arguments between Mr. and Mrs. Munsen. (6) Increase in frequency of pleasant conversation. (7) Increase in amount of time and frequency per week Mr. Munsen spends with Mrs. Munsen and the children watching television, going on trips, and talking to each other. (Chapters 9 and 16.)

(2) 2. In behavioral terms, describe the rationale for the procedure involved in Mrs. Munsen's drawing up two lists of topics.

Answer: Mrs. Munsen made a list of topics to discuss with Mr. Munsen (S^D), and a list of topics not to discuss with Mr. Munsen. (S^Δ). Items on the S^D list (List A) were S^Ds for Mrs. Munsen's speaking that was reinforced by the counselor in role-play situations. Items on the S^Δ list (List B) were not reinforced by the counselor. The counselor used a discrimination-training procedure to teach Mrs. Munsen to talk only about S^D topics to increase the frequency of pleasant conversation with Mr. Munsen and to decrease the frequency of their arguments involving List B topics. (Chapter 7.)

(2) 3. State two measures that could be used to evaluate the effectiveness of the discrimination-training procedure employed by the counselor.

Answers:

1. Increase in frequency of speaking about List A topics.
2. Decrease in frequency of speaking about List B topics. (Chapters 7 and 16.)

(1) 4. How was Mr. Munsen's leaving the house negatively reinforced?

Answer: By leaving the house, Mr. Munsen terminated Mrs. Munsen's nagging and criticizing. Thus, his response of leaving the house was negatively reinforced. (Chapter 13.)

ANSWERS FOR CASE STUDY 5

(2) 1. State two desired behaviors that could be included in treatment goals appropriate to Mr. Lewis's problem of nonassertion.

Answers: The following would be appropriate desired behaviors for Mr. Lewis: (1) Mr. Lewis asks his boss for a raise. (2) Mr. Lewis states his opinions to his boss. (3) Mr. Lewis speaks to his boss in a clear, firm voice, with his hands at his side. (4) Mr. Lewis speaks to a woman in a clear, firm voice with his hands at his side. (5) Mr. Lewis appropriately defends his rights in a conversation with his boss. (Chapter 9.)

(2) 2. Describe two role-playing techniques that could be used as part of Mr. Lewis's treatment if he were participating in group therapy.

Answers: The following role-playing techniques could be used as part of Mr. Lewis's treatment: (1) Modeling—a group member demonstrates appropriate behaviors in role plays of problematic situations; Mr. Lewis appropriately imitates the modeled behaviors (and is positively reinforced). (2) Role reversal—Mr. Lewis role plays the part of his boss, for example, and another group member role plays Mr. Lewis to demonstrate appropriate behaviors and to demonstrate how Mr. Lewis's nonassertive behaviors serve as antecedents for his boss's responses. (3) Behavioral rehearsal—Mr. Lewis practices appropriate behaviors in role plays of problematic situations and is reinforced by the therapist and group members for appropriate performance. (Chapter 11.)

(2) 3. Describe a procedure that Mr. Lewis could use to establish himself as a conditioned reinforcer for his dates.

Criteria for correct answer: Your answer should show Mr. Lewis's arrangement of conditions so that he is associated as an S^D with a variety of unconditioned and conditioned positive reinforcers delivered on a noncontingent basis.

Sample answer: Mr. Lewis could invite a woman out for dinner, bring her flowers or candy, talk about her interests during the meal, and take her dancing afterwards. He does these things noncontingently, that is, no specific behaviors are required of the woman to obtain these rewards. As these items appear to be rewarding to the woman, Mr. Lewis becomes associated with their delivery; he is the S^D for her responses that lead to the availability of the reinforcers. Mr. Lewis thus begins to acquire reinforcing value for the woman. (Chapter 10.)

ANSWERS FOR CASE STUDY 6

(2) 1. State the inappropriate behaviors emitted by Mr. Potts during criticism.
Answers:

Mr. Potts:

1. rapped his knuckles against each other and
2. made excuses. (Note: The other behaviors were elicited, not emitted.) (Chapters 2 and 14.)

(3) 2. How could a modeling-plus-reinforcement procedure have been used to help Mr. Potts obtain a new job?

Answer: Group members could model appropriate behaviors for Mr. Potts in role plays of job interviews. When Mr. Potts imitated these appropriate behaviors in role plays, he would receive positive reinforcement from the group members and therapist. (Chapter 11.)

(2) 3. What reinforcement was arranged for Mr. Potts in the treatment situation, and what were the conditions for its delivery?

Answer: The therapist and group members praised Mr. Potts as soon as he responded appropriately in role plays. (Chapter 2.)

(4) 4. List Mr. Potts's respondent behaviors elicited by criticism.

Answers: The following respondent behaviors were elicited during criticism: (1) Mr. Potts's hands trembled, (2) his breathing became more rapid, (3) he perspired heavily, and (4) his face turned red. (Chapter 14.)

(2) 5. Identify the behavioral procedures that were used to promote generalization of desired behavior change from the group treatment setting to Mr. Potts's natural environment.

Answers:

1. Behavioral rehearsal was used in the group treatment setting to provide Mr. Potts with an opportunity to become more skillful in performing appropriate behaviors in his natural environment.

2. Behavioral assignments were given to Mr. Potts so that he would practice appropriate behaviors learned in the group setting in his natural environment. (Chapter 15.)

ANSWERS FOR CASE STUDY 7

(5) 1. List five contingencies Mrs. Drake carried out with Stephen and Dianne.

Answers: (1) If Dianne teased and made faces at Stephen, she would lose privileges such as watching television and having a bedtime snack. (2) If Stephen hit Dianne, he was told to go to his room. (3) If Stephen refused to go to his room, Mrs. Drake would physically move Stephen to his room where he was to remain for fifteen minutes. (4) If Stephen kicked or cursed Mrs. Drake, the time in the room was extended by five minutes. (5) If he screamed or made loud noises while in the room, his time was extended by five minutes. (Chapters 4 and 12.)

(3) 2. Name the behavioral principle that was the basis for the punishment administered to Stephen and Dianne. Name the reinforcers involved for Stephen and Dianne.

Answers: Both procedures involved response-contingent removal of positive reinforcers. The positive reinforcers for Stephen were Mrs. Drake's attention and Dianne's crying when Stephen hit her. The positive reinforcers for Dianne were privileges such as television and bedtime snacks. (Chapter 12.)

(2) 3. The therapist told Mrs. Drake to spend time with Stephen in the evenings and to play cards with him. The goal was to increase social behaviors

performed by mother and son that would be positively reinforced by each other. Describe two possible situations that would indicate that this goal was being achieved.

Criteria for correct answers: Your answers should include information that some behaviors related to time spent together by Mrs. Drake and Stephen have increased over their previous rate. The behaviors should be positive or rewarding in contrast to the verbal reprimands and physical punishment by Mrs. Drake and the cursing and kicking by Stephen that characterized their past interactions.

Sample answers: (1) Mrs. Drake reports that Stephen is telling her many things about his school activities that he never talked about before. (2) Stephen asks Mrs. Drake to read to him. (3) Mrs. Drake reports speaking in a mild tone of voice to Stephen more often. (4) Mrs. Drake reports that she puts her arm around Stephen more often. (Chapter 12.)

(6) 4. Describe a shaping procedure Mrs. Drake could have used to establish cooperative play behaviors between Stephen and Dianne.

Criteria for correct answer: Your answer must include the following steps of a shaping procedure: (1) specification of the terminal behavior, (2) specification of reinforcers, (3) specification of initial and intermediate responses, (4) reinforcement of initial response until it occurs consistently, (5) shift criteria for reinforcement to next intermediate response, (6) continue to reinforce one response, then shift criteria to next intermediate response until terminal behavior is achieved, (7) reinforce the terminal behavior.

Sample answers: The terminal behavior is that Stephen and Dianne play a game together for fifteen minutes without physical or verbal attacks. Reinforcers used are pennies and gumdrops. The initial response is they are both in the same room engaged in separate activities. Intermediate responses include their sitting next to each other, playing different games; asking and agreeing to play a game together. Initially, Mrs. Drake would reinforce Stephen and Dianne when they were both in the same room playing different gaes. When those responses occurred consistently, Mrs. Drake would shift the criterion for reinforcement to the next intermediate response, sitting next to each other playing different games. When these responses occurred consistently, Mrs. Drake would shift the criterion for reinforcement to the next intermediate response. This procedure of reinforcing one response until it occurs consistently, then shifting the criterion for reinforcement to the next intermediate response continues until the terminal behavior is performed. The terminal behavior is reinforced. (Mrs. Drake could also model appropriate behaviors or use verbal instructions in conjunction with a shaping procedure.) (Chapter 6.)

ANSWERS FOR CASE STUDY 8

(4) 1. Specify the target behaviors and their negative consequences for Mrs. Gomez and Mr. Terry.

Answers: The target behaviors were: (1) asking questions and making comments unrelated to topics being discussed; (2) talking continuously for five minutes or more without pausing for others to respond.

The negative consequences were: (1) ridicule and (2) exclusion from conversations held by other group members. (Chapter 8.)

(3) 2. State three measurable goals of the procedure carried out by the psychiatric nurse.

Answers: Goals of the treatment procedure were: (1) to decrease inappropriate questions and comments, (2) to increase Mrs. Gomez's and Mr. Terry's appropriate speech during conversations, (3) to decrease the amount of time each spoke without a pause, and (4) to increase Mrs. Gomez's and Mr. Terry's participation in appropriate conversations with staff and relatives. (Chapter 9.)

(2) 3. Describe two behavioral techniques the psychiatric nurse could use to help Mrs. Gomez and Mr. Terry generalize appropriate verbal behavior outside the group.

The nurse could give Mrs. Gomez and Mr. Terry behavioral assignments in which they would be required to practice the desired verbal behaviors outside the group setting; behavioral rehearsal could also be used in the group setting to allow Mrs. Gomez and Mr. Terry to practice appropriate verbal behavior with reinforcement. (Chapter 15.)

(2) 4. Describe (a) a reinforcer that was given in the group to Mrs. Gomez and Mr. Terry contingent on appropriate speech and (b) a possible reinforcer that would maintain their appropriate speech outside the group.

Answers: (a) The nurse and group members complimented and praised Mrs. Gomez and Mr. Terry when they made appropriate statements during the conversation exercise. (b) Reinforcers outside the group could include other persons involving them in their conversations; staff or relatives reinforcing appropriate speech with praise, attention, interest. (Chapters 2 and 15.)

Total Possible: 89
Criterion Score: 80

APPENDIX

1

CASE STUDIES

CASE STUDY 1

Behavioral Assessment of Drug Abuse

Harold, a twelve-year-old junior high school student, started smoking marijuana six months ago at a party given by one of his friends. He enjoyed that experience and continued his experimentation with other drugs, including amphetamines and barbiturates. During the past few months, Harold has failed to complete his class assignments, sometimes handing in a blank sheet of paper. His midterm report card showed four Fs and one C in a crafts course. Harold's parents, Mr. and Mrs. Townsend, were concerned that he might drop out of school or not pass to the next level. About this time, Mrs. Townsend found a marijuana cigarette and some of her diet pills in Harold's desk drawer. When confronted with this evidence, Harold admitted to taking drugs, but argued that they did not interfere with his functioning in school or at home.

Shortly after the midterm grades came out, a teacher referred Harold to the school social worker, describing Harold as being "inattentive in the classroom, poorly motivated, and having a negative attitude toward learning." He was failing most of his classes.

Harold complained to the school social worker that his parents frequently grounded him, nagged him, withheld his allowance, and denied him privileges such as watching television and going out with his friends. Upon further questioning, Harold revealed that his parents' disciplinary measures were applied because of his failing grades. Harold admitted that he, too, was worried about flunking out of school, and conceded that his drug taking might be interfering with his studying. When asked to describe his drug taking, Harold indicated that he smoked pot regularly with his friends and took pep pills and downers occasionally. Harold indicated that when he started studying, his friends often invited him over to listen to records and get stoned. He also spent many evenings at his girlfriend's home and they usually began the evening by taking some pills. When he was home alone, Harold would look in his notebook for his class assignments, smoke two or three joints before beginning them, and complete only part of his assignments or none of them at all.

After several sessions, Harold said that he was beginning to recognize the relationship between his poor school performance and drug taking.

CASE STUDY 2

Decreasing Tantrum Behaviors

In a group of parents who were learning child management skills, Carla's mother, Mrs. Hernandez, told the social worker that almost every time she told Carla to put her toys away, Carla screamed. Mrs. Hernandez would attempt to placate her by promising to buy her new clothes and by putting Carla's toys away herself.

Mrs. Hernandez was instructed to stop making promises to Carla when she screamed about putting away her toys, and to walk away from Carla when she did this. She was told that Carla's screaming might get worse before it got better, but that if she held firm, Carla's screaming would gradually decrease. Mrs. Hernandez carried out these instructions for five days, during which time Carla's screaming gradually decreased. By the sixth day, Carla no longer screamed when told to put her toys away.

The social worker also instructed Mrs. Hernandez to praise Carla and give her reinforcers, such as gum or cookies, when she put her toys away. Mrs. Hernandez followed these instructions and Carla began putting her toys away more frequently.

CASE STUDY 3

Conditioning Verbal Behavior

Mr. Clark was a 45-year-old patient who had been on a back ward of a mental hospital for eleven years. He was described by ward staff as mute and withdrawn. He spent much of the day sitting in a chair looking at the floor or pacing up and down the halls of the ward. Mr. Clark remained silent when spoken to and did not initiate conversation with patients or staff.

The treatment procedure consisted of placing Mr. Clark in a room where slides of animals, people, and landscapes were shown to him through a slide projector. Mr. Clark was asked to talk about the pictures when he saw a green light appear on a panel. When the green light was off, the psychologist spoke about the pictures and Mr. Clark was asked to silently look at them. When the green light was turned on, Mr. Clark was instructed to speak. When Mr. Clark made any speech sound he was given a piece of candy. A counter registered one point for each sound that Mr. Clark made. In addition, the psychologist said "good" immediately after each sound. An automatic recorder counted each second of speech as one response.

Mr. Clark made no speech sounds during the initial treatment session, only 5 responses the second session, and 48 responses during the fifth session. During the tenth treatment session, Mr. Clark said 76 words, such as "boy and girl," "cat," "house and yard." During the next five sessions, the psychologist asked Mr. Clark specific questions about the content of the slides and gave Mr. Clark hints that facilitated correct responding. On the fifteenth session Mr. Clark appropriately described a slide as follows: "A boy and girl are playing on the swing."

After 15 sessions, ward staff reported that for the first time in many years Mr. Clark had spoken to several persons and had made short replies to comments directed to him by staff.

CASE STUDY 4

Stimulus Control of Marital Interaction

Mrs. Munsen consulted a marriage counselor about her marital difficulties. Her husband refused to see the counselor with her. Mrs. Munsen complained that her husband ran around town drinking with his male friends during the evenings and spent little time with her and their children. They rarely went to the movies or to other entertainment, and Mrs. Munsen did all the food shopping by herself. She had stopped making his breakfast as a result of their frequent arguments before he left for work.

Mrs. Munsen berated her husband for going out with his friends, for not helping her around the house, and for not spending time with her and their children. Mr. Munsen responded to her criticism by swearing at her and telling her to mind her own business. Mrs. Munsen became so upset during these arguments that she ran into her room and locked the door, remaining there until Mr. Munsen left the house.

In her interviews with Mrs. Munsen, the marriage counselor determined that Mr. and Mrs. Munsen rarely discussed topics of mutual interest. Their conversations revolved around Mrs. Munsen's complaints and Mr. Munsen's abusive responses to them. Mrs. Munsen said that she would like to have more satisfying conversations with her husband and felt that improvement in this area was her primary concern.

In order to initiate changes in the focus of their interactions from complaints and arguments to more pleasant conversation, the counselor instructed Mrs. Munsen to make a list of topics that she should discuss with her husband (List A). These topics included his work, the two children, and camping. Mrs. Munsen made a second list of topics that she should not discuss with her husband (List B). Topics on the second list included complaints such as his staying out late at night, watching television at his friends' homes, not taking Mrs. Munsen shopping or to the movies, and not spending time with his family. Mrs. Munsen was also instructed to greet Mr. Munsen with a kiss when he came home from his job, and to ask him how his work had gone.

In the counselor's office, when Mrs. Munsen discussed topics from List A, the counselor praised her and engaged in conversation with her. When Mrs. Munsen discussed topics on List B, the counselor did not reply. Mrs. Munsen's talking about topics on List A increased in frequency, while her talking about topics on List B decreased in frequency.

CASE STUDY 5

Behavioral Assessment of Nonassertiveness

Mr. Lewis is a 30-year-old unmarried man who seeks assistance for his difficulty in establishing and maintaining satisfying relationships with women. He complains that women find him unpleasant to be around, and he never knows what to say in their presence. Of the last four women Mr. Lewis has taken out, all have refused a second date. Mr. Lewis only has one male friend.

Mr. Lewis is a bookkeeper for a clothing manufacturer. He has worked for the same firm for nine years. Although he was promised a promotion and raise two years ago, he still earns the same salary and is at the same position he was in when he first began with the company. He has never discussed his feelings about being treated unfairly with his boss, although other employees in similar circumstances have benefited from doing so.

The therapist asked Mr. Lewis to describe his experience on the last date he had. Mr. Lewis said that they were having coffee in a restaurant after seeing a movie, and he could not think of interesting things to say to his date. He concluded that he just "bored her to death" talking about his work. When the therapist asked Mr. Lewis to describe his date's conversation, Mr. Lewis said he couldn't remember much about what she said, since he was so concerned about making a good impression. On one occasion, Mr. Lewis said a young woman fell asleep while he was trying to explain a complicated bookkeeping procedure. The therapist observed that Mr. Lewis kept his head down during the interview, and often held his hand in front of his mouth when speaking so that his speech was difficult to understand. He sometimes drifted from one topic to another without waiting for the therapist's response to what he had said, and he frequently spoke in a monotone.

The therapist asked Mr. Lewis to describe his last conversation with his boss. Mr. Lewis was seated across the desk from his boss who asked him what he wanted. Mr. Lewis mumbled, looked down at the floor, and began to talk about his financial problems. When the boss responded by asking Mr. Lewis why he could not manage his finances properly, Mr. Lewis stammered and tried to defend his way of managing money. Finally, Mr. Lewis mumbled, "I'm sorry," and walked out, without raising the issues of his promotion and salary increase.

Upon further questioning, Mr. Lewis indicated that he often found himself being taken advantage of in situations in which he should have stated his opinions or defended his rights. Mr. Lewis said that he hoped to improve this situation through therapy and would cooperate with the therapist's recommendations. The therapist gave Mr. Lewis an assignment to record significant information about the situations in which he felt exploited.

CASE STUDY 6

Developing Appropriate Behaviors in Group Treatment

At a group therapy meeting, Mr. Potts complained of frequent "anxiety and depression." He had recently been laid off from his job, was bored, and had no outside interests. He spent most of his time sleeping or watching television.

In asking Mr. Potts to specify the behavioral components of his anxiety and depression, it was found that Mr. Potts felt "anxious" in situations where he was criticized by his wife or employer. He often felt "depressed" after these encounters. In a role play of these situations, Mr. Potts perspired heavily, his face turned red, his breathing became more rapid, and he rapped his knuckles against each other. His hands trembled and he made excuses as he replied to the criticism.

Mr. Potts and members of the group role played situations in which Mr. Potts was criticized by his employer and his wife in order to assess his current behavior patterns. When Mr. Potts disagreed with the group members' analysis of his situation, role plays were conducted to allow Mr. Potts to observe someone else demonstrating his problematic behaviors and their effects on others.

In order to demonstrate appropriate responses to criticism, several group members played the part of Mr. Potts in role plays and responded appropriately to criticism. Afterwards, Mr. Potts played himself in role plays of the criticism situations. When Mr. Potts had difficulty imitating the appropriate behaviors, the therapist prompted him in making the appropriate responses. Mr. Potts practiced responding appropriately in role plays and received praise from the therapist and group members as soon as he demonstrated appropriate behaviors. Assignments were given to Mr. Potts to perform the behaviors practiced in the group in his natural environment.

Similar procedures were used to help Mr. Potts prepare for an interview for a new job. He soon completed a successful job interview and was hired as a bus driver.

To deal with Mr. Potts's "boredom," the group assigned him to pursue an outside interest or hobby. Mr. Potts decided to reestablish his interest in bowling. The therapist instructed Mr. Potts to go to a bowling alley, to observe people bowling, and to discuss his experience with two persons. Shortly thereafter, he and his wife joined a bowling league.

CASE STUDY 7

The Parent as a Behavior Modifier

Mrs. Drake complained to a therapist at a community mental health center that she found it impossible to discipline her 9-year-old son, Stephen. He frequently hit his younger sister Dianne, making her cry and inflicting bruises. He sometimes broke her toys during these incidents. When Mrs. Drake intervened to stop Stephen from hitting Dianne, Stephen cursed and kicked Mrs. Drake. Verbal reprimands, threats, and attempts to physically punish Stephen failed to eliminate his undesired behaviors.

The therapist instructed Mrs. Drake to monitor situations in which the hitting occurred. Mrs. Drake reported that Dianne often teased or made faces at Stephen prior to his hitting her. Mrs. Drake's report also indicated that she spent most of her time in the evenings trying to discipline Stephen.

Treatment consisted of Mrs. Drake telling Dianne to stop teasing and making faces at Stephen, with the contingency arranged that if she teased and made faces she would lose privileges, such as watching television or having a bedtime snack. On two subsequent occasions, Dianne lost television privileges and a bedtime snack. After these two experiences, Dianne stopped teasing and making faces at Stephen.

Treatment further consisted of instructing Mrs. Drake to tell Stephen to go to his room when he hit Dianne. If he refused to obey, Mrs. Drake would physically carry or move Stephen to his room, where he was required to remain by himself for 15 minutes. If he kicked or cursed Mrs. Drake, the time was extended 5 minutes. If he screamed or made loud noises while in his room, the time was also extended 5 minutes.

The first time Mrs. Drake took Stephen to his room, he kicked and cursed. He also screamed while in the room. Stephen remained in his room for 25 minutes. The same thing happened the second time. The third time Mrs. Drake instituted the treatment procedure, Stephen stopped cursing and kicking her. The fourth time the procedure was applied, Stephen went to the room by himself and quietly remained there until his time was up. After the fifth time the procedure was employed, Stephen no longer hit his sister.

Mrs. Drake was also instructed to spend leisure time with Stephen in the evenings. Since Stephen liked to play cards with his mother, she was to play cards with him in the evenings.

CASE STUDY 8

Developing Appropriate Conversation

Mrs. Gomez and Mr. Terry were elderly participants in an outpatient treatment group for discharged mental patients. In social situations they often asked questions and made comments that were unrelated to the topic being discussed. For example, when several group members were discussing a recent film, Mr. Terry asked the person speaking if he was going grocery shopping that afternoon. In addition, Mrs. Gomez and Mr. Terry were frequently observed talking continuously for five minutes or more without pausing for responses from others. These speech patterns resulted in their being ridiculed and excluded from many conversations held by other group members.

The psychiatric nurse devised a conversational exercise to be played by the six members of a group in which Mrs. Gomez and Mr. Terry participated. The nurse began the exercise by making a statement, and each of the other group members added a statement to her introduction. Each statement was required to bear logical connection to the previous statement.

At first Mrs. Gomez and Mr. Terry both added inappropriate statements to the previous ones. On these occasions they were stopped by the nurse or group members, who required them to make appropriate statements and complimented or praised them for doing so. Group members prompted Mrs. Gomez and Mr. Terry, offering hints and suggestions for correct statements. As they practiced the exercise on subsequent occasions, both Mrs. Gomez and Mr. Terry made fewer inappropriate remarks and increasingly more appropriate ones. The frequency of their appropriate remarks during conversations outside the group was also observed to increase. Appropriate speech was reinforced by staff and relatives.

APPENDIX

2

COURSE PRETEST

QUESTIONS FOR CASE STUDY 2
(SEE PAGE 200)

(2) 1. What were the two goals of the program carried out by Mrs. Hernandez?

(2) 2. What were the measures used to determine movement toward the goals?

(1) 3. What phenomenon was the social worker describing when he told Mrs. Hernandez that Carla's screaming might increase in severity at first?

(2) 4. What two conditions were maintaining Carla's screaming prior to treatment?

QUESTIONS FOR CASE STUDY 6
(SEE PAGE 228)

(2) 1. State the inappropriate behaviors emitted by Mr. Potts during criticism.

(3) 2. How could a modeling-plus-reinforcement procedure have been used to help Mr. Potts obtain a new job?

(1) 3. What was the rationale for the bowling assignment as a way to treat Mr. Potts's boredom?

(2) 4. What type of reinforcement was planned for Mr. Potts in the treatment situation and what were the conditions for its delivery?

(2) 5. Identify the behavioral procedures that were used to promote generalization of desired behavior change from the group treatment setting to Mr. Potts's natural environment.

QUESTIONS FOR CASE STUDY 7
(SEE PAGES 228–229)

(5) 1. List five contingencies Mrs. Drake carried out with Stephen and Dianne.

(3) 2. Name the procedure that describes Mrs. Drake's interventions with Dianne. Describe an incident in which this procedure might be used.

(2) 3. The therapist told Mrs. Drake to spend time with Stephen in the evenings, and to play cards with him. The goal was to increase social behaviors performed by mother and son, which would be positively reinforced by each other. Describe two possible situations that would indicate that this goal was being achieved.

APPENDIX

3

COURSE PRETEST ANSWERS

ANSWERS FOR CASE STUDY 2

(2) 1. What were the two goals of the program carried out by Mrs. Hernandez?

Answers: The goals of the program were (1) to decrease the frequency of Carla's screaming about putting her toys away and (2) to increase the frequency of Carla's putting her toys away.

(2) 2. What were the measures used to determine movement toward the goals?

Answers: The measures used to determine movement toward the goals were (1) the decrease in frequency of Carla's screaming and (2) the increase in the frequency of Carla's putting her toys away.

(1) 3. What phenomenon was the social worker describing when he told Mrs. Hernandez that Carla's screaming might increase in severity at first?

Answer: The social worker informed Mrs. Hernandez about a typical *extinction* phenomenon, the increase in severity of a target behavior when the extinction procedure is first instituted.

(2) 4. What two conditions were maintaining Carla's screaming prior to treatment?

Answers: Carla's mother was maintaining Carla's screaming by (1) promising to buy her new clothes and (2) putting her toys away.

ANSWERS FOR CASE STUDY 6

(2) 1. State the inappropriate behaviors emitted by Mr. Potts during criticism.

Answers: During criticism, Mr. Potts (1) rapped his knuckles against each other and (2) made excuses. (Note: The other behaviors were elicited, not emitted; they constitute incorrect answers if included.)

(3) 2. How could a modeling-plus-reinforcement procedure have been used to help Mr. Potts obtain a new job?

Answer: Group members could model appropriate behaviors for Mr. Potts in role plays of job interviews. When Mr. Potts imitated these appropriate behaviors in role plays, he would receive positive reinforcement from the group members and therapist.

(1)   3.   What was the rationale for the bowling assignment as a way to treat Mr. Potts's boredom?

Answer: The bowling assignment was a way to establish appropriate behaviors that could be reinforced in Mr. Potts's natural environment. These behaviors would be incompatible with boredom, that is, sleeping and watching television all day.

(2)   4.   What type of reinforcement was planned for Mr. Potts in the treatment situation and what were the conditions for its delivery?

Answer: The therapist and group members praised Mr. Potts as soon as he responded appropriately in role plays.

(2)   5.   Identify the behavioral procedures that were used to promote generalization of desired behavior change from the group treatment setting to Mr. Potts's natural environment.

Answers:

1.   Behavioral rehearsal was used in the group treatment setting to provide Mr. Potts with an opportunity to become more skillful in his ability to perform appropriate behaviors in his natural environment.

2.   Behavioral assignments were given to Mr. Potts so that he would practice appropriate behaviors learned in the group setting in his natural environment.

ANSWERS FOR CASE STUDY 7

(5)   1.   List five contingencies Mrs. Drake carried out with Stephen and Dianne.

Answers: (1) If Dianne teased and made faces at Stephen, she would lose privileges such as watching TV or having a bedtime snack. (2) If Stephen hit Dianne, he was told to go to his room. (3) If Stephen refused to go to his room, Mrs. Drake would physically move Stephen to his room where he was to remain for 15 minutes. (4) If Stephen kicked or cursed Mrs. Drake, the time in the room was extended by 5 minutes. (5) If he screamed or made loud noises while in the room, his time was extended by 5 minutes.

(3)   2.   Name the procedure that describes Mrs. Drake's interventions with Dianne. Describe an incident in which the procedure might be used.

Answer: Response-contingent punishment by removal of positive reinforcers was the procedure used by Mrs. Drake with Dianne. If Dianne teased or made faces at Stephen, she would lose privileges such as watching television or having a bedtime snack.

(2)   3.   The therapist told Mrs. Drake to spend time with Stephen in the evenings, and to play cards with him. The goal was to increase social behaviors performed by mother and son, which would be positively reinforced by each

other. Describe the two possible situations that would indicate that this goal was being achieved.

Criterion for correct answers: Your answers should include information that some behaviors related to time spent together by Mrs. Drake and Stephen have increased over their previous rate. The behaviors should be positive or rewarding, in contrast to the verbal reprimands and physical punishment by Mrs. Drake and the cursing and kicking by Stephen that characterized their past interactions.

Sample answers: (1) Mrs. Drake reports that Stephen is telling her many things about his school activities that he never talked about before. (2) Stephen asks Mrs. Drake to read to him. (3) Mrs. Drake reports speaking in a mild tone of voice to Stephen more often. (4) Mrs. Drake reports that she puts her arm around Stephen more often.

The total point value of this Course Pretest is 27. For guidelines in scoring your answers, see page xviii.

Criterion score for this test is 24.

APPENDIX

4

CHAPTER PRETEST ANSWERS

CHAPTER 1

(2) 1. State two essential criteria for specifying a response.

Answers:

Two essential criteria for specifying a response are:

(1) the response is stated in *positive* terms and

(2) it refers to *observable* actions; that is, what the individual says or does.

(6) 2. A. Indicate with a (+) which of the following statements are written in behaviorally specific terms, and indicate with a (−) statements that are vague and require further specification.

Criteria for correct answers:

Responses describe what the person *says* or *does* in *positively stated, observable* terms. Responses stated negatively are incorrect. Sample answers follow those statements that required further specification.

Answers: Statements a and c are correct as written; statements b and d require further specification.

B. After completing 2A above, rewrite in specific terms only those statements in which the responses are not described behaviorally.

+ a. Ted saw three clients today and made four phone calls.

− b. Bob is becoming a drug addict.

Sample answer:

Bob takes sleeping pills at night and amphetamines in the morning.

+ c. Bruce kissed Sally on the cheek.

− d. She acted out her anger toward him.

Sample answer:

She threw his new fishing rod in the garbage.

(1) 3. Name the most commonly used measure of response strength.

Answer: Frequency per time unit or rate.

The total point value of this test is 9. Score one point for each of the two parts of question 1; score one point for each correctly identified statement in question 2A and one point for each correctly rewritten statement in question 2B. Score one point for a correct answer to question 3. For guidelines in scoring your answers, see page xviii.

Criterion score for this test is 8. If your score is at least 8, you may take the post-test for this chapter. If you score less than 8, read the chapter before you take the post-test.

CHAPTER 2

(1) 1. In order to maximize the effectiveness of a positive reinforcer for a specific response, when should the positive reinforcer be delivered?

Answer: The reinforcer should be delivered *immediately after* the response is performed.

(4) 2. List the four outcomes or directions in which a target behavior can be modified.

Answers:

Modification techniques can be applied so that a behavior is (1) acquired or established, (2) increased or strengthened, (3) maintained at a particular strength or pattern of occurrence, or (4) decreased or weakened.

(1) 3. It has been demonstrated that presentation of a certain event following a behavior can increase the likelihood that the behavior will recur. Name the behavioral principle to which this statement refers.

Answer: Positive reinforcement.

(3) 4. In the example that begins this chapter, what behavior did the caseworker positively reinforce? What were the reinforcers?

Answers: The caseworker reinforced Mr. Mosley's coming late to his appointments. The reinforcers were the warm greeting and extra time at the end of the session.

The total point value of this test is 9. The distribution of points is indicated next to each question.

Criterion score: 8

CHAPTER 3

(4) 1. Renumber the following steps so that they are in the correct order to carry out the procedure that you would use to determine if a specific stimulus served as a positive reinforcer for a target behavior.

Answers:

_____2_____ 1. Withhold the stimulus continuously, that is, each time the target response occurs.

<u>   1   </u>   2. Determine the frequency of target behavior.

<u>   3   </u>   3. Observe decrease in frequency of target behavior.

<u>   4   </u>   4. Present stimulus after the target behavior occurs and observe an increase in its frequency.

(2)   2. What are two practical difficulties you might encounter in applying an extinction procedure to decrease the frequency of an undesired response?

Answers:

1. Withholding the reinforcer each time the response occurs.

2. Making sure that the client is not reinforced for the behavior by someone else.

(1)   3. What is spontaneous recovery?

Answer: The recurrence of an extinguished response at a future time in a situation similar to the one in which the behavior was reinforced.

(2)   4. Describe the extinction procedure and its effect.

Answer: The extinction procedure consists of withholding the positive reinforcer each time the target response is performed. The effect is a decrease in frequency of the target response to zero or a prespecified rate.

Criterion score: 8

CHAPTER 4

(4)   1. Which of the following are statements of positive reinforcement contingencies? (Circle the correct ones.)

    (a.) Finish your math assignment, and you may play outside.

    (b.) If you wash the dishes, I'll give you an ice cream cone.

    c. If you fight with your brother, you will get a spanking.

    d. He completed his chores in three hours.

(1)   2. Briefly describe how superstitious behavior is acquired.

Answer: Superstitious behavior is the result of an accidental relationship between a behavior and a reinforcer. An individual makes a response that is followed by an unplanned reinforcer that coincidentally strengthens the response.

(3)   3. Give an example of a positive reinforcement contingency you could establish to help Harold (Case Study 1) complete his class assignments.

Criteria for correct answer: Your answer must state a specified amount of school work to be completed in order for Harold to receive a specified positive reinforcer.

Sample Answer: Harold, after you complete one of your assignments, you can turn on your stereo.

(1) 4. Intermittent reinforcement makes a well-learned response more resistant to extinction. (Circle one.)

(a.) True

b. False

(1) 5. When is it more appropriate to use continuous reinforcement rather than intermittent reinforcement?

Answer: It is more appropriate to use continuous reinforcement to establish a response or to strengthen a response that occurs with low frequency.

Criterion score: 9

CHAPTER 5

(1) 1. What is the effect of increasing a ratio too quickly on a fixed-ratio schedule?

Answer: The response will extinguish (straining the ratio).

(2) 2. In fixed-interval and variable-interval schedules, what two events are required in order for reinforcement to be delivered?

Answers:

1. Passage of designated time, followed by

2. the individual making the appropriate response.

(2) 3. State two characteristics of responses maintained on ratio schedules.

Answers: Ratio schedules are characterized by (1) high rates of responding and (2) minimal hesitation between responses.

(1) 4. State one way in which fixed-ratio and variable-ratio schedules generate different behavior patterns.

Answer: Fixed-ratio schedules generate a postreinforcement pause and variable-ratio schedules do not.

(4) 5. Match the following schedules in Column A with their examples in Column B.

A		*B*
1. fixed-ratio	b	a. deadlines
2. variable-ratio	c	b. piecework
3. fixed-interval	a	c. slot machines
4. variable-interval	d	d. waiting for a taxi

Criterion score: 9.

CHAPTER 6

(1) 1. In Case Study 3, pages 49–50, Mr. Clark's speech could be developed by (circle one correct answer):

   a. extinction
   b. intermittent reinforcement
   c. shaping with successive approximations
   d. differential reinforcement of approximation of incompatible responses

(1) 2. In order to shape a new behavior, you would not use differential reinforcement. (Circle one.)

   a. True
   b. False

(2) 3. For the response class "talking about sports," name two responses.

   Criterion for correct answers: Each member of the response class must have the same effect on the environment, for example, reinforced by conversation.

   Sample Answers:

   Discussing players' batting averages.

   Talking about the hockey game coming up.

   Discussing football strategy.

(2) 4. How are positive reinforcement and extinction involved in differential reinforcement?

   Answer: Responses that meet specific criteria are *positively reinforced,* while reinforcement is withheld continuously from other responses, that is, they are *extinguished.*

(2) 5. Give an example of a DRO procedure that could be used to decrease Carla's screaming (Case Study 2).

   Answer: Carla's mother could reinforce any behaviors Carla performed other than screaming, such as helping her mother put groceries away, fixing a broken toy, or playing quietly by herself. Reinforcement is thus withheld for the undesired screaming and appropriate behaviors are strengthened.

   Criterion score: 7

CHAPTER 7

(2) 1. What is an S^D for a response? What is an S^Δ?

   Answers: An S^D is a discriminative stimulus that signals or sets the occasion for a response made in its presence to be reinforced. An S^Δ is a discriminative stimulus that signals or sets the occasion for a response made in its presence not to be followed by a reinforcer.

(1) 2. What is the effect of a discrimination procedure involving two discriminative stimuli (S^D and S^Δ) and one response?

Answer: Stimulus control; the response rate in the presence of S^D increases, and the response rate in the presence of S^Δ decreases.

(1)   3.   In Case Study 3, what function did the green light serve?

Answer: When the green light was on, Mr. Clark's speech was reinforced; when the green light was off, his speech was not reinforced. The green light on, therefore, served as an S^D for Mr. Clark's speech.

(6)   4.   In the following examples, identify the discriminative stimulus, the response and the reinforcer by labeling the S^D, R, and S^+, in the paradigms.

   a.   Bob sees Joe walking down the street. Bob says, "hello," and Joe says, "good morning."

Answer:

S^D
sight of Joe walking down the street
R ——————————————————————→ S^+
Bob says "hello"   Joe says "good morning"

   b.   Shirley hears the ice cream truck, asks her aunt for a quarter, and buys an ice cream cone.

Answer:

S^D
sound of ice cream truck
R ——————————————————————→ S^+
Shirley asks her aunt for a quarter   ice cream cone

(1)   5.   True or False. When a response is reinforced in the presence of one S^D, it will not occur in the presence of other similar stimuli.
Answer: False

Criterion score: 10

CHAPTER 8

(2)   1.   Rewrite the following sentences so that the strength of the response is stated in measurable terms.

Criterion for correct answers: The sentence must state the strength of the response in measurable terms such as frequency/time (rate), duration, intensity, or latency.

   a.   Hortense has repeatedly phoned the adoption agency.

Sample answer: Hortense phoned the adoption agency 10 times this month.

b.   Roger rarely kisses his wife.

Sample answer: Roger kissed his wife 2 times last week.

(2)   2.   In Case Study 8 (see Appendix 1), what were the behavioral excesses shown by Mrs. Gomez and Mr. Terry?

Answers: The behavioral excesses shown by Mrs. Gomez and Mr. Terry were (1) asking questions and making comments unrelated to topics being discussed, and (2) talking continuously for 5 minutes or more without pausing for responses from others.

(2)   3.   What were the negative consequences of these behaviors?

Answers: Mrs. Gomez and Mr. Terry were (1) ridiculed and (2) excluded from many conversations.

(3)   4.   From the information given in the following paragraph, identify Henry's target responses, the antecedent, and the negative consequences.

When someone comes over to talk to Henry or ask him a question, he mutters and speaks in a low voice so that the person has difficulty hearing what he is saying. The person typically stops talking and walks away from Henry soon after he begins to mutter.

Answers:

Henry's target responses: Henry mutters and speaks in a low voice. Antecedent: Someone starts talking to Henry or asks him a question. Negative consequences: The person stops talking and walks away.

(2)   4.   State two criteria that can be used in establishing problem priorities for treatment.

Answers: The following four criteria can be used in establishing problem priorities for treatment:

1.   the problem that is the most immediate expressed concern of the client or significant others.

2.   the problem that has extensive negative consequences for the client, significant others, or society if not handled immediately,

3.   the problem that can be corrected most quickly, considering resources and obstacles, and

4.   the problem that requires handling before other problems can be treated.

Criterion score: 10

CHAPTER 9

(1)   1.   Which of the following statements best describes the purpose of behavioral assessment? (Circle the correct answer.)

a.   Reconstruct an individual's personality.

b.   Help a person learn to accept him or herself.

       c.   Specify appropriate behaviors.

       (d.) Identify target behaviors and their controlling conditions, and formulate behavioral change goals.

(3) 2. Using the information from Case Study 7 (see Appendix 1), state (a) two of Stephen's target responses, (b) the probable positive reinforcer that maintained them, and (c) the antecedent to the target responses.

    Answers:

    a.   Target responses: Stephen hit Dianne; Stephen broke Dianne's toys.

    b.   Probable reinforcer: Mrs. Drake's attention; that is, she spent most of her time trying to discipline Stephen.

    c.   Antecedent: Dianne teased, made faces at Stephen.

(1) 3. In order to determine controlling antecedents of the target behavior, an appropriate question to ask a client is (circle a or b):

    (a.) Where does this problem occur?

    b.   Why do you continue to engage in this behavior?

(3) 4. Using the information from Case Study 5 (see pages 105–106), state an intermediate treatment goal for Mr. Lewis specifying (a) a desired response and (b) a relevant antecedent.

    Criteria for correct answer: Your answers must indicate that Mr. Lewis makes an assertive response in the presence of an antecedent that previously served as an S^D for nonassertive behaviors. This response should be less difficult for Mr. Lewis to perform than the terminal goal.

    Sample answers:

    Intermediate goal: Mr. Lewis makes a legitimate request of his boss.

    Desired response: Mr. Lewis looks directly at his boss and says, "I would like to take a week off at the end of June."

    Relevant antecedent: Mr. Lewis is seated across the desk from his boss.

(1) 5. How is behavioral reenactment used in behavioral assessment?

    Answer: Behavioral reenactment is used to obtain RAC-S assessment information on the client's behaviors in the problematic situation. It is particularly useful in validating the accuracy of a client's verbal report of the target behaviors and their controlling conditions.

    Criterion score: 8

CHAPTER 10

(2) 1. Which is usually more effective, a simple conditioned reinforcer or a generalized conditioned reinforcer? Support your answer.

    Answer: Generalized conditioned reinforcers are more effective than simple conditioned reinforcers because they are associated with a wide variety of reinforcers, while simple conditioned reinforcers are associated with just one reinforcer. (Generalized conditioned reinforcers are less susceptible to the effects of satiation. If an individual is satiated with regard to one reinforcer, there are usually other reinforcers of which he or she is sufficiently deprived to ensure the effectiveness of the generalized conditioned reinforcer.)

(1) 2. What is the difference between an unconditioned reinforcer and a conditioned reinforcer?

Answer: An unconditioned reinforcer increases reponse strength without prior association with other reinforcers. A conditioned reinforcer is a neutral or nonreinforcing stimulus that becomes a reinforcer through association with a reinforcing stimulus.

(4) 3. Give two examples of generalized conditioned reinforcers and two examples of unconditioned reinforcers.

Answers: Examples of generalized conditioned reinforcers include praise ("That was very good."), money, affection (kisses, hugs, "I love you."), tokens. Examples of unconditioned reinforcers include food, water, sex, warmth, tactile stimulation.

(1) 4. True or False. In order for a neutral stimulus to function as a conditioned reinforcer, a minimum of 100 pairings is necessary.

Answer: False.

(3) 5. Identify the components of one unit of a stimulus-response chain.

Answer: The components of one unit of a stimulus-response chain consist of a discriminative stimulus (S^D), a response (R), and a conditioned reinforcer (S^{r+}) that also serves as the S^D for the following response in the chain.

Criterion score: 10

CHAPTER 11

(3) 1. Describe how a modeling-plus-reinforcement procedure can be used to develop a child's imitation of an adult using a fork correctly.

Answer: The adult models or demonstrates the proper use of a fork. The adult's behaviors serve as the modeled stimulus. When the child imitates the modeled stimulus, the adult gives the child a reinforcer. Thus, the child's imitation of the adult's behaviors is strengthened.

(3) 2. Indicate True (T) or False (F) beside each of the following statements:

a. ___F___ If an individual does not perform a response after he or she has observed someone else perform it, the individual has not learned it.

b. ___T___ It is more difficult to teach a song to a child who has no imitative skills than to a child who imitates excessively.

c. ___F___ Imitated behavior cannot be conditioned through reinforcement when the client has no imitative skills as, for example, a severely retarded child.

(3)   3.   Using the information from Vignette 6 below, how could modeling and reinforcement have been used to help Mr. Potts obtain a new job?

Answer: Group members could model appropriate job interview behaviors, e.g., speaking clearly, making eye contact, which Mr. Potts observes. He then imitates their appropriate behaviors. The therapist and group members praise Mr. Potts when he appropriately imitates desired behaviors.

Criterion score: 8

CHAPTER 12

(2)   1.   Name the two types of punishment procedures that can be used to suppress a response.

Answers:

1.   Response-contingent presentation of a punishing stimulus.

2.   Response-contingent removal of a positive reinforcer.

(1)   2.   Briefly describe a time-out procedure.

Answer: A time-out procedure consists of removing an individual from a reinforcing situation immediately after performance of an inappropriate behavior and placing him or her in an environment with minimal availability of reinforcement for a fixed, brief period of time.

(2)   3.   Briefly describe two disadvantages of punishment procedures.

Answers: Any two of the following are acceptable:

1.   The punished response is likely to reappear in the absence of the punisher.

2.   Aggression against the punisher.

3.   Aggression toward someone or something that is in no way related to the delivery of the punishment.

4.   Punishment could also suppress appropriate behaviors occurring immediately prior to its delivery.

5.   The person administering the punishment can become a conditioned aversive stimulus through association with the punisher.

6.   The person administering the punishment may be imitated by observers.

7.   The punishing stimulus can serve as an S^D for responses that are positively reinforced.

(4)   4.   Mrs. Kelly asked Sharon to fold the laundry after it had been washed and dried. When Mrs. Kelly returned, Sharon was talking to her friend on the phone and the laundry had not been folded. What should Mrs. Kelly do to demonstrate her knowledge of the necessary conditions to maximize the effectiveness of punishment?

Criteria for correct answer: Your answer must include the following points: (1) delivery of a punisher immediately after performance of the inappropriate response; (2) a punisher of sufficient intensity to suppress the inappropriate response; (3) specification of appropriate responses; and (4) positive reinforcement for appropriate responses.

Sample answer: Mrs. Kelly should tell Sharon to get off the phone and immediately punish her by telling her that she cannot visit her friends as scheduled that afternoon. Mrs. Kelly should then tell Sharon to fold the laundry and praise her for carrying out this task.

Criterion score: 8

CHAPTER 13

(1) 1. What is a major advantage of avoidance conditioning in maintaining a response?

Answer: A response that is conditioned through an avoidance procedure is highly resistant to extinction.

(3) 2. Give an example of the behavioral procedure that produces escape behavior.

Criteria for correct answer: Your answer must specify (1) a negative reinforcer that remains in effect until (2) a response is made that (3) terminates or reduces the effect of that stimulus (negative reinforcer).

Sample answer: Mr. Jackson comes home drunk and repeatedly demands that his wife have sex with him. Mrs. Jackson gives in, which silences Mr. Jackson's demands.

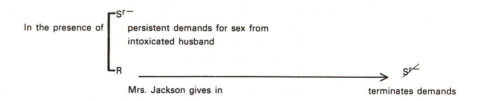

(4) 3. Give an example of the behavioral procedure that results in avoidance behavior.

Criteria for correct answer: Your answer must specify (1) a conditioned negative reinforcer that is presented as a cue for (2) a response made in its presence that (3) terminates the conditioned negative reinforcer and (4) avoids or prevents the onset of another negative reinforcer.

Sample answer: Jimmy tells Billy that he will have him investigated unless he tells him where he got the money. Billy then tells him that Libby gave it to him.

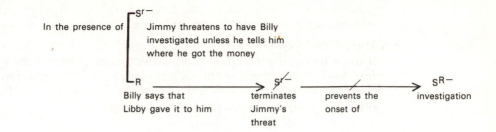

In the presence of [S^r-

Jimmy threatens to have Billy
investigated unless he tells him
where he got the money

R ———————————→ S^r- —————/————→ S^R-
Billy says that   terminates   prevents the   investigation
Libby gave it to him   Jimmy's   onset of
                         threat

(2) 4. Give an example of (a) a primary aversive stimulus that could be used as a negative reinforcer and (b) a conditioned aversive stimulus that could be used as a negative reinforcer.

Answers:

1. Primary negative reinforcers: shock, physical attacks (e.g., hitting, kicking, pinching), intense light, noise or temperature. The stimulus does not require prior pairing or association with another stimulus.

2. Conditioned negative reinforcers: threats, fines, demerits, failing grades, harsh or demeaning words, such as "idiot." The stimulus requires pairing or association with another stimulus before it can act as a negative reinforcer.

Criterion score: 9

CHAPTER 14

(1) 1. Describe a procedure for extinguishing a classically conditioned response.

Answer: Present the conditioned stimulus repeatedly without presenting the unconditioned stimulus until the conditioned stimulus no longer elicits the conditioned response.

(8) 2. Given the following information, specify operant and respondent behaviors: A man gets in his car and drives home. As he walks in the door, the aroma of dinner cooking makes his mouth water. He runs to the kitchen, panting, kisses his wife and sits down at the table.

Answers: Operants: gets in his car; drives home; walks in; runs to the kitchen; kisses his wife; sits down.

Respondents: mouth waters; panting.

(1) 3. Explain the persistence of emotional respondent behavior in the absence of identifiable reinforcing consequences for the individual.

Answer: Respondent behavior is not controlled by its consequences as is operant behavior. It is controlled by antecedents and, therefore, persists regardless of consequences, as long as the conditioned stimulus is occasionally paired with the unconditioned stimulus.

(1)   4.   How can a phobia be treated?

Answer: By pairing relaxation stimuli with the conditioned stimuli that elicit fear until the relaxation stimuli are capable of eliciting physiological responses incompatible with fear (systematic desensitization). Flooding is another technique that can be used to treat a phobia.

Criterion score: 10.

CHAPTER 15

(2)   1.   a.   You are treating an alcoholic client. As part of the treatment program to decrease his drinking, you suggest several nondrinking behaviors appropriate in the social situations where he usually drinks. These behaviors are new to him, but he agrees to try them out. What is the most likely obstacle to success for this part of therapy?

Answer: He is unlikely to perform these nondrinking behaviors in social situations either because he has never been reinforced for them, or because he does not have the skills required to perform them.

b.   What can you do to counteract this effect or to plan for this problem?

Answer: You can use behavioral rehearsal and reinforce alternative behaviors to maximize successful generalization from the treatment setting to the problematic social situations. Behavioral assignments, beginning with simple ones, can also be used to introduce these nondrinking behaviors gradually into the client's actual problematic situations.

(1)   2.   Using the information from Case Study 6, page 228, describe how behavioral rehearsal was used with Mr. Potts to facilitate generalization of appropriate responses to criticism.

Answer: The therapist and group members showed Mr. Potts how to make appropriate responses to criticism. Mr. Potts role played situations where he was criticized by his employer and his wife, demonstrating appropriate behaviors. He was praised by the therapist and group members for performing appropriately in these role plays.

(1)   3.   Behavioral assignments are given (circle the correct answer(s)):

a.   to structure the client's activities between therapy sessions.

b.   to help the client apply in her natural environment what she has learned in treatment.

c.   so the client can receive feedback from the therapist based on a specific behavior he has attempted to perform.

d.   all of the above.

(1)   4.   True or False: It is usually more difficult for a desired behavior to generalize beyond the practice setting when more than one therapist is involved in developing the behavior.

Answer: False

(3)   5.   Turn to pages 225–226 to see Case Study 3. State three ways you could maximize successful generalization of Mr. Clark's speech.

Answers: Successful generalization from therapy to ward can be promoted by:

1.   reinforcing ward staff for reinforcing Mr. Clark's speech on the ward,
2.   shifting reinforcement for Mr. Clark's speech from a continuous to an intermittent schedule,
3.   the therapist reinforcing Mr. Clark's speech on the ward,
4.   using more than one therapist to reinforce Mr. Clark's speech in the treatment setting,
5.   having the psychologist conduct additional sessions to maintain Mr. Clark's speech at a high level after Mr. Clark has achieved criterion peformance in speaking about the slides,
6.   Ward staff reinforcing Mr. Clark's speech in the treatment setting.

Criterion Score: 7

CHAPTER 16

(1)   1.   What does informed consent in a behavioral-change program refer to?

Answer: Informed consent means that the client understands the proposed treatment and voluntarily agrees to participate.

(1)   2.   An intervention plan for teaching a hospitalized mental patient self-care skills could include: (circle one)

a.   covert sensitization and modeling
b.   positive reinforcement and systematic desensitization
c.   positive reinforcement, shaping, and chaining
d.   none of the above.

(3)   3.   State three ways in which the client's progress can be evaluated.

Answers:
1.   Behavioral changes in the desired direction from baseline measures.
2.   Client's subjective perceptions of improved circumstances.
3.   Reports of significant others of improvement in the client's target behaviors.
4.   Client satisfaction with practitioner services.

(2) 4.   What is the purpose of a treatment contract?

Answer: The purpose of a treatment contract is to make explicit the client's expectations for service and the practitioner's assessment of what is required of the client and significant others.

Criterion score: 6

APPENDIX

5

CHAPTER POST-TEST ANSWERS

CHAPTER 1

(10) 1. A. Indicate with a (+) which of the following statements are written in behaviorally specific terms, and with a (−) the statements that are vague and require further specification.

Criteria for correct answers: Responses describe what the person *says* or *does* in *positively stated, observable* terms. Responses stated negatively are incorrect. Sample answers follow those statements that required further specification.

  1. B. After completing 1A above, rewrite in specific terms only those statements in which the responses are not described behaviorally.

+ a. Eddy took two cans of beer from the refrigerator.

− b. Johnny expressed his feelings of inadequacy at the ball game.

Sample answer: After striking out, Johnny threw down his bat and ran home.

− c. Norman showed hostile feelings toward his probation officer this week.

Sample answer: Every time Norman's probation officer asked him a question about school, Norman said, "Mind your own business."

− d. Mr. Smith asserted his authority over use of the car.

Sample answer: Mr. Smith kept both sets of keys to the car in his pocket.

− e. He thinks of his girlfriend often.

Sample answer: He writes letters to his girlfriend daily.

+ f. Mr. Foster said, "I can't earn enough money to make you happy."

(1) 2. In Case Study 1, pages 7-8, Harold is described as having a "negative attitude toward learning." Specify a behavior that might have led the teacher to describe him in that way.

Criterion for correct answer: Your answer must state an observable behavior emitted by Harold.

Sample answers:

1. Harold turns in incomplete assignments or blank sheets of paper.
2. Harold throws paper airplanes at other students.

(1) 3. Rewrite the following statement to include a frequency-per-time-unit (rate) measure of response strength: Mr. Foster ordered a drink from the bar.

Criterion for correct answer: Your answer must state the number of times Mr. Foster ordered a drink from the bar within a specified time period.

Sample answers:

1. Mr. Foster ordered 6 drinks from the bar in the past 45 minutes.
2. Mr. Foster ordered 1 drink from the bar in the past 6 hours.

The total point value of this test is 12. Score 1 point for each correctly identified statement in Question 1A, 1 point for each correctly written statement in Question 1-B, 1 point for a correct answer to Question 2, and 1 point for a correct answer to Question 3. For guidelines in scoring your answers, see page xviii.

Criterion score for this test is 11. If your score is at least 11, you have mastered this chapter and should go on to chapter 2. If you scored less than 11, review the chapter until you can answer the questions correctly.

CHAPTER 2

(2) 1. Define the positive reinforcement procedure and its effect on the strength of a response.

Answer: The presentation of a stimulus contingent on performance of a response (procedure) that increases the strength of that response (effect).

(2) 2. Give one example of an object or event that you think acts as a positive reinforcer for you. State your proof.

Criteria for correct answer: Any object or event is correct if evidence is given that the response increases in strength after presentation of the stimulus.

Sample answer: You go to a new hair stylist to get your hair cut. You are pleased with the results. You now go only to this hair stylist once a month.

Response: Going to new hair stylist.

Positive Reinforcer: Hair cut the way you like.

Baseline Rate of going to this hair stylist: 0 times/month

Current Rate: Once/month for the past eight months.

(3)   3.   From Case Study 1, pages 7–8, draw a paradigm showing how positive reinforcement could be used to increase the frequency of Harold's completing his class assignments, labeling the appropriate components. What evidence could be used to evaluate the effect of this procedure?

Criteria for correct answer: The positive reinforcement paradigm should be given, specifying the reinforcer used. Each component of the paradigm should be labeled as shown below. Evidence for the reinforcement effect must show that the rate of the response increased over its baseline rate.

Sample answer:

R ————————————————————————→ s⁺

| Harold shows his mother one complete assignment | is followed by | Harold receives television privileges for the evening |

Watching television serves as a positive reinforcer if the rate of Harold's completing his assignments increases over the baseline rate.

(4)   4.   Rewrite the following statements, specifying the target behaviors and indicating the baseline rates.

Criteria for correct answers: Behaviors must be specified in positively stated, observable terms and include a baseline measure of response rate (frequency/time).

a.   Hank is always annoying his brother.

Sample answer: Three times last week, Hank read the newspaper aloud while his brother practiced the violin.

Target Behavior: Reading the newspaper aloud.

Baseline Measure: Three times last week.

b.   Mary was often depressed.

Sample answer: Mary cried alone in her room four nights this week.

Target Behavior: Cried alone in her room.

Baseline Measure: Four nights this week.

(2)   5.   Correct these statements so that the effectiveness of the candy bar and the movies as positive reinforcers can be maximized.

Criteria for correct answers: The candy bar and the movies must follow the desired responses (walking the dog and washing the car) immediately.

a.   Mrs. Jones gave Edward a candy bar and asked him to take her dog for a walk.

Sample answer: As soon as Edward returned from walking the dog, Mrs. Jones gave him a candy bar.

b.   Harvey washed his father's car and his father took him to the movies three weeks later.

Sample answer: Harvey washed his father's car and his father took him to the movies immediately after he finished.

(1)   6.   Lillian goes shopping immediately after she completes her housework. How could baseline data be used to determine if going shopping served as a positive reinforcer for doing housework?

Answer: The baseline rate of Lillian's doing housework (without going shopping) is compared with the rate of doing housework and going shopping immediately after. If shopping is a positive reinforcer for housework, Lillian will do housework more frequently than during a baseline period when housework is not followed by going shopping.

Criterion score: 13.

CHAPTER 3

(3)   1.   Describe the procedure for extinguishing a response by giving an example in which you specify the response and its reinforcer.

Criteria for correct answer:

An observable response and a specific reinforcer must be stated. Your answer must state that this reinforcer is withheld each time the response is performed.

Sample answer:

Response: Client stares at the ceiling while talking to you.

Positive Reinforcer: Attention in the form of conversing with the client, looking at the client and smiling.

Extinction Procedure: Each time the client stares at the ceiling while talking to you, you remain silent, that is, you withhold your attention (conversing, looking at, smiling).

(3)   2.   After observing a mother hug her son when he cried, what would you do to determine whether or not the mother's hugging served as a positive reinforcer for the child's crying?

Answer:

1.   Determine the rate of the child's crying.
2.   Tell the mother to refrain from hugging her child each time he cried. If the child's crying decreases (even after an initial increase), it is likely that the mother's hugging served as a positive reinforcer for her son's crying.
3.   If it is important to demonstrate that the hugging did reinforce the crying, the mother should reinstate hugging her son when he cried. If the crying increases again, the mother's hugging served as a positive reinforcer for her son's crying.

(1)   3.   Describe the effects of extinction on the rate of a target response.

Answer: There is usually an initial increase or burst in the rate of responding and then a gradual decrease in the rate of the target response to its baseline rate or to a prespecified level.

(2) 4. Using the information from Case Study 2, page 30, indicate how positive reinforcement played a part in the following:

   a. Increasing the frequency of an undesired behavior.

   Answer: Mother provided positive reinforcement—she promised to buy new clothes and put the toys away—for Carla's undesired behavior of screaming when told to put her toys away.

   b. Increasing the frequency of a desired behavior.

   Answer: Mother provided positive reinforcement—praise and concrete rewards—for Carla's desired behavior of putting her toys away.

(1) 5. How is spontaneous recovery considered in a treatment plan?

   Answer: The behavior modifier can anticipate the possible recurrence of the target response at a later date when the client is in a situation that is similar to the one in which the target response was reinforced. The behavioral practitioner, client, and/or significant others can then arrange for reinforcement to be consistently withheld should the target behavior recur.

   The total point value of this test is 10. The point distribution is indicated next to each question.

   Criterion score: 9.

CHAPTER 4

(2) 1. Reexamine Case Study 1 on pages 7–8. State a positive reinforcement contingency related to that case study that you could use to help Harold complete his class assignments. Specify a reinforcer and a response.

   Criteria for correct answer: Your answer must state a specified amount of school work to be completed in order for Harold to receive a specified positive reinforcer. The response and reinforcer must be stated in positive terms.

   Sample answer: You could tell Harold, "After you complete one of your assignments, you can play your stereo for half an hour."

(2) 2. As described in this chapter, self-control reinforcement contingencies are more desirable than accidental contingencies. What is the difference between an accidental contingency and a self-control reinforcement contingency?

   Answer: In a self-control reinforcement contingency, the individual arranges conditions so that his or her behavior is predictably followed by reinforcement. The reinforcer is made available contingent on performance of the response. In an accidental contingency, an individual makes a response that is followed by a noncontingent reinforcer that coincidentally strengthens the response.

(1) 3. When is it more appropriate to use continuous reinforcement rather than intermittent reinforcement?

   Answer: To establish a response or to strengthen one that occurs with low frequency.

(1) 4. What evidence indicates that intermittent reinforcement makes a response more resistant to extinction than continuous reinforcement?

Answer: If a response is maintained on an intermittent reinforcement schedule, an individual will emit a greater number of responses during extinction than if the response had been maintained on a continuous schedule of reinforcement.

(3) 5. State three advantages of using intermittent reinforcement over continuous reinforcement.

Answers:

1. Intermittent reinforcement requires fewer reinforcements to maintain the behavior after it has been established, resulting in more efficient use of available reinforcers.

2. An intermittent schedule makes the response more resistant to extinction.

3. Intermittent reinforcement resembles most reinforcement schedules that maintain behavior in the individual's environment.

4. The reinforcer is effective longer because satiation is gradual.

(3) 6. Define the Premack Principle and give an example of its use and effect.

Answer: The Premack Principle states that a response that occurs more frequently than another response (high-probability response) can serve as a reinforcer for a response that occurs less frequently (low-probability response).

Criteria for correct example: Your example must specify two behaviors, one occurring with greater frequency than the other. The high-frequency behavior is made contingent on performance of the low-frequency behavior. The effect is an increase in performance of the low-frequency behavior.

Sample answer: Betty Jones frequently invites her friends for coffee in the morning but rarely gives her children breakfast. She can increase the frequency of giving her children breakfast if inviting her friends over is made contingent on making breakfast for her children. The effect of using the Premack Principle should be an increase in the frequency of Betty's giving the children breakfast.

Criterion score: 11.

CHAPTER 5

(1) 1. Give an example of straining the ratio.

Criterion for correct answer: Your example must show that a response has extinguished because the number of responses required for reinforcement was increased too rapidly.

Sample answer: A teacher established a positive reinforcement contingency for a child who scribbled on his math work sheets instead of solving the problems. On the first day of the procedure, she gave the child a gold star immediately after each math problem that he completed. The child earned twelve gold stars. The second day of this procedure, she required that he complete ten math problems in order to receive one gold star. On that day, the child completed three problems and scribbled on the rest of the work sheet.

(3) 2. Using the information from Case Study 3, pages 49–50, how could you schedule reinforcement to maintain Mr. Clark's increased vocalizations after session 15?

Criteria for correct answer: Your answer must include the following three points:

1. After a consistent rate is established on a continuous reinforcement schedule (CRF), shift to a small fixed-ratio schedule, FR 2, for example.
2. Gradually shift from FR 2 to progressively larger schedules, such as FR 3, FR 4, FR 6, FR 8. . . .
3. Gradually shift from FR to VR schedules (VR 4, VR 7, VR 10 . . .) to approximate reinforcement availability in the client's environment.

(10) 3. Match the various schedules in Column A with their characteristics from Column B. (Items from Column B can be used 0, 1 or more times in Column A and each schedule in Column A can have 1 or more characteristics from Column B.)

Column A		*Column B*
Fixed-Interval	1, 6, 8	1. Initial low rate of responding, terminal high rate of responding.
Variable-Interval	3, 10	
Fixed-Ratio	2, 5, 9	2. Postreinforcement pause.
Variable-Ratio	4, 5	3. Consistent, moderate rate of responding; no postreinforcement pause.

4. Characteristic slot machine schedule.
5. Very high response rate with minimal hesitation between responses.
6. Scallop.
7. Initial burst of responding, tapering off to low rate of responding.
8. Deadlines.
9. Piecework.
10. Waiting for a taxi.

Criterion score: 13.

(4) 1. Define a response class and give an example of one, describing two of its members.

Criterion for correct answer: Members of the response class specified must have the same or similar effect on the environment.

Sample answer:

Response Class: talking about sports

Effect: other person talks about sports with you

Member: discussing a player's batting average

Member: describing a touchdown pass

(7) 2. The seven steps involved in shaping a behavior are listed below. Fill in the specific responses and/or reinforcers related to each step, using your own example of shaping a motor (nonverbal) behavior.

Fill in with examples

Sample answer:

1. Specify terminal response.

2. Specify reinforcer(s).

3. Specify initial and intermediate responses directed toward achieving terminal response.

4. Differentially reinforce initial response until it is performed consistently.

5. Shift criterion for reinforcement to next intermediate response.

6. Continue the procedure of differential reinforcement and shifting the criterion for reinforcement until the terminal behavior is performed.

7. Reinforce terminal behavior.

1. An autistic child throws a ball.

2. Raisins and praise ("Good").

3. Movement toward the ball with any part of the body; touching the ball with the hands; holding the ball in the hands; moving the ball around in the air.

4. Any movement toward the ball with any part of the body was reinforced until it was performed consistently.

5. Reinforcement was given only when the child was touching the ball with her hands.

6. When the child was consistently touching the ball with her hands, the criterion for reinforcement was shifted and given only when the child was holding the ball in her hands. Reinforcement was then given only for moving the ball around in the air.

7. Continue praising and giving raisins when the child throws the ball.

(2) 3. Two second-grade students fight whenever they are together in school. Describe how a DRO procedure can be used to decrease the frequency of their fighting.

Answer: Reinforcement is given only when the students are doing something *other than* fighting. The teacher praises the students and gives them points for interacting in a positive manner, for doing their school work while sitting next to each other, and for any other behaviors except fighting. The teacher ignores them when they fight. Thus, fighting is extinguished while other appropriate behaviors are reinforced.

(3) 4. Give an example of response differentiation, specifying a response class, the differentiated response, and the reinforcer.

Criteria for correct answer: Your answer must include (1) a class of responses whose members can be reinforced; (2) a specific response in that class that has been selectively reinforced over the others and is performed with greater frequency; and (3) the specific reinforcer involved.

Sample answer: When Joe speaks to his stepfather about his problems, his stepfather rarely answers him. When Joe talks about sports, however, his stepfather pays attention; that is, he sits down with Joe and listens to him.

Response Class: talking to his stepfather.

Differentiated Response: Joe talks more frequently about sports.

Reinforcer: stepfather's attention—he sits down and listens to Joe.

(2) 5. Using the information from Case Study 3, pages 49–50, describe how the psychologist could use a DRO procedure to determine if it was the candy and points that served as reinforcers for Mr. Clark's increased speech, and not the attention he received in the experimental situation.

Answer: The psychologist could employ a DRO procedure in which Mr. Clark is given candy and points for any behavior *other than* speaking. If Mr. Clark's speech decreased when these reinforcers were presented after the other behaviors, then the candy and points had acted as effective reinforcers for Mr. Clark's speech. The psychologist could further demonstrate the effectiveness of the candy and points by increasing Mr. Clark's speech using these reinforcers.

Criterion score: 16.

CHAPTER 7

(3) 1. Using the information from Case Study 4, pages 69–70, answer the following: (1) Describe the discimination-training procedure that was used. (2) How were reinforcement and extinction involved in this procedure? (3) Describe the effects of this procedure.

Answers:
1. In Case Study 4, the counselor employed a discrimination-training procedure with Mrs. Munsen in which list A topics functioned as S^Ds and list B topics were S^{Δ}s.

2. List A topics were reinforced with praise by the counselor. Talking about topics on list B was ignored and extinguished.

3. The frequency of talking about topics on list A increased and the frequency of talking about list B topics decreased.

(3) 2. Jim, a retarded teenager, does not discriminate the men's restroom sign from the ladies' sign; that is, he sometimes walks into the ladies' restroom, and sometimes into the men's. Give an example of a stimulus-fading procedure you could use to teach Jim the appropriate discrimination.

Criteria for correct answer: Your answer must include (1) identification of the stimuli, men's restroom sign in large letters (S^D), ladies' restroom sign in small letters (S^Δ), and the novel stimulus, men's sign in small letters; (2) specification of the stimulus dimension to be varied gradually or faded; (3) specification of the correct response and its reinforcer; and (4) reinforcement for correct responses while changing the original S^D to the novel stimulus.

Sample answer: (1) the S^D is the men's restroom sign in large letters; the S^Δ is the ladies' restroom sign in small letters; and the novel stimulus is the men's sign in small letters. (2) Letter size was selected as the stimulus dimension to be varied. Jim had been previously taught to discriminate large letters from small letters; that is, when shown two words, one written in small letters and one writen in large letters, he chose the word written in large letters. (3) When Jim chose the men's sign, the counselor praised him and gave him a token. The counselor showed Jim two signs, the men's restroom sign written in very large letters (S^D) and the ladies' restroom sign written in small letters (S^Δ). (4) The size of the letters of the men's restroom sign was gradually decreased until the letters were the same size as those on the ladies' sign. Jim continued to choose the men's sign.

(5) 3. Describe a procedure for establishing a discrimination. In your example, include one S^D, one S^Δ and one response. Specify the reinforcer. How would you know when stimulus control has been achieved?

Criteria for correct answer: Your answer must specify a response, an S^D, and an S^Δ, and the reinforcer. The procedure consists of reinforcing the response in the presence of S^D and allowing the response to be performed initially in the presence of S^Δ while withholding reinforcement. Stimulus control is achieved when the response is performed in the presence of the S^D and not in the presence of the S^Δ. An additional characteristic of stimulus control is that the latency between the S^D and the response is short.

Sample answer: Teaching a small child to call his father "daddy" and not to call his uncle "daddy." The father is the S^D for the child's saying "daddy," a response that leads to reinforcement such as the father saying "good" or hugging the child. The uncle is an S^Δ for the child's saying "daddy." Reinforcement is withheld when the child says "daddy" upon seeing the uncle. When the child called his father (S^D) "daddy" immediately upon seeing him, and did not call his uncle (S^Δ) "daddy," stimulus control was achieved.

Criterion score: 10.

CHAPTER 8

(4) 1. Give two examples of behavioral deficits and two examples of behavioral excesses.

   Criteria for correct answers: Behavioral deficits refer to the absence or low frequency of appropriate behaviors. Behavioral excesses refer to high frequency of inappropriate behaviors.

   Sample answers:

   Behavioral Deficits:

   1. When someone compliments Joy, she puts her head down and remains silent.
   2. A ten-year-old retarded child only speaks three words.

   Behavioral Excesses:

   1. Bill throws rocks at other children.
   2. Carol runs away from home when she is disciplined.

(4) 2. A caseworker tells her supervisor that a client is always late for appointments.

   a. Which of the following two questions should the supervisor ask her in order to obtain baseline measures of the complaint? (Circle the correct answer(s).

      1. Why do you think the client is always late?
      2. How many minutes late is the client?
      3. How many times has the client been late this month?
      4. What do you think the client's lateness means?

   b. Give one hypothetical answer to each of the questions you chose above that would provide baseline data of the target behavior.

      Criteria for correct answers: Your answers must provide specific data on the frequency and/or duration of the problematic behavior.

      Sample answers:

      He is fifteen minutes late.

      She has been late three times this month, and we have had only four appointments.

(3) 3. From the information given in the following paragraph, identify Shirley's target response, its antecedents, and its negative consequences.

   Shirley's boss frequently asks her to work late. Last week, he made four such requests. When her boss makes these requests, Shirley holds her head down and says, "Okay." Shirley had unpleasant arguments with her husband twice over working late, and on another night they arrived late to a play.

   Answers:

   Shirley's Target Response(s): She holds her head down, says "okay."

   Antecedent: Shirley's boss asks her to work late.

Negative Consequences: Shirley had unpleasant arguments with her husband; they were late in arriving to a play.

(3) 4. From the information given in the paragraph below, identify the target response, its antecedent, and the probable positive reinforcer.

Children are talking in a group. No one is talking to Howard. When Howard tells jokes about himself, the other children gather around and laugh at him. The social worker observes that the other children rarely speak to Howard unless he is making fun of himself.

Answers:

Target Response: Howard tells jokes about himself.

Antecedent: Children are talking in a group. No one is talking to Howard.

Probable Reinforcers: Children gather around and laugh at him.

Criterion score: 13.

CHAPTER 9

(4) 1. Using the information from Case Study 5, pages 105–106, state four of Mr. Lewis's target behaviors.

Answers: Mr. Lewis (1) mumbled, (2) looked down at the floor, (3) held his hand in front of his mouth, (4) spoke in a monotone, (5) drifted from one topic to another without waiting for a response, and (6) talked only about his job on dates.

(1) 2. Specify one antecedent related to Mr. Lewis's conversation with his employer.

Answer:

1. Mr. Lewis is seated across the desk from his boss.
2. Boss asks Mr. Lewis what he wants.

(2) 3. State two negative consequences of Mr. Lewis's nonassertive behaviors.

Answers:

1. Mr. Lewis does not have satisfying relations with women; for example, his second dates are refused, and one woman fell asleep while he was talking to her.
2. Mr. Lewis does not get a raise and promotion, remains in same position at same salary.

(1) 4. Now turn to pages 7–8 to see Case Study 1. Using the information from that case study, state a probable reinforcer maintaining Harold's drug use.

Answer: Probable reinforcers maintaining Harold's drug use include:

1. He listens to records with his friends.
2. He spends time with his girlfriend.
3. He avoids doing his homework.
4. He avoids the nagging of his parents.

(3)   5.   State an intermediate behavioral change goal for Mr. Lewis based again on the information from Case Study 5, specifying (1) a desired response, (2) a relevant antecedent, and (3) a possible positive reinforcer.

Criteria for correct answers: Your answers must indicate that Mr. Lewis makes an alternative response in the presence of an antecedent that previously served as an S^D for nonassertive behaviors. This response should be less difficult for Mr. Lewis to perform than his final goal. A possible reinforcer must be delivered after performance of the desired response.

Sample Answers:

Intermediate Goal with a Woman: Mr. Lewis talks about a topic of mutual interest with his date.

Desired Response: Mr. Lewis speaks in a pleasant tone of voice about a mutually interesting topic, such as a recent movie both he and the woman saw.

Relevant Antecedent: Having coffee in a restaurant with a woman.

Possible Reinforcer: The woman responds favorably to Mr. Lewis; she smiles at him.

Intermediate Goal with Boss: Mr. Lewis makes a legitimate request of his boss.

Desired Response: Mr. Lewis looks directly at his boss, speaks in a pleasant tone of voice, and clearly states his request or business.

Relevant Antecedent: Sitting across the desk from his boss.

Possible Reinforcer: Boss agrees to Mr. Lewis's stated request or business, or boss acknowledges the legitimacy or reasonableness of the request.

Criterion score: 10

CHAPTER 10

(2)   1.   An institutionalized mental patient, Mr. Clark, was given money during a verbal conditioning study. He dropped one coin on the floor and left the rest of the coins he had earned on the table. The psychologist concluded that money did not function as a generalized conditioned reinforcer for Mr. Clark in the way that it does for most adults in our society. What could the psychologist do to establish money as a reinforcer for Mr. Clark?

Criteria for correct answer:

Your answer must describe a procedure in which the psychologist pairs money with the delivery of known reinforcers. The money must serve as the S^D for Mr. Clark's response of handing the money to the psychologist which is followed by delivery of an established reinforcer.

Sample answer:

The psychologist showed Mr. Clark a variety of items including chewing gum, magazines, and cookies that were placed on a table. He told Mr. Clark to point to an item he would like to have. After Mr. Clark pointed to an item, the psychologist gave Mr. Clark a coin(S^D) and asked Mr. Clark to hand him the coin (R). The psychologist gave Mr. Clark the item (S^{R+}) as soon as Mr. Clark gave him the coin. The psychologist repeated this procedure until Mr. Clark took the money during the study.

(3) 2. You are a social worker in a community setting, and adolescents who have had one or two contacts with the police and juvenile authorities are referred to you. You station yourself in the low-socioeconomic neighborhood where these youths live because you plan to engage a group of them in activities that will help them stay out of trouble with the law, improve their academic performance, interview for and successfully hold jobs, and solve various interpersonal and family difficulties. Give two examples that indicate what you could do to establish yourself as a generalized conditioned reinforcer.

Criteria for correct answer:

Your answer should include two examples that show the worker's arrangement of conditions so that he or she is associated as an S^D for client responses that are followed by delivery of a variety of unconditioned and conditioned positive reinforcers.

Sample answer:

The social worker could invite the youths to a meeting and provide a variety of refreshments such as soft drinks, cookies, and popcorn. The only behavior required of the youths is attendance at the meetings. The worker could also take them for rides in the agency van and to activities such as bowling. These items and events become paired with the worker who is the S^D for client responses that lead to food and activities. If these events are reinforcing for the clients, the worker will acquire reinforcing value for them.

(1) 3. Now turn to pages 49–50 to see Case Study 3. In this case study, the green light served as an S^D for Mr. Clark's speech. It was paired with candy and praise from the psychologist. How could the psychologist determine if the green light had become a conditioned reinforcer?

Answer: If presentation of the green light after any response other than speaking increased the strength of the other response, it would be a conditioned reinforcer. An alternative test would be for the psychologist to withhold the candy and praise until Mr. Clark's speaking decreased. Then the psychologist would present the green light immediately after Mr. Clark spoke. If Mr. Clark's speech increased, the green light would be a conditioned reinforcer. The second test is not recommended for ethical reasons in a clinical setting. Since the goal of treatment is to increase Mr. Clark's speaking, any test that involved decreasing his speech would be of questionable value to him.

(2) 4. State two advantages of using conditioned reinforcement over primary reinforcement in maintaining behavioral change in a client's environment.

Answers:

1. An individual is less likely to satiate on a conditioned reinforcer if it is a generalized conditioned reinforcer.

2. Conditioned reinforcers are more commonly presented for desired behaviors than primary reinforcers in the client's environment. Generalization of desired behavior is, therefore, more likely to occur the more

similar the reinforcers in the treatment environment are to reinforcers in the client's natural environment.

(4) 5. Give an example of a problem that can be analyzed as a stimulus-response chain. Include at least two stimulus-response units, and label the appropriate components.

Criteria for correct answer:

Your answer must include a series of behaviors linked by conditioned reinforcers that also serve as S^Ds for the following responses, and a terminal reinforcer that maintains the chain.

Sample answer:

At parties, Joe is always either drinking or getting himself a drink. Some behaviors in this chain are shown in the following diagram:

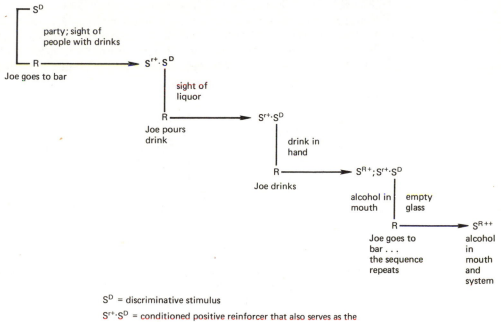

S^D = discriminative stimulus

$S^{r+} \cdot S^D$ = conditioned positive reinforcer that also serves as the discriminative stimulus for the following response

R = response

$S^{R++}; S^{r++}$ = positive reinforcer that terminates the chain.

Criterion score: 11.

CHAPTER 11

(3) 1. Give an example that describes how a modeling-plus-reinforcement procedure is used to develop and strengthen a response.

Criteria for correct answer:

Your answer must include the following points: (1) a model (S^m) who demonstrates appropriate behavior for a person, (2) a person who imitates the S^m, and (3) a reinforcer delivered contingent on appropriate imitation.

Sample answer:

In Case Study 6, page 228, Mr. Potts observed group members role playing him and demonstrating appropriate responses to criticism. These models demonstrated appropriate responses that served as S^{m}s (modeled stimuli) for Mr. Potts to imitate. When Mr. Potts imitated these behaviors in role-plays he received positive reinforcement in the form of praise and encouragement from the group members and therapist.

(4) 2. Give an example of the use of modeling in developing assertive behaviors in a group setting.

Criteria for correct answer: Your answer must include: (1) specification of target and assertive responses, (2) the use of a group member as a model (S^m) who demonstrates assertive responses, (3) imitation of the modeled stimulus by the client, and (4) a reinforcer presented by group members contingent on appropriate imitation.

Sample answer:

Neil has a hard time getting girls to go out with him. He typically approaches them with statements such as, "You wouldn't like to go to the movies Saturday night, would you?" "I have two tickets to a play, if you wouldn't mind going?" Neil speaks in a pleading, whining voice. These inappropriate behaviors were observed by group members during a behavioral reenactment of Neil's last attempt to get a date. The therapist asked Nick, a group member, to model assertive responses for Neil. Neil imitated the behaviors Nick demonstrated, and gradually learned to perform assertive behaviors in a variety of role plays. Group members reinforced Neil with praise for appropriate imitation.

(4) 3. Describe the use of a modeling procedure with prompts, reinforcement, and fading, given the following information: A social worker is trying to teach a retarded child to answer questions about his family. When the social worker asks the child, "How many brothers do you have?" the child does not answer. The child can talk and can say all the words necessary to answer the question.

Criteria for correct answer:

Your answer must include the following points: (1) the social worker models the correct response; (2) if the child still does not respond, the social worker models the correct response and prompts the child; (3) a specific reinforcer is given when the child correctly imitates the model; and (4) the prompt is faded out when the child answers on his own.

Sample answer:

The social worker asks the child, "How many brothers do you have?" When the child does not answer, the social worker demonstrates the correct response, "I have four brothers." If the child still does not respond, the social worker models the correct answer again and prompts the child, for example, "Now you say it, Tony." When the child imitates the model (S^m), the social worker gives the child a raisin and praises him saying, "That's very good, Tony." Gradually, the social worker fades out the prompt by saying it in a softer voice each time until the child says, "I have four brothers," in response to the question "How many brothers do you have?"

Criterion score: 10.

CHAPTER 12

(3) 1. Give an example of the two types of punishment procedures and indicate how you would evaluate their effectiveness.

Criteria for correct answer:

One example should specify a punishing stimulus that is presented contingent on performance of a response. The second example should specify the withdrawal of a positive reinforcer contingent on performance of a response. In both cases, the effectiveness of the punishment is evaluated by observing a decrease in the strength of the punished response as compared with baseline measures.

Sample answers:

1. Mrs. Jones said to Mr. Jones, "You spend all your money on booze." Mr. Jones slapped Mrs. Jones across the face. *Effect:* Mrs. Jones stopped complaining to Mr. Jones about his spending money on liquor.
2. Last week Bert came home a half-hour late and his mother told him he couldn't drive the car for 3 days. *Effect:* Since then Bert has come home on time.

(2) 2. Give an example that contrasts extinction with punishment by response-contingent removal of a positive reinforcer.

Criteria for correct answer:

Your example must include the following two points: (1) Punishment is the removal of a reinforcer other than that which maintains the target response; extinction is the withdrawal of the positive reinforcer maintaining the target response. (2) Punishment results in a rapid decrease or suppression of the target response; extinction results in the gradual decrease in strength of the target response.

Sample answer:

Mr. Barnes criticized his wife for being overweight while they got ready for bed. Mrs. Barnes became angry and yelled at him. This happened several times a week during the past month.

Punishment: When Mr. Barnes criticized Mrs. Barnes, she refused to have sexual intercourse with him.

Effect: Mr. Barnes stopped criticizing Mrs. Barnes about her weight.

Extinction: When Mr. Barnes criticized Mrs. Barnes, she turned away from him and continued whatever she was doing.

Effect: Mr. Barnes gradually criticized her less frequently, as Mrs. Barnes continued to ignore him.

(5)　3.　Give an example of how you could maximize the effectiveness of punishment with a highly talkative client who frequently gets off the subject during your interviews and rambles on other topics.

Criteria for correct answer:

Your answer should include the following points: (1) delivery of a punisher immediately after rambling responses; (2) punisher delivered each time rambling occurs; (3) punisher of sufficient intensity to suppress rambling; (4) specification of alternative appropriate behavior; (5) positive reinforcement of appropriate behavior; (6) removal of reinforcement for inappropriate behaviors; and (7) arrangement of the punishment contingency so that escape is not possible.

Sample answer:

Each time the client begins to ramble, the therapist immediately says, "Stop! You are off the subject." The therapist should then specify what the client should talk about, thus providing S^Ds for client responses that the therapist can reinforce. For example, the therapist could ask, "What were you doing when the problem occurred?" If answered appropriately, the therapist says, "That's getting at the problem. Please continue." This reinforces the client for staying on the topic.

Effect: Client rambling stops or decreases in frequency.

(3)　4.　Using the information from Case Study 7, pages 143–144, name the punishment procedure administered to Stephen by Mrs. Drake. Draw a paradigm of an incident that would lead her to use this procedure. Label the appropriate components.

Answers:

1.　The procedure used was time-out.

2.　A representative incident can be diagrammed as follows:

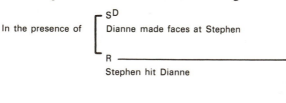

(1)　5.　Give an example of punishment applied in a self-control contingency.

Criteria for correct answer:

Your example must include self-administered punishment, either response-contingent removal of a positive reinforcer or response-contingent presentation of a punishing stimulus.

Sample answers:

1. If I smoke more than one pack of cigarettes this week, I will send $50 to the American Cancer Society (removal of a positive reinforcer).

2. An individual carries an electronic cigarette case that is set to deliver a slight shock if opened at intervals of less than 30 minutes (presentation of a punishing stimulus).

Criterion score: 13.

CHAPTER 13

(2) 1. Give an example contrasting the effects of punishment and negative reinforcement. Specify relevant responses and stimuli involved in each procedure.

Criteria for correct answers:

Your example must demonstrate the effects of punishment in decreasing the strength of the punished response and negative reinforcement in increasing the strength of the escape or avoidance response.

Sample answers:

Punishment: A program evaluator requested data on client outcomes from treatment staff (R). They told him that they were too busy to get the data for him (S^{r-}). The program evaluator stopped asking for the data.

Negative Reinforcement: A program evaluator repeatedly requested data on client outcomes from treatment staff (S^{r-}). They finally gave her the data she requested (R), thus terminating the requests (S^{r-}). The likelihood is increased that staff will comply with similar requests made in the future.

(3) 2. Give an example of escape behavior developed by negative reinforcement. Label relevant responses and stimuli.

Criteria for correct answer:

Your example must indicate: (1) that a negative reinforcer is presented until (2) a specific response is made that reduces its effect or terminates it, and (3) there must also be evidence that the frequency of the escape response increases.

Sample answer: Mrs. Munsen nagged and criticized her husband (S^{r-}). Mr. Munsen left the house (R) more often, which removed the nagging and criticism (S^{r-}).

(2) 3. Now turn to page 225 to see Case Study 2. Describe the interaction between Carla and her mother in terms of positive and negative reinforcement, prior to the social worker's intervention.

Answers:

Positive Reinforcement for Carla: Mother put the toys away and promised to buy her new clothes.

Negative Reinforcement for Mrs. Hernandez: Carla screamed (S^{r-}) until her mother put the toys away and promised to buy her new clothes (R), the responses that terminated the screaming (S^{R-}).

(4)   4.   Sylvia told Harold, "Buy me a new car or I'll leave you." Harold bought her a new car, and she stopped threatening to leave him. Draw a paradigm that describes the avoidance behavior, labeling relevant components.

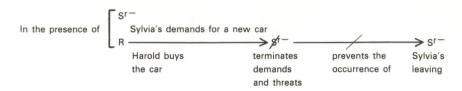

Criterion score: 10.

CHAPTER 14

(3)   1.   Turn to pages 226–227 to see Case Study 4. Using information from that case, state one operant behavior and two possible respondent behaviors involved in Mrs. Munsen's "being upset."

Answers: The operant behaviors involved in Mrs. Munsen's "being upset" included: (1) running into her room and (2) locking the door.

Possible respondent behaviors include any autonomic responses, such as increased heart rate, perspiration, face flushed, or tears, that were elicited by antecedent stimuli.

(7)   2.   The following examples include operant and respondent behaviors. Place an O in the space of those italicized behaviors that are operant, and an R for those that are respondent.

    a.   1.   __O__   A teenager in a treatment group *swears* at another boy.

        2.   __R__   The second boy's face *turns* red.

    b.   1.   __O__   You *ask* a client a question about his brother; you observe that his

        2.   __R__   breathing *quickens* and perspiration

        3.   __R__   *appears* on his forehead.

    c.   1.   __O__   You *give* Janet a piece of candy for completing her assignment.

        2.   __O__   Carol observes this and *starts whining.*

(2)   3.   Draw a paradigm showing respondent conditioning of the following phobia:

A child is afraid of dentists. When he approaches a dentist's office he begins to tremble, turns pale, breathes rapidly, then turns and runs away. This child has dental problems that must be taken care of soon, or he may lose many of his teeth.

Criteria for correct answer: Your answer must include a paradigm showing the pairing of pain (US) with a previously neutral stimulus (dentist's office) until the neutral stimulus acquires the ability to elicit anxiety (CR). (If the US was very intense, conditioning the CR could be accomplished on the basis of a single pairing).

Sample answer: A paradigm showing respondent conditioning of the child's fear of dentists looks like this:

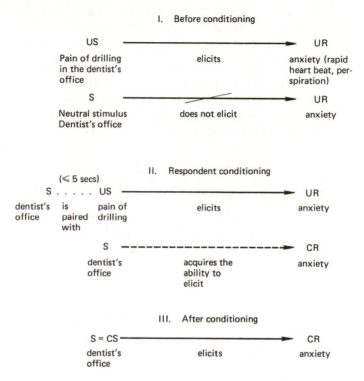

(2) 4. Describe an operant procedure for treating both operant and respondent features of the phobia described in Problem 3.

Criteria for correct answer: The operant procedure used to treat this phobia must involve the development of operant behaviors that are incompatible with escape and avoidance in the phobic situation, as well as conditioning respondent behaviors incompatible with anxiety.

Sample answer: Shaping with successive approximations can be used to develop operant behaviors incompatible with running away from the dentist's office. The therapist arranges treatment conditions so that the child gradually approaches the phobic stimulus (the dentist's office) and receives positive reinforcement for behavioral approximations. The therapist could also laugh and talk about pleasant topics with the child in order to establish physiological responses that are incompatible with trembling, rapid breathing, and turning pale in the feared situation.

Criterion score: 13.

(3)   1. List three obstacles to generalization of desired responses from the practice setting to the client's natural environment.

Answers:

1. Lack of similarity between antecedent stimuli (S^{D}s and CSs) in the practice setting and the client's environment.

2. Reinforcement of undesired responses in the natural environment.

3. Lack of reinforcement for desired responses in the client's environment.

4. Desired responses were not sufficiently practiced in the practice setting.

(1)   2. Turn to pages 225–226 to see Case Study 3. Mr. Clark's speech was developed in a laboratory-like situation. State one reason his speech might not generalize from the treatment setting to the ward.

Answer:

Mr. Clark's speech might not generalize from the treatment setting to the ward for any of the following reasons:

1. Ward staff do not reinforce Mr. Clark's speech, so that his speaking will be extinguished.

2. S^{D}s for speech on the ward might be different from S^{D}s for speech in the treatment setting (for example, there is no green light for speaking on the ward).

3. Ward staff might reinforce quiet, inactive patient behaviors emitted by Mr. Clark.

4. Mr. Clark's speaking might not have been sufficiently practiced in the treatment setting.

(2)   3. State two ways you could maximize successful generalization of Mr. Clark's speech.

Answers:

Successful generalization from therapy to ward can be promoted by:

1. Reinforcing ward staff for reinforcing Mr. Clark's speech on the ward.

2. Shifting reinforcement for Mr. Clark's speech from a continuous to an intermittent schedule.

3. The therapist could reinforce Mr. Clark's speech on the ward.

4. Using more than one therapist to reinforce Mr. Clark's speech in the treatment setting.

5. Having the psychologist conduct additional sessions to maintain Mr. Clark's speech at a high level, after Mr. Clark has achieved criterion performance in speaking about the slides.

6. Ward staff reinforcing Mr. Clark's speech in the treatment setting.

(2)   4. Turn to pages 226–227 and review Case Study 4. State two behavioral assignments the marriage counselor gave Mrs. Munsen in that study.

Answers:

The counselor gave Mrs. Munsen the following behavioral assignments:

1. To make two lists of topics: one to discuss with her husband (list A), the other not to discuss with her husband (list B).

2. To kiss Mr. Munsen when he came home from work and ask him how his work had gone.

(2)   5. State two reasons for using behavioral assignments in implementing a behavioral change program.

Answers:

The following are reasons for using behavioral assignments in implementing a behavioral change program:

1. Behavioral assignments give the client the opportunity to try out behaviors that are discussed and rehearsed in the practice setting.

2. Behavioral assignments structure a client's activities between meetings to follow steps toward attainment of behavioral change goals in the natural environment.

3. Behavioral assignments promote generalization of desired responses from the practice setting to the client's natural environment.

(1)   6. Refer to Case Study 8 on pages 189–190. How was behavioral rehearsal used to help Mrs. Gomez and Mr. Terry converse appropriately with their peers?

Answers:

The psychiatric nurse required them to make appropriate statements during the group conversation exercise. They were reinforced with praise for doing so, and were corrected and told to try again when they made inappropriate statements.

(1)   7. What is the rationale for using behavioral rehearsal?

Answer:

The rationale for using behavioral rehearsal is to provide an opportunity for the client to become more skilled in his or her ability to perform appropriate behaviors. Behavioral rehearsal promotes generalization of desired responses from the practice setting to the client's natural environment by insuring that the desired behaviors are first well learned in the practice setting.

Criterion score: 11.

CHAPTER 16

(2)   1. Turn to pages 227–228 to see Case Study 5. Now state one possible resource and one possible barrier to goal attainment, given the following behavioral change goal for Mr. Lewis: Mr. Lewis assertively asks his employer for a salary increase.

Answers:

Possible Resources: Mr. Lewis's stated cooperation and desire to improve his situation; support of co-workers; favorable employment record with the company.

Possible Barriers: Co-workers discourage him; Mr. Lewis is reluctant to make an appointment to see his boss.

(4)   2.   Develop an intervention plan for teaching Mr. Wallenta (see page 200) how to brush his teeth. He has never been observed to brush his teeth. Include two behavioral techniques and outline the procedure you would follow to achieve the goal.

Criteria for correct answers: Behavioral techniques should be selected from those in Table 16-1 that can (1) establish the response and (2) maintain the response. The procedure for implementing the techniques must be described.

Sample answer: Modeling and positive reinforcement are selected as the behavioral techniques. The nurse would demonstrate toothbrushing to Mr. Wallenta, and tell him to do it the same way. When Mr. Wallenta picked up the toothbrush, he would be reinforced with a token. The nurse would continue to model each step of toothbrushing, reinforcing Mr. Wallenta for correct imitations.

Shaping could also be used in conjunction with modeling. In this case, Mr. Wallenta would be reinforced for any approximations he made to the modeled stimulus. Standing near the sink, reaching for the toothbrush or toothpaste, and putting the toothbrush in his mouth might be approximations that would be reinforced.

Still another possibility could be chaining or backward chaining, used with modeling and positive reinforcement.

(2)   2.   Describe a method for evaluating the effectiveness of an assertiveness training procedure that could be used with Mr. Lewis.

Criteria for correct answer: Your evaluation method must include a measure of the strength of assertive behaviors before, during, and after treatment, both in the treatment situation and in the client's environment.

Sample answer: One way to obtain an objective measure of behavioral change would be to have Mr. Lewis role play a situation with the therapist or a female secretary. Mr. Lewis would be observed by the therapist in a similar situation before, during, and after treatment. The therapist records assertive behaviors and their frequency in order to provide measures for evaluating the effectiveness of the intervention program. The second source for obtaining this information would be data provided by Mr. Lewis before, during and after treatment, concerning the frequency of performing assertive behaviors in his natural environment.

(3)   4.   State three evaluation criteria you could use to determine if marital arguments were effectively treated.

Answers:

1. Number of arguments decreases.
2. Duration of arguments decreases.
3. Intensity of arguments decreases.
4. Satisfaction with regard to arguments increases.
5. Greater reported satisfaction with marriage.

Criterion score: 10.

APPENDIX

6

NOTATIONAL SYMBOLS AND PARADIGMS

NOTATIONAL SYMBOLS

R = response

S = stimulus

$S+$ = presentation of a positive reinforcer

S^{R+} = presentation of an unconditioned positive reinforcer

S^{r+} = presentation of a conditioned positive reinforcer

$S-$ = presentation of a punisher or a negative reinforcer

S^{R-} = presentation of an unconditioned punisher or an unconditioned negative reinforcer

S^{r-} = presentation of a conditioned punisher or a conditioned negative reinforcer

US = unconditioned stimulus
UR = unconditioned response

$\longrightarrow$ = is followed by (operant)
$\longrightarrow$ = elicits (respondent)

$\lceil$ = in the presence of

S^{Δ} = discriminative stimulus signaling nonreinforcement

S^D = discriminative stimulus signaling reinforcement

S^m = modeled stimulus

$\cancel{S^+}$ = removal of a positive reinforcer

$\cancel{S^{R+}}$ = removal of an unconditioned positive reinforcer

$\cancel{S^{r+}}$ = removal of a conditioned positive reinforcer

$\cancel{S^-}$ = termination, removal, or reduction of a negative reinforcer

$\cancel{S^{R-}}$ = termination, removal, or reduction of an unconditioned negative reinforcer

$\cancel{S^{r-}}$ = termination, removal, or reduction of a conditioned negative reinforcer

CS = conditioned stimulus
CR = conditioned response

$\nrightarrow$ = is not followed by (operant)
$\nrightarrow$ = does not elicit (respondent)

BEHAVIORAL PARADIGMS

R ⟶ s^+ R ⟶ s^+

Procedure: positive reinforcement   *Procedure:* extinction

Effects: increase in strength of R   *Effects:* decrease in strength of R

In the presence of $\left[\begin{array}{l} s^D \\ R \longrightarrow s^+ \end{array}\right.$

In the presence of $\left[\begin{array}{l} s^\Delta \\ R \longrightarrow s^+ \end{array}\right.$

Procedure: discrimination training

Effects: increase in strength of R in the presence of S^D; decrease in strength of R in the presence of S^Δ

In the presence of $\left[\begin{array}{l} s^{D_1} \\ R_1 \longrightarrow s^+ \end{array}\right.$

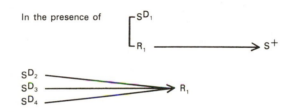

Procedure: stimulus generalization

Effects: strength of R_1 increases in the presence of S^{D_1}; the likelihood of R_1 occurring in the presence of S^{D_2}, S^{D_3}, and S^{D_4} increases

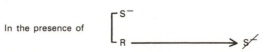

R ⟶ S^- R ⟶ $\cancel{s}$

Procedure: punishment by presentation   *Procedure:* punishment by removal of a
                of a punisher   positive reinforcer; response cost

Effects: decrease in strength of R   *Effects:* decrease in strength of R

In the presence of $\left[\begin{array}{l} S^- \\ R \longrightarrow \cancel{s} \end{array}\right.$

Procedure: negative reinforcement; escape conditioning

Effects: increase in strength of the escape response, R

In the presence of

Procedure: negative reinforcement; avoidance conditioning

Effects: increase in strength of the avoidance response, R

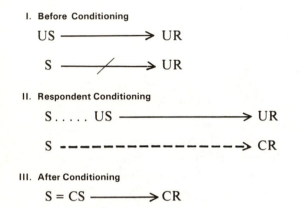

I. **Before Conditioning**

$$US \longrightarrow UR$$

$$S \longrightarrow\!\!\!/\longrightarrow UR$$

II. **Respondent Conditioning**

$$S \ldots US \longrightarrow UR$$

$$S \dashrightarrow CR$$

III. **After Conditioning**

$$S = CS \longrightarrow CR$$

Procedure: respondent conditioning

Effects: neutral stimulus becomes a conditioned stimulus capable of eliciting a conditioned response

GLOSSARY

Accidental Reinforcement Contingency   A coincidental relationship between a response and a reinforcer. The response is strengthened by an unplanned reinforcer. The likelihood that the response will recur under similar conditions is increased. Superstitious behavior is established under this contingency.

Antecedent   A stimulus event that precedes or accompanies a response and could influence its occurrence.

Anxiety   An intense emotional response frequently characterized by physiological changes such as increased heart rate, perspiration, rapid breathing, and subjective statements of ill ease or fear. Anxiety may generate escape or avoidance behaviors.

Assertiveness Training   A behavioral-change procedure for improving deficient social or interpersonal skills. Usually involves instructions, role playing, behavioral rehearsal, behavioral assignments, and reinforcement. Relaxation training techniques may also be used to decrease anxiety related to under- or overassertive behaviors. For example, assertiveness training can help an individual decrease mumbling, looking at the floor when conversing, or inappropriately agreeing with someone, and to increase appropriate behaviors such as speaking in a clear voice, looking at the person to whom one is speaking, and stating divergent views or opinions when appropriate. Also called social skills training.

Aversive Stimulus   An object or event identified as unpleasant, annoying, or painful; when given the opportunity, the individual will usually escape or avoid it. Aversive stimuli can be used as punishers or negative reinforcers.

Avoidance Behavior   A behavior that results in termination, removal, or reduction of a negative reinforcer and that prevents the onset of a second, established negative reinforcer.

Backward Chaining   A behavioral change technique used to teach a complex series or sequence of behaviors. The last stimulus-response unit of the chain is established first, and the other units are added in reverse order until the desired chain is complete.

Baseline Data   Measures of response strength recorded prior to intervention, including rate, duration, intensity, latency and/or magnitude. Response rate or frequency per time unit (operant) and magnitude (respondent) are the most common measures recorded.

Baseline Rate; Baseline Level   The strength of a behavior prior to intervention or modification as measured by its rate, duration, intensity, latency, and/or magnitude.

Behavior; Response   Any observable, measurable movement or activity of an individual. The terms behavior and response are used interchangeably throughout the text.

Behavioral Assessment   The approach and procedures used to evaluate a client's problem(s) or circumstances. Behavioral assessment provides the basis for goal setting and establishing an intervention plan.

Behavioral Assignment   A specific task involving behaviors to be performed by the client outside the practice setting between treatment sessions.

Behavioral Contingency   A statement that specifies the behaviors to be performed in order for certain consequences to follow.

Behavioral Contract   An agreement between two or more individuals in which the expected behaviors of each are specified along with the consequences for their performance and nonperformance.

Behavioral Deficit   Absence or low frequency of appropriate behaviors.

Behavioral Excess   High frequency of inappropriate behaviors.

Behavioral Medicine   Interdisciplinary field that applies behavioral analysis and technology to problems of physical health such as, asthma, headaches, insomnia, and hypertension.

Behavioral Reenactment   A role-playing technique used to obtain RAC-S information regarding the client's behaviors in the problematic situation by observing him or her role play an incident that simulates the problem.

Behavioral Rehearsal   A role-playing technique in which the client practices desired behaviors that have been suggested and/or demonstrated by the therapist or group members in a structured situation with feedback.

Behavior Modification   The application of principles and techniques derived from the experimental analysis of behavior to a wide range of human problems. Behavior modification emphasizes the methods of applied behavior analysis, the principles of operant conditioning, and the concepts of social learning theory. The goals of behavior modification are to improve the human condition and to advance the scientific knowledge base of human behavior and its determinants. Basic features of the behavior modification approach include (1) specificity in describing problems, goals and interventions, and (2) systematic planning, implementation, and evaluation of interventions and programs.

Behavior Therapy   Generally used as synonymous with the term behavior modification. The term behavior therapy connotes the provision of behavior modification services to individuals in a client-therapist setting. Historically, behavior therapy referred to treatment methods based primarily on classical conditioning.

Biofeedback   A process that allows an individual to monitor and influence his or her physiological responses using auditory, visual, and/or other sensory feedback regarding physiological states, such as heart rate, muscle tension, brain waves, and skin temperature. Biofeedback is used in the operant control of autonomic functions and is often applied in conjunction with self-control procedures and relaxation training techniques.

Chains   (See stimulus-response chains.)

Classical Conditioning; Respondent Conditioning   Development or establishment of a response through pairing a neutral stimulus with an unconditioned stimulus until the neutral stimulus acquires the ability to elicit a conditioned response.

Conditioned Aversive Stimulus   An unpleasant, annoying, or painful stimulus that has acquired these properties through pairing or association with an established aversive stimulus. When given the opportunity, the individual will usually escape or avoid it.

Conditioned Negative Reinforcer   A stimulus that sets the occasion for an escape or avoidance response that terminates or removes the effect of the stimulus. The removal of this stimulus increases the likelihood that the escape or avoidance response will be performed again. The conditioned negative reinforcer acts in this way through pairing or association with an established negative reinforcer.

Conditioned Response (CR)   In the respondent conditioning paradigm, a measurable activity elicited by a conditioned stimulus (CS). The CR is similar to the unconditioned response.

Conditioned Stimulus (CS) In the respondent conditioning paradigm, a previously neutral event that acquires the ability to elicit a conditioned response through pairing with an unconditioned stimulus.

Consequence   A stimulus that follows a behavior and can influence the future likelihood of the behavior. Consequences can be reinforcing, punishing, or neutral.

Contingency   (See behavioral contingency.)

Continuous Reinforcement Schedule (CRF)   A reinforcement schedule in which a reinforcer is delivered each time the response is performed.

Covert Sensitization   An anxiety-eliciting technique utilizing imagined stimuli to weaken maladaptive approach behaviors; it involves respondent pairing of an aversive stimulus with the maladaptive situation. The client is often instructed to make appropriate escape and avoidance responses that can be negatively reinforced by termination of the imagined aversive stimulus.

Deprivation   A condition in which a reinforcer has been unavailable to an individual for a specified period of time. A reinforcer is most effective in increasing the strength of a response when a high level of deprivation exists.

Differential Reinforcement   A procedure in which a certain response is reinforced while reinforcement is withheld from other members of the response class. When the reinforced response occurs frequently, to the exclusion of responses from which reinforcement is withheld, we say that the response has become differentiated.

DRO Procedure   Differential reinforcement of behaviors other than the target behavior. Used to decrease the rate of a target behavior. This procedure can be used to determine if a stimulus serves as a reinforcer for a target respone.

Discriminative Stimulus, S^D   An antecedent stimulus that signals or sets the occasion for a response made in its presence to be followed by a reinforcer.

Discriminative Stimulus, S^Δ   An antecedent stimulus signaling that a response made in its presence will not be followed by a reinforcer.

Discrimination Training   A behavioral procedure in which a response is reinforced in the presence of the S^D and extinguished in the presence of the S^Δ. Results in stimulus control; the response occurs during S^D and never or rarely during S^Δ.

Duration   A measure of response strength. The length of time a response occurs.

Errorless Learning   (See stimulus fading.)

Escape Behavior   Behavior that results in the termination, removal, or reduction of a negative reinforcer. Removal of the negative reinforcer increases the strength of this behavior.

Ess-Dee (S^D)   (See discriminative stimulus, S^D.)

Ess-Delta (S^Δ)   (See discriminative stimulus, S^Δ).

Extinction   Operant extinction—the positive reinforcer for a response is withheld continuously (that is, each time the response occurs) until the response decreases in frequency to zero or a prespecified level. In avoidance conditioning, the established negative reinforcer is no longer presented. Respondent extinction—the conditioned stimulus is presented repeatedly, without presenting the unconditioned stimulus, until the conditioned stimulus no longer elicits the conditioned response.

Fading   (See stimulus fading.)

Fixed-Interval Schedule   An intermittent reinforcement schedule in which a reinforcer is delivered for a response performed after a designated period of time. For example, *FI 2 min.* means that a reinforcer is delivered when a response is made after 2 minutes have passed.

Fixed-Ratio Schedule   An intermittent reinforcement schedule in which a prescribed number of responses must be performed in order for a reinforcer to be delivered. For example, *FR 10* indicates that a reinforcer is delivered after 10 responses have been performed.

Flooding   A technique for treating problem behaviors by extinction of avoidance responses. Flooding consists of exposing the individual directly, or in imagination, to the phobic stimulus (CS) for a prolonged period of time, while preventing any escape or avoidance responses. The CS is presented continuously until it no longer elicits anxiety (CR).

Frequency   The number of times a response is performed; frequency per time interval (response rate) is the most common measure used in recording response strength.

Generalized Conditioned Reinforcer   A previously neutral or nonreinforcing stimulus that has acquired the ability to increase response strength through association with established reinforcers. It usually refers to an object that can be exchanged for a variety of conditioned or unconditioned reinforcers such as money.

Imitated Response   A response performed after observing a modeled stimulus. The imitated response is physically similar to the modeled stimulus with regard to an observable dimension(s) such as position or movement.

Intensity   A measure of response strength that is indicated in units such as grams, pounds, decibels. Measures the severity of an operant response.

Intermittent Reinforcement   Any schedule of reinforcement that is less than continuous. A response is reinforced on some occasions, and reinforcement for that response is withheld on other occasions.

Latency   A measure of response strength. The interval between presentation of a stimulus and performance of a response. In operant conditioning, the interval between presentation of the S^D and performance of the response. In respondent conditioning, the interval between presentation of the US or CS and elicitation of the UR or CR, respectively.

Magnitude   A measure of the strength of a respondent; usually obtained by measuring secretion of a gland or contraction of a muscle or blood vessel.

Model   An individual whose behavior serves as a cue or modeled stimulus (S^m) for another person's imitated response.

Modeling Procedure; Model Presentation   A modeled stimulus is presented that is intended to influence performance of an imitated response. The imitated response is similar to the modeled stimulus.

Modeled Stimulus (S^m)   The behavior of a model that is intended to influence performance of an imitated response.

Natural Environment   The physical and social surroundings in which the target behavior was reinforced and in which behavioral changes are designed to be performed and maintained.

Negative Reinforcement   The strengthening of a response through escape or avoidance conditioning. (1) Escape conditioning—a procedure in which a response that terminates, removes, or reduces the effect of a stimulus is strengthened. (2) Avoidance conditioning—a procedure in which a response that terminates, removes, or reduces the effects of a negative reinforcer and prevents the onset of a second negative reinforcer is strengthened.

Negative Reinforcement Contingency   A statement that specifies the response that must be performed in order to terminate, remove, or reduce the effect of a stimulus.

Negative Reinforcer   A stimulus whose termination, removal, or reduction increases the strength of the escape or avoidance response that terminates, removes, or reduces its effect.

Neutral Stimulus   Operant: A stimulus that does not increase or decrease the strength of a response it follows. Respondent: An antecedent stimulus that does not elicit a UR or a CR.

Operant Behavior   Behavior that is controlled by its consequences.

Paradigm   A stimulus-response model using notational symbols to depict relationships between stimuli and responses.

Phobia   Maladaptive anxiety or fear attached to a specific object; it involves a conditioned avoidance response.

Positive Reinforcement   A procedure to increase the strength of a response by presenting a stimulus contingent on performance of the response.

Positive Reinforcement Contingency   A statement specifying the behavior that must be performed in order for a positive reinforcer to be delivered.

Positive Reinforcer   A stimulus presented after a response that increases the strength of that response and the likelihood that it will be performed again.

Premack Principle   A positive reinforcement contingency named for its originator. It states that a higher probability behavior can reinforce a lower probability behavior. That is, a behavior occurring more frequently than another behavior can serve as a reinforcer for the behavior that occurs less frequently.

Primary Aversive Stimulus   (See unconditioned aversive stimulus.)

Primary Negative Reinforcer   (See unconditioned negative reinforcer.)

Primary Positive Reinforcer   (See unconditioned positive reinforcer.)

Primary Punisher   (See unconditioned punisher.)

Punisher; Punishing Stimulus   A stimulus presented after a response that suppresses or decreases the strength of that response. Removal of a positive reinforcer contingent on a response is also referred to as a punisher or punishing stimulus.

Punishment   Procedures applied to suppress or decrease the strength of behaviors. Includes (1) response-contingent presentation of a punisher and (2) response-contingent removal of a positive reinforcer.

Punishment Contingency   A statement specifying the response that must be performed in order for a punisher to be presented.

RAC-S   Acronym for *R*esponse, *A*ntecedents, *C*onsequences, *S*trength; the behavioral assessment framework used in this text.

Rate   The most common measure of response strength; response frequency per time unit.

Reinforcer   A stimulus whose presentation or removal contingent on a response increases the strength of that response and the likelihood that it will be performed again. (See positive reinforcer; negative reinforcer.)

Resistance to Extinction   The number of responses performed after reinforcement has been discontinued. The greater the number, the higher the resistance.

Respondent Behavior   Behavior that is elicited by a preceding or antecedent stimulus.

Respondent Conditioning; Classical Conditioning   Development or establishment of a response by pairing a neutral stimulus with an unconditioned stimulus until the neutral stimulus acquires the ability to elicit a conditioned response.

Response; Behavior   Any observable, measurable movement or activity of an individual.

Response Class   A group of behaviors of which each member or response produces the same or similar effect on its environment, for example, reinforcement.

Response Cost   The punishment technique of removing or withdrawing a positive reinforcer contingent on performance of the target response. Also called punishment by response-contingent removal of a positive reinforcer.

Response Differentiation   The refinement of a response or the narrowing of a response class through differential reinforcement.

Response Strength   For operant behavior, measured by (1) frequency per time unit (rate), (2) duration, (3) intensity, and/or (4) latency. For respondent behavior, measured by (1) latency and/or (2) magnitude.

Reward   An object or event that is identified as pleasant, satisfying, or desirable, or one that an individual will seek out or approach. A reward may or may not act as a positive reinforcer.

Role Reversal   A role-play technique in which an individual role plays the part of another person while the therapist or group member role plays his or her part.

Satiation   A condition in which a reinforcer has been continuously available to an individual until it loses its reinforcing effect.

Schedule of Reinforcement   A contingency that specifies the conditions under which reinforcement is delivered for a response. Types of reinforcement schedules include continuous, fixed-interval, fixed-ratio, variable-interval, and variable-ratio.

S-Dee (S^D)   (See discriminative stimulus, S^D.)

S-Delta (S^Δ)   (See discriminative stimulus, S^Δ).

Secondary Aversive Stimulus   (See conditioned aversive stimulus.)

Secondary Negative Reinforcer   (See conditioned negative reinforcer.)

Secondary Positive Reinforcer   (See conditioned positive reinforcer.)

Secondary Punisher   (See conditioned punisher.)

Self-Control Reinforcement Contingency   An individual arranges conditions so that the desired response is followed by self-administered reinforcement.

Shaping with Successive Approximations   A behavioral procedure used to develop a new behavior or one that rarely occurs. Differential reinforcement is used to strengthen members of one response class. When these responses are performed consistently, the criterion for reinforcement is shifted to the next response class. Each successive response class more closely approximates the desired terminal response.

Simple Conditioned Reinforcer   A previously neutral or nonreinforcing stimulus that has acquired the ability to increase response strength through pairing or association with one particular established reinforcer, for example, a bus token.

Social Reinforcer   A reinforcing stimulus that becomes available through interaction with another individual. Attention, praise, and approval are examples of social reinforcers.

Social Skills Training   (See assertiveness training.)

Spontaneous Recovery   The recurrence of an extinguished response at a future time when stimulus conditions are similar to those in which the response was reinforced.

Stimulus (plural, Stimuli)   Any measurable object or event. It can include physical features of the environment as well as an individual's own behaviors or the behaviors of others. Stimuli can be discriminative, eliciting, reinforcing, punishing, or neutral.

Stimulus Control   A response occurs in the presence of S^D and never or rarely in the presence of S^Δ. Additionally, the interval between presentation of the S^D and the occurrence of the response (latency) is short.

Stimulus Fading   A procedure used to transfer stimulus control of a behavior from an original S^D to a novel stimulus. The S^D is gradually altered along one dimension until it resembles the new stimulus. The individual responds appropriately and is reinforced in the presence of S^D throughout its changes with no errors or responses to S^Δ. Stimulus fading is also called errorless learning.

Stimulus Generalization   A response reinforced in the presence of one stimulus, S^D, US, or CS will also be performed in the presence of other similar stimuli.

Stimulus-Response Chains   Units of stimuli and responses that comprise complex sequences or patterns of behavior. Each unit consists of an S^D, a response, and a conditioned reinforcer that also serves as the S^D for the next response. The chain terminates with delivery of a reinforcer.

Straining the Ratio   A phenomenon occurring when a fixed-ratio schedule is increased too rapidly. A response will extinguish if the number of responses required for reinforcement is increased too rapidly.

Superstitious Behavior   The result of an accidental contingency. Behavior is strengthened by an unplanned reinforcer that follows it. (See accidental contingency.)

Systematic Desensitization   A respondent procedure for treating phobias. It involves deep muscle relaxation to suppress anxiety by pairing phobic or anxiety-eliciting stimuli with relaxation stimuli in the client's imagination. A hierarchy of items related to the feared stimulus is constructed, and the client is presented with the items on the hierarchy from the least anxiety-eliciting item to the most anxiety-producing event until no anxiety is elicited.

Target Behavior; Target Response   The behavior or response to be observed or counted; the behavior selected for analysis or modification.

Time-out   A form of punishment by response-contingent removal of positive reinforcement. The individual is removed from the reinforcing situation immediately after the target behavior is performed and placed for a brief period in an environment with minimal availability of reinforcement.

Token Economy   A planned reinforcement program in which individuals earn tokens or points for performing desired behaviors. These tokens or points can be exchanged for a variety of objects or privileges.

Transfer of Change   The generalization or transfer of behavioral change from the practice setting to a client's natural environment.

Treatment Contract   A written or verbal statement of commitment between the practitioner and client that defines the roles of the client and practitioner so that each agrees to perform certain activities that can lead to attainment of the client's goals.

Treatment Planning   The process of developing and structuring interventions based on the assessment of an individual's problem and the goals that have been established. It includes the design of the intervention plan, selection of behavioral techniques, and the procedures for implementing the plan. The treatment plan should be prepared and implemented in a manner that allows for systematic evaluation.

Unconditioned Aversive Stimulus   A stimulus that is identified as unpleasant, annoying, or painful. It does not require pairing or association with another stimulus to acquire these properties. When given the opportunity, the individual will usually escape or avoid it.

Unconditioned Negative Reinforcer   A stimulus that signals an escape or avoidance response that terminates or reduces the effect of the stimulus. The removal of this stimulus increases the likelihood that the escape or avoidance response will be performed again. The unconditioned negative reinforcer acts in this way without requiring prior pairing or association with another stimulus.

Unconditioned Positive Reinforcer   A stimulus whose presentation contingent on a response increases the strength of that response, without requiring prior pairing or association with another stimulus.

Unconditioned Punisher   A stimulus whose presentation contingent on a response suppresses or decreases the strength of that response without requiring prior pairing or association with another stimulus. Also the removal of an unconditioned positive reinforcer.

Unconditioned Response (UR)   In the respondent conditioning paradigm, the response that is elicited by an unconditioned stimulus.

Unconditioned Stimulus (US)   In the respondent conditioning paradigm, an object or event that elicits an unconditioned response without requiring prior pairing or association with another stimulus.

Variable-interval Schedule   An intermittent reinforcement schedule in which a reinforcer is delivered when the response is made after an average amount of time has passed. The interval is randomly varied around a given time value. For example, *VI 5 min.* means that reinforcement is made available for a response performed after an average of 5 minutes has passed, although the interval might range from 2 to 9 minutes.

Variable-ratio Schedule   An intermittent reinforcement schedule in which a reinforcer is delivered after an average number of responses is emitted. The ratio is randomly varied around a given value. For example, *VR 8* means that reinforcement is delivered after an average of 8 responses has been performed, although the number of responses required for reinforcement might range from 1 to 20.

AUTHOR INDEX

Agras, W.S., 78
Alberti, R.E., 135
Allen, K.E., 35, 60, 65
Anderson, J., 121
Anrep, G.V., 181
Antonitis, J.J., 121
Armstrong, E., 176, 182
Austin, J.B., 177, 181
Ayllon, T., 24, 35, 65, 116, 121
Azrin, N.H., 65, 116, 121, 144, 145, 146, 150, 151

Bachrach, J., 23
Baer, D.M., 24, 35, 128, 135, 151
Bandura, A., 130, 135
Barber, T.X., 182
Bailey, J.S., 35
Barlow, D.H., 28, 31, 35, 78, 92, 177, 181
Bellack, A.S., 180
Bernstein, D.A., 173, 180
Bersch, P.J., 121
Bijou, S.W., 191
Birnbrauer, J., 35
Blanchard, E.B., 175, 180
Bolstad, O.D., 92
Borkovec, T.D., 173, 180
Boudewyns, P.A., 174, 182
Brion-Meisels, L., 19
Briscoe, R.V., 35
Britles, C.J., 163
Brown, G.D., 151
Bucher, B.D., 151
Burchard, J., 65
Burchard, S., 65
Butterfield, W.H., 78, 207

Callahan, E.J., 176, 180
Campbell, L.M., 178, 180
Castro, L., 151
Cautela, J.R., 16, 17, 19, 24, 91, 92, 177, 178, 180
Chaplin, E.W., 174, 180
Churchill, D.W., 129, 135
Churchill, S.R., 107
Commons, M.L., 56
Corriveau, D.P., 208
Corsini, R.J., 135
Corwin, L., 192
Coulter, S.K., 129, 135
Craighead, W.E., 192
Csanyi, A.P., 44

Dangel, R.F., 191
Davidson, P.O., 91, 92, 180
Davidson, S.M., 91, 92, 180
Davis, J.R., 162
Dawley, H.H., 173, 182
DeLange, J., 192

Earnhart, T., 192
Eisler, R.M., 181
Ellis, W.D., 122
Epstein, L.H., 175, 180
Erwin, W.J., 23
Everett, P.M., 35
Eysenck, H.J., 174, 180

Fantino, E., 121
Feldman, M.P., 163, 176, 180
Feldman, R.A., 93
Ferster, C.B., 56, 65

287

Milton, O., 107
Mohr, J.P., 23
Monti, P.M., 208

Neuringer, C., 163
Nevin, J.A., 56

O'Banion, D.R., 44
O'Flaherty, K., 93
Ollendick, T.H., 144
Osborne, J.G., 192, 206, 208

Palumbo, A., 192
Patel, U.A., 176, 182
Patterson, G.R., 163, 192
Paul, G.L., 206, 208
Pavlov, I.P., 2, 165, 167, 181
Pear, J., 31, 35, 88, 93
Pedi, S.J., 93
Peterson, L., 65
Peterson, R.F., 128, 135, 191
Phelps, R., 192
Phillips, D., 24, 178, 182
Phillips, E., 121
Pinkston, E.M., 35
Polster, R.A., 44, 191
Pope, K., 181
Powers, M.A., 145, 151
Premack, D., 41, 44

Rachlin, H., 151
Radin, N., 107
Ramp, E., 56
Rayner, R., 166, 182
Rechs, J.R., 44
Reese, N.M., 35
Reid, J.B., 163
Rescorla, R.A., 182
Rimm, D.C., 177, 178, 181, 182
Risley, T., 129, 136, 140
Rogers, C.R., 107
Rose, S.D., 192
Russell, M.A.H., 176, 182
Russell, R.K., 177, 182

Salzberg, H., 162
Sanok, R.L., 78
Sarbin, T., 93
Sarri, R., 85, 93, 107, 202, 208
Schaefer, H.H., 107
Schaeffer, B., 162
Schoenfeld, W.N., 121
Schweid, E., 191

Schwartz, G., 182
Sechrest, L.B., 188, 191
Seidner, M.C., 208
Semb, G., 56
Semb, S., 56
Shapiro, D., 175, 182
Sherman, J.A., 128, 135
Shipley, R.H., 174, 182
Shorkey, C., 78
Simmons, J.Q., 140, 151, 162, 191
Singer, J.L., 181
Singh, R., 24
Sipich, J.F., 177, 182
Skinner, B.F., 2, 24, 43, 44, 56, 65, 78, 107
Sloane, R.B., 206, 208
Smith, D.E.P., 192
Smith, J.M., 192
Solomon, R.L., 151, 163, 182
Spencer, C.J., 135
Stachnik, T., 35, 192
Staddon, J.E.R., 121
Stalgaitis, S.J., 151
Stebbins, W.C., 166, 181
Stein, T.J., 192
Stoyva, J., 175, 182
Striefel, S., 78
Strupp, H.H., 121
Stuart, F., 91, 93
Stuart, R.B., 44, 91, 93
Sundel, M., 78, 85, 91, 93, 99, 107, 131, 135, 136, 192, 202, 208
Sundel, S.S., 91, 93, 107, 131, 133, 136, 208

Taylor, J., 78
Terdal, L.G., 93
Terrace, H.S., 78
Thomas, E.J., 93
Thomas, J., 65
Thoresen, C.E., 44, 149, 151
Tillema, M., 135
Tobias, L.L., 177, 182
Turkat, I.D., 107, 208
Turner, K.D., 35
Tyler, V.O., 151

Ullmann, L.P., 23, 24
Ulrich, R., 35, 192

Vasta, R., 122
Vattano, A.J., 44
Vinter, R., 85, 93, 107, 202, 208
Voetglin, W., 176, 181

SUBJECT INDEX

A-B-A-B experimental design, 28–29, 30
Accidental contingencies, 40, 279
  and negative reinforcement, 160
Aggressive behavior (*see* Overassertive behaviors)
Airplane phobia, 173–174
  respondent method for treating, 173–174
Alcoholism, 176, 177, 178, 186
Antecedent, 69, 70–75, 279
  in behavioral assessment, 90
  controlling, 90
  gradual alteration of, in fading, 75
  in RAC-S paradigm, 98
  in respondent conditioning, 165
Anxiety, 279
  operant components, 169
  and respondent behaviors, 168
Assertiveness, and human service practitioners, 131
Assertiveness training, 130–134, 198, 199, 279
  and anxiety, 130
  and behavioral assignments, 132, 133–134
  and behavioral reenactment, 132, 133
  and behavioral rehearsal, 134, 190
  in groups, 132–134
    assessment, 133
    evaluation, 134
    goal formulation, 133
    leader's role, 133–134
    planning and implementing, 133–134
    and relaxation training, 130
    stages of, 133–134
  hierarchy in, 132
  and modeling, 130, 132
  and overassertive behaviors, 130–131

  and role playing, 132, 133–134
  and underassertive behaviors, 130, 131–132
Assessment Form, 100
  example of, 102
Aversion relief, 176–177
  and avoidance conditioning, 176–177
Aversion therapy, 176, 199
  and treatment of child molester, 176
Aversive consequences, 90–91
  and intensity of target behavior, 89
Aversive stimulus, 138–139, 154–155, 279
  in covert sensitization, 177–178
  as a negative reinforcer, 154–155, 156–157
  and punishers, 138–139
  as a punisher, 156
  in respondent conditioning techniques, 176
  role in establishment of phobia, 159
Avoidance behaviors, 157–160, 279
  and anxiety, 169
  constructive aspects of, 161
  in covert sensitization, 177–178
  extinction of, 159
  and intermittent reinforcement, 159
  and negative reinforcement, 157–160
  in phobias, 159–160
    resistance to extinction, 159
  role in establishment of phobia, 159
Avoidance conditioning, 157–159
  effect, 158
  paradigm, 158
  procedure, 157–158
  use in aversion relief, 176–177
Autistic children, 206